D0776789

In Defense of Liberal Democracy

Manuel Hinds

IN DEFENSE OF LIBERAL DEMOCRACY

WHAT WE NEED TO DO TO HEAL A DIVIDED AMERICA

MANUEL HINDS

imagine!

An Imagine Book
Published by Charlesbridge
9 Galen Street
Watertown, MA 02472
(617) 926-0329
www.imaginebooks.net

Library of Congress Cataloging-in-Publication Data
Names: Hinds, Manuel, author.
Title: In defense of liberal democracy : what we need to do to heal a divided
    America / Manuel Hinds.
Description: [Watertown] : Charlesbridge Publishing, [2021] | Includes
    bibliographical references. | Summary: "A warning call and rebuttal to the
    growing body of world opinion that liberal democracy and its foundation,
    capitalism, are decadent and ineffective, and that a new social order must be
    found to replace it"—Provided by publisher.
Identifiers: LCCN 2020028551 (print) | LCCN 2020028552 (ebook) |
    ISBN 9781623545093 (hardcover) | ISBN 9781632892263 (ebook)
Subjects: LCSH: Capitalism—United States. | Liberalism—United States. |
    Democracy—United States. | United States—Politics and government—1989-
Classification: LCC HC110.C3 H56 2021 (print) | LCC HC110.C3 (ebook) |
    DDC 330.973—dc23
LC record available at https://lccn.loc.gov/2020028551
LC ebook record available at https://lccn.loc.gov/2020028552

Jacket design by Ronaldo Alves
Interior design by Mira Kennedy

Printed in the United States of America
(hc) 10 9 8 7 6 5 4 3 2 1

Para Carmen Beatriz, Eleonora, Eva María, Thomas, Renee,
Marco, Natalia y Sebastián y Martin y Mathew

*We did not think the ideal of liberal democracy, the open society,
would have to be fought for all over again.*

Darryl Pinkney

*The crisis consists precisely in the fact that the old is dying and the
new cannot be born; in this interregnum a great variety
of morbid symptoms appear.*

Antonio Gramsci

★ CONTENTS ★

Introduction   1

Part I   9

  1 Far from Equilibrium   11
  2 Ghosts from the Past   21
  3 The Economic Effects of Change   43
  4 The Legitimation of Destructiveness   64
  5 The Magnetic Fields   75

Part II   93

  6 The Birth of the Two Orders   95
  7 France and England   109
  8 The Gilded Age: The United States and Germany   129
  9 Darkness at Noon   158
  10 The Welfare State and Communism   183

Part III   209

  11 Toward Complexity   211
  12 The Individual and Society   222
  13 The Appeal of Slavery   237
  14 Our 1776 Moment   249

Bibliography   277

Endnotes   289

Epigraph Sources   311

Acknowledgments   313

Index   315

About the Author   323

INTRODUCTION

These are the times that try men's souls.
Thomas Paine

Early in the afternoon of November 18, 1863, a tall, ungainly man stood up in a landscape of rolling hills in Pennsylvania to deliver a short address. He wanted to summarize the essence of the history of his country—past, present, and future—in a few words that would also spell out the rationale for the civil war that was bleeding it. In an unforgettable first paragraph, he chiseled, as in rock, the concepts of liberty and equality as fundamental to the nation:

> Four score and seven years ago our fathers brought forth on this continent, a new nation, conceived in Liberty, and dedicated to the proposition that all men are created equal.

He then described the crisis the country was facing as a test of these foundational ideas:

> Now we are engaged in a great civil war, testing whether this nation, or any nation so conceived and so dedicated, can long endure. We are met on a great battle-field of that war. We have come to dedicate a portion of that field, as a final resting place for those who here gave

their lives that that nation might live. It is altogether fitting and proper that we should do this.

Finally, this man, who within two years would also give his life that his nation might live, the last full measure of devotion, gave an all-encompassing description of the past and future history of his country:

> But in a larger sense, we can not dedicate—we can not consecrate— we can not hallow—this ground. The brave men, living and dead, who struggled here, have consecrated it, far above our poor power to add or detract. The world will little note, nor long remember what we say here, but it can never forget what they did here. It is for us the living, rather, to be dedicated here to the unfinished work which they who fought here have thus far so nobly advanced. It is rather for us to be here dedicated to the great task remaining before us—that from these honored dead we take increased devotion to that cause for which they gave the last full measure of devotion—that we here highly resolve that these dead shall not have died in vain—that this nation, under God, shall have a new birth of freedom—and that the government of the people, by the people, for the people, shall not perish from the earth.

President Abraham Lincoln then sat, taking by surprise the audience, which had expected a much longer address, especially as the main orator that day, Edward Everett, had taken two hours to deliver his speech. Staring at the president before applauding, the audience created a moment of awkwardness that gave Lincoln the impression that the meaning of his message had not reached them. Yet within a few hours, the Gettysburg Address was well on its way to becoming one of the greatest pieces of oratory in history.

In this extraordinary speech, Lincoln portrayed American history as an eternally unfinished business, a work that would continue to be in progress through the ages, a struggle to ensure that the government of the people, by the people, and for the people would evolve and change in accordance with circumstances—but would not die. In this approach, he followed the path of the Founding Fathers, who saw the social order they were creating not as a static framework but as a dynamic vessel that would lead the United States into an extraordinary adventure of freedom, democracy, and equality. Like all adventures, this grand experiment could produce good or bad results, depending on what Americans did with their free lives.

Lincoln's Gettysburg Address echoed the words John Adams had written on June 6, 1826, in response to an invitation to dine with the citizens of his beloved hometown of Quincy, Massachusetts, on the fiftieth anniversary of the Declaration of Independence. In a short letter to the organizing committee, he excused himself on grounds of poor health but then offered this piece of his wisdom about the American Revolution:

> A Memorable epoch in the annals of the human race; destined, in future history, to form the brightest or the blackest page, according to the use or abuse of those political institutions by which, they shall, in time to come, be Shaped, by the human mind.[1]

Like Lincoln thirty-seven years later, Adams put the responsibility for the outcomes of the new American social order squarely on the shoulders of American citizens. He and his comrades did not pretend to have created a perfect system, a static structure, a utopia that would automatically direct its citizens to do the right thing and attain perfection. Having been conceived, as Lincoln said, in liberty, the entire social order was designed to guarantee precisely the freedom that would allow its citizens to act in good or bad faith, to make mistakes and recover from them, or not. In that short paragraph, Adams had made clear that the social order would be flexible by saying that the institutions they had created would be subject to change in an unfathomable future. They knew that crises would come and the world would change, requiring institutional transformations, and that keeping the country on the right track defined by the Declaration of Independence and the US Constitution would require work and sacrifice by generations to come.

By choosing freedom over direct authority, and flexibility to adjust and correct over a search for a perfect utopia that would remain unchanged through time, the Founding Fathers designed an incredibly adjustable and resilient social order. No political system from that period survived without change into the twenty-first century—except the one they established in the United States. Loose enough to allow for unprecedented freedom, the American social order has resisted three great crises, each followed by momentous and unforeseeable changes that radically transformed the life of the country. The crisis of the 1770s and 1780s led to the creation of the institutional setting of American liberal democracy, the social order that would hold the country together through the first stage of the industrial revolution. This social order then survived the second crisis, the Civil War, and with substantial institutional changes prepared the country to absorb successfully the second stage of the industrial revolution, driven by heavy machinery, electricity, the internal combustion engine, and ultimately air travel and advanced telecommunications. Of course, Lincoln did not know this change was coming, but he trusted the flexibility of the spirit of freedom to handle whatever might follow.

The third crisis, the Great Depression, again put the United States in danger of being split apart, not geographically but socially, economically, and politically. That economic disaster pushed people in the United States and throughout the world to consider changing the basis of liberal democracy, abandoning freedom for stability, perpetual dynamism for static order. Many countries moved in these directions with disastrous results. The United States sailed into this dark storm not knowing what it would find on the other side, yet it continued to trust that the legacy of freedom, equality, and individual rights inherited from the Founding Fathers and maintained by generations since would keep its citizens safe and creative while navigating these treacherous waters.

The sailing was not easy. Production and employment fell by a quarter in the early 1930s, recovered only weakly in the middle years of the decade, and then again plunged in 1937 and 1938. It seemed that the country had lost its knack of creating wealth in the midst of freedom. In 1937, when the country was sinking into a depression within the Great Depression after a weak recovery, Henry Morgenthau Jr., the treasury secretary, feeling the fear taking hold of the country again, told President Roosevelt that his son had asked him what exactly would be the correct New Deal response to this second floundering. What had the New Deal achieved, exactly?

Morgenthau told Roosevelt that he had told his son that "the United States had come through this terrific turmoil and . . . the individual in this country still had the right to think, talk, and worship as he wished."[2] This point was the essence of the American dream, which had remained unaltered since the inception of the country.

Yet the crisis did not end there. There were still eight years of economic hardship and world war to endure. But by that time, it was already clear that the social order created by the Founding Fathers had succeeded again, and that democracy was progressing toward ever greater triumph. The world that emerged from World War II was radically different from that which had preceded the Great Depression.

Again, the country's institutional setting changed to accommodate this new world, which witnessed the United States becoming the most powerful country on the planet. The vessel invented by the Founding Fathers had delivered what was expected from it, not automatically, but because the people had trusted it and fought for it.

A fourth crisis is brewing. The United States, in fact the entire world, is again facing "times that try men's souls." Like the first three crises, this one is emerging from deep changes taking place in society, so deep that they demand changes in the institutional setting. As happened in the last two, in the second half of the nineteenth century and during the 1920s and 1930s, the current crisis is being driven by a technological revolution that is deeply altering the relationships between different members and strata of society. These relationships have been strained even further by the COVID-19 pandemic, a global crisis that, like a world war, combines the fear of massive loss of life with the economic disruptions of a global depression, and thus has accelerated the changes that had been taking place in the previous decades, further pressuring the social order, nationally and internationally. And again, doubts about the ability of liberal democracy to face these changes without breaking are becoming increasingly common.

In Defense of Liberal Democracy is an argument for that noble vessel, which has served well not just the United States but many other countries, the most advanced in the world. Not just the vessel of liberal democracy but also the entire conception of life as an adventure that cannot be predicted or controlled, only sailed in full freedom and in equality with all our fellow human beings. I defend liberal democracy for two reasons. First, the memory of all those who gave their lives, not just in so many battlefields but also in their working places, homes, and communities to be able to transfer the baton of freedom that they had received from their parents to the next generation. Seen from today's perspective, part of Lincoln's genius at Gettysburg was to look ahead to this process of passing the baton when he said, "It is for us the living, rather, to be dedicated to the unfinished work which they who fought here have thus notably advanced."

His words apply as much today as in 1863. The honored dead are all the preceding generations that kept the ideals of liberal democracy as their compass in their journeys. They have relived the lives of the Founding Fathers as they have adapted themselves to differing circumstances in order to keep the nation's vessel on the course of freedom, equality, and individual rights. In this sense, the nation has been founded as many times as there have been generations, all of which have kept intact the sacred legacy. Our generation cannot be the one that ends this ennobling tradition.

But there is another fundamental reason to defend liberal democracy. As it did during the previous crises, liberal democracy remains the best social order in the face of dramatic change and crisis, not just because it protects the rights of the individual but also because it is the most flexible and creative system, the best to deal with uncertainty—and not with a false sense of security but with true security that offers creativity and the ability to correct mistakes when the vessel is about to enter a dark storm.

~

Our challenges are similar to those faced by the Founding Fathers in 1776 as they worked to design a new society that should live in freedom and progress in a future they could not foresee. At that moment, they were not looking for policies but for institutions best suited to attain their objectives over the long life of the nation.

Today, we are faced with our 1776 moment. Our challenge is to create the pillars that will structure social life during the twenty-first century without knowing what challenges this century will pose. To grasp the nature of our quest, we must understand what differentiates societies that react positively to the dissolution of the old order and those that react negatively to it. We must also understand the effects of change itself in the social order.

As the economist John Maynard Keynes once wrote, "Economists set themselves too easy, too useless a task if in the tempestuous seasons they simply tell us that when the storm is past the ocean is flat again."[3] In this book, I don't look at the calm that follows the storm but at the storm itself, which is the process of economic, social, and political actions and reactions that the industrial revolution triggered in the industrializing nations during the nineteenth and twentieth centuries, and which the connectivity revolution is triggering in our times. In the midst of tempests, ships may navigate upstream and end up miles away from where they should have rested had they just followed the flow of the river in calm weather.

Our current storm is the result of a profound technological revolution. How we respond to that revolution could be the key to creating a flexible, horizontal social order in the spirit of the Founding Fathers, or it could result in a vertical social order capable of the destruction of liberty and equality. Look at the political manipulation of data, the misuse of social media, fake news, and even the creation of parallel versions of political realities spanning not just a few instances of false stories but the entire political environment. Confusion and destructiveness do not arise from the technologies. They arise from the tensions of the transformation. They are responses to change.

Understanding this choice is essential if we are to make wise decisions in the difficult years ahead. The only certainty is that we will face storms as violent as those of the industrial revolution. When making decisions regarding our direction, we must take into account that the storms will be there and will obstruct whatever action we take.

Will we have to go through wars and domestic conflicts like those of the twentieth century? Of course, we don't know. But the answers I found in history, and which I explore in this book, provide a stern warning about the dangers lurking in our future, dangers that we thought had disappeared when in fact they were just hiding. These answers are only obliquely related to economics. They are anchored in values and culture, which in turn give shape to institutions, economic and noneconomic. As it has been in the past, it will be in the future: our values will shape the future.

PART I

But the crisis unfolds today ever more strikingly, and no cosmopolitan rhetoric can prevent or eliminate it. It is, in its depths, the inescapable contradiction of liberal individualism and democratic homogeneity.

Carl Schmitt

1

FAR FROM EQUILIBRIUM

[A] population undergoing drastic change is a population of misfits, and
misfits live and breathe in an atmosphere of passion . . .
Eric Hoffer

The worlds of the nineteenth and twentieth centuries had a strange encounter in a small German city in the midst of World War I. On April 9, 1917, the train of the imperial crown prince of Germany, which enjoyed high priority in the railroad traffic system, had to stop at Halle for two hours to let a train with higher priority go through. The reason for this unusual priority was that, seated in that train, in a wagon marked as sealed, was Vladimir Lenin—a citizen of one of the countries at war with Germany who was being carried back to Russia from his exile in Switzerland. The German high command hoped that his presence in Russia would change the course of the war in favor of the Central Powers.[4] The priority given to his train seemed dictated by the protocols of history, for the crown prince would never be crowned emperor of Germany, while the plebeian Lenin was on his way to inherit the tsardom of Russia.

As Lenin rode toward his destiny, the old order of Europe was collapsing. Within a year of his trip, by the end of the war, revolutions would spring up all over Europe; long-lasting autocratic dynasties would come to an end in Germany, Russia, the Ottoman Empire, and Austria-Hungary; the British Empire—the backbone of established world order—would be fatally weakened; and the redoubtable Second Reich created by Bismarck to unify Germany would fall into a state of dissolution that threatened the very existence of the country. The proximate cause of all these events was the chaotic disruption caused by World War I. Beneath such chaos, however, a trend seemed unstoppable. The age of socialism was dawning, spreading hope and terror in millions of people around the world.

There was an idea driving this trend: capitalism was dead, killed by the wide differences in wealth and income that emerged from it, by the rough instability it elicited in economic activities, and by the secular stagnation that led to high levels of unemployment. A new vision was emerging to substitute for the dying system, and it was based on the ideas of Karl Marx, a German philosopher and revolutionary who had died in 1883. The chaotic world created by individual economic freedom was to be replaced by a well-ordered socialist world where the means of production would be owned by the state. Without private property, greed would disappear, allowing the government to make rational economic decisions for the good of all members of society. In this way, the huge benefits of industrial progress would be shared by everyone, in a stable environment that would stand in sharp contrast to the series of booms and depressions characteristic of capitalism. It would be the triumph of reason over chaos.

Lenin believed that liberal democracy would die along with capitalism. He saw democracy as a gigantic farce mounted by capitalists to conceal and justify the exploitation of the poor. It would be replaced by what he called the dictatorship of the proletariat, whose historic role would be to eliminate private ownership and its associated greed. Once this objective had been attained, the state would disappear because, without greed, people would not need its guidance or protection. A new human being would have emerged to live in the upcoming utopia, the communist paradise.

Communism, however, was not the only doctrine that rose in those tempestuous days to threaten capitalism and liberal democracy. Within a few months, Benito Mussolini, a defector from the Italian Socialist Party, and Adolf Hitler, an Austrian who had become a corporal in the German army, came to the same conclusion as the Marxists. Capitalism was a source of corruption and decay. Redemption could be attained only through the rationalizing power of the state. They hated the concept of class struggle that underpinned Marxist doctrine, however; they dreamed of an ideal society unified under the old Roman and German values of discipline and devotion to the state.

Hitler and Mussolini remained socialists, but for them socialism did not mean state ownership of the means of production. It simply meant that what they considered to be the interests of the state should prevail over those of individuals. Private capitalists would still own the means of production, but they would not interact with each other and with the rest of society in an environment of free-market competition. Instead, they would act in accordance with the commands of the government. That is, society would remain capitalistic in form, but its soul would have been taken by socialism.

These leaders were incredibly successful in the 1920s and 1930s, taking over three of the most powerful countries in the world and enabling their followers to take over many other countries in Eastern and Southern Europe. The world that they created, however, was different from that which they had promised. Rather than a new world of rationality, the new leaders created infernos of destruction.

These men had more in common than their contempt for capitalism and liberal democracy: each (like Joseph Stalin) came from obscure corners of society, and while they used structured ideas as a vehicle to attain power, they imposed personal, arbitrary tyrannies. The most important similarity, however, was the method they used to attain power and increase it: the encouragement and deliberate shaping of divisiveness in the population. They each defined a specific minority as the culprit of their society's problems; they whipped up hatred in the majority against this minority; and they turned the former against the latter in what they described as an apocalyptic war of extermination, portraying themselves as the leaders of the people in this fight. In the case of Lenin and Stalin, the minority was the bourgeoisie; in the case of Hitler, it was the Jews and other people the Nazis considered inferior. These ideas turned their doctrines into mechanisms of destruction.

The surge of communism was incredibly bloody. It killed 65 million people in China and 20 million in the Soviet Union. It also killed 4 million in Cambodia and North Korea, 1.7 million in Africa, 1.5 million in Afghanistan, a million each in the communist states of Eastern Europe and Vietnam, and 150,000 in Latin America (mainly in Cuba). Altogether, communism was accountable for almost 100 million deaths in the twentieth century. Add to these the 25 million killed in the name of Nazism, and these ideologies of destruction took

125 million lives in the twentieth century—and this doesn't include the many millions who died in international and civil wars in the midst of these conflicts.[5] The two world wars alone accounted for another 40 to 45 million military deaths.

In the end, the evil that Nazi-fascists and communists unleashed against their victims turned against the perpetrators. Nazi Germany destroyed itself in 1945 in its suicidal confrontation with the rest of the world. Almost fifty years later, the Soviet Union sank under the weight of its bloody past. The huge empire that was associated in the minds of the world with iron and steel, with unbending will and sweeping power, was prostrate. No other empire in history had fallen that fast, except for those destroyed by foreign invasions. In this case, it was clear that it had fallen from within. The world was astonished to see its demise.

After its fall, it became evident that the Soviet Union had been a mighty military power but an economic dwarf. Its industries were obsolete and inefficient, its agriculture was disastrous, services barely existed, and healthcare and social security were comparable to those of developing countries. The only sector that worked was the industrial-military complex aimed at turning the country into a superpower.

There had been no gain for the Soviet population from their self-inflicted tragedies. People had made terrible sacrifices for decades on end, thinking that they were building a paradise on earth, only to discover, generations later, that their country had remained as backward, relative to the developed capitalist countries, as it had been when the regime had started in 1917. The capitalist countries had not gone through the murderous periods the Soviets had endured, had not surrendered their freedoms, and had not been isolated from what was going on outside their borders. They were richer and enjoyed a level of social services that far surpassed those of the communist countries. In the early 1990s, Soviet citizens found that they had to rebuild their country along the lines of the system they had learned to despise.

On the other side, capitalism did not die. Instead, it had thrived. The wide differences in wealth and income, the rough economic instability, and the secular stagnation that Marx and Lenin had denounced disappeared at the end of World War II. For many decades, the problems that Lenin, Mussolini, and Hitler had exploited to open their road to power suddenly gave way to an egalitarian, stable, and sustained expansion of liberal democracy. Then, at the end of the 1980s, communism collapsed and liberal democracy stood alone as the victor in this long struggle. Few thought it would ever be challenged again.

At the peak of its prestige, liberal democracy was for several years the only viable social order. Its position seemed unassailable. But events began to unfold that challenged the vision of the Founding Fathers, events driven by problems similar to those that had led to the rise of tyrants in Europe a century ago.

These events have not been isolated. They are evidence of trends that started well before the COVID-19 pandemic, which has just accelerated them. Gradually first, and then quite rapidly, our times have begun to show increasingly vivid similarities to the first three decades of the twentieth century, so much so that by the 2020s, our problems have come to mirror those that besieged that era. These problems include widening gaps in the distribution of income and wealth, economic instability, growing political polarization, stiff divisiveness over a broad range of social and political issues, the fragmentation of world order, and a shift in the social and political mood toward pessimism. In many quarters, these problems are being blamed on liberal democracy.

We are now witnessing the rise of authoritarian leaders who obtain power by fostering hatred against minorities. For most of the latter half of the twentieth century, political success was based on unifying societies, but now there are many politicians who believe that the path to power is based on creating divisiveness—like the leaders of the destructive regimes of the past. The COVID-19 pandemic has enabled many hitherto democratic governments to acquire power over the citizenry that can only be compared to those wielded by the dictators of the early twentieth century. In April 2020, the *Economist* published a list of ten governments that were taking advantage of the pandemic to grab more power—Hungary, Cambodia, Serbia, Turkey, China, India, El Salvador, Uganda, Togo, and Azerbaijan. In the United States, President Trump claimed to have "absolute power" to decide on actions to be taken to face the pandemic, though he was soon forced to abandon this position. The Hungarian parliament, however, passed a law giving the prime minister almost unlimited power to rule by decree, and in Turkey, at least eight journalists had been arrested and charged with "spreading misinformation." In Bolivia, the president decreed that those who "misinform or cause uncertainty to the population" can be jailed from one to ten years. And so on.[6] The past has indeed come back to haunt us.

These old problems, appearing out of the past like ghosts, are taken as evidence by many that liberal democracy has failed and must be replaced. But the fact that they appeared a hundred years ago, disappeared after the end of World War II, and reappeared at the turn of the new millennium suggests not failure of the system but a new cycle of changing circumstances, similar to what the world has experienced before: disruptions from a technological revolution that is changing our social order as deeply as the industrial revolution had.

Profound technological advances, while opening the road for a better future in the long run, are terribly disruptive in the short term. They render obsolete the capital accumulated in physical assets; in human knowledge and skills; and, even more fundamentally, in the shape of the institutions linking the fabric of society. Such disruption, particularly the erosion of social order, elicits a strong resistance to change in any society, which in many past instances has led to terrorism, violent revolution, and the installation of fundamentalist regimes that impose a retrograde social order of the past on the emerging society.

Although the current technological revolution started in the third quarter of the twentieth century, its economic, political, and social effects have only recently become apparent. Many people refer to it as the fourth industrial revolution, based on Klaus Schwab's enumeration of the products that have spearheaded each of the four.[7] The first was the mechanization of economic activities, including agriculture and textile production, starting around 1765. The symbol of this revolution is the invention of the steam engine. The second was the emergence of new sources of energy (electricity, gas, and oil) and the introduction of massive returns due to the increased scale of production. Inventions emerging from this revolution, which began around 1870, included the internal combustion engine, the airplane, and telecommunications. The third revolution started toward the end of the 1960s and leveraged significant advances in nuclear energy, electronics, telecommunications, biotechnology, and computers. The fourth revolution, starting at the dawn of the third millennium, arose from the spread of the internet and various communication technologies that use its power.

In terms of aims, however, I argue that there are only two revolutions: the industrial revolution (with a first and a second stage coinciding with the first and second revolutions in Schwab's classification) and the connectivity revolution. We can visualize the difference between a "normal" innovation and one that triggers a technological revolution by picturing progress as a straight line leading from lesser to higher development. A "normal" innovation accelerates the speed at which society moves along that line. A technological revolution shifts the direction of the line, redefining the direction of progress. The industrial revolution changed the world by multiplying the power of the muscle. This new one is multiplying the power of the mind.

These effects take place only when technological change is deep enough to affect the social order. There were substantial technological advances from the end of World War II to the beginning of the connectivity revolution, but they did not cause substantial disruption because they were all in the direction of multiplying the power of muscle. Disruption increased exponentially when the direction of progress changed from multiplying the power of the muscle to multiplying the power of the mind.

I use the term *connectivity revolution* because its revolutionary power comes from the intimate connection that the new technologies establish between people, people with machines, and machines with machines. While the industrial revolution was concerned with things, the connectivity revolution is concerned with relations. In this way, the world is moving from a technological revolution, in which the main challenge was to submit nature to the human will, to one where the main challenge is to deal with a growing proximity to each other—around the world and in the same neighborhood. The adjustment is more intimate, it is more complex, and it is more difficult.

Before the connectivity revolution, people could ignore the presence of those who lived far away. The morals, mores, and customs of other cultures were of little interest except for curiosity. Now the interactions between distant cultures are much closer, requiring adjustment if peace is to be maintained. These adjustments have to be made by individuals, the most difficult for a culture to effect. And all this is happening while the economy is changing at the speed of a hurricane. The new relationships that the new technologies are creating and the ones they are destroying will necessitate a new social order—as happened a hundred years ago.

The industrial revolution gathered steam at the end of the eighteenth century because of several interrelated currents. As the pace of scientific and engineering progress increased exponentially, a technological revolution unfolded in two main waves. The first wave started in the late eighteenth century with the industrialization of textile production and the invention of the steam engine; proceeded with the application of the latter to industrial processes, railways, and steamships; and ended with the introduction of the telegraph and the submarine cables that tied together the entire globe. The second stage continued from 1870 with the invention of electric machinery and the internal combustion engine and the development of steel and industrial chemistry, and culminated in the early twentieth century with the invention of the telephone, automobile, airplane, radio, and television. Each of these waves sent ripples throughout society, establishing new industries, destroying or transforming old ones, and changing the living conditions of succeeding generations.

As production became increasingly dependent on these new inventions, machines rather than people became the most important factor of production. The massive use of machinery led to the development of economies of scale: the larger the scale of production, the lower the unit cost of produced goods. Everything became massive. Large-scale methods of production, introduced in agriculture, industry, commerce, and services, displaced the artisan activities that had provided employment for the majority of the people, thus changing the shape of society from one where most people were self-employed (even sharecroppers) into one in which most of them worked in industries owned by others.

The combination of the increasing rate of population growth with the displacement of many agricultural workers (productivity per agricultural worker radically improved as a result of industrialization) caused massive migration to developing and unpopulated countries, mainly the United States, Canada, Argentina, Australia, and New Zealand.

The physical wealth of European countries increased exponentially as newly created industrial enterprises accumulated investments of unprecedented magnitude in machinery and equipment. Progress was unevenly distributed, however; while the fortunes of those that took advantage of the revolution increased rapidly, the living standards of large numbers of people declined catastrophically, creating a kind of urban poverty that had never existed before. Financial crises devastated the economy with almost predictable regularity, and unemployment became a permanent problem. The problems described by Marx besieged the newly industrialized countries.

As the industrial revolution progressed, the complexity of economic relations increased: in terms of the variety and volume of the inputs needed for industrial activities, the geographic origin of such inputs, and the size of the markets that were needed to sustain industrial production. The focus of economic activity shifted from the local to the national and international. This process made obsolete not only the capital embodied in the tools and abilities of craftspeople but also the entire set of preindustrial institutions that had regulated the economy. As these events eroded the feudal and autocratic systems that had controlled preindustrial societies, Europe started the traumatic process of finding a new social order.

The industrial revolution created a more horizontal society because industrialization increased the complexity of economic relations to a point that the vertical control of local and national governments of the feudal age was no longer practical. The dimensions of economic life that had been controlled in the previous decades and centuries—prices, wages, production volumes, imports, hiring, and firing—could be controlled no longer. It also became impossible to tie peasants to the land. In this more dynamic industrial economy, people had to change jobs, often moving to other places. The growing volume of national and international transactions pushed for the elimination of barriers to trade, not just between the petty localities of the feudal world but across countries as well. The economy became a network of equals.

A decentralized mechanism was needed to coordinate the new economy. Gradually, webs of contracts between private parties replaced the strict commands of both feudal lords and guilds as the main mechanism to introduce order in the new economy. This web of contracts created the basic infrastructure of modern capitalism.

Financial markets, which had existed primarily to finance the princes of the preindustrial age, became the centerpieces of the new capitalism, financing all stages of production as a result of the decisions of numerous individuals who bought and sold financial instruments to fund specific activities. Traders also moved center stage, as providers of inputs and as outlets for the massive commercialization of industrial goods. Eventually, entrepreneurs and workers who were organized in trade unions became the third and fourth pillars of capitalism. Through their collective ability to manage the immense complexity of the economic relations of the new society, they became the center of the new, more horizontal society where decisions were made collectively via myriads of individual decisions.

Politically, democracy—also a network of equals—became the logical response to the complexities of life in this new society. As the population flowed into overcrowded cities, and urban life became unbearably miserable for many, discontent was easily mobilized, ideas were easily exchanged, and politics assumed a mass character that was new to Europe. People reclaimed their right to govern themselves and wanted improvements in their standard of living. The old autocratic institutions were not ready to manage these new political relations.

Initially, by pushing countries toward a horizontal social order, the industrial revolution opened the door for the development of capitalism and liberal democracy. But it also opened the door for communist and Nazi-fascist systems because many reacted against the surface unfairness and permissiveness of capitalism and liberal democracy, which they believed would lead to the collapse of newly industrializing countries. Many people thought that the only system that could ensure the survival of order was autocracy, either as it had existed previously or as presented in communism and Nazi-fascism. In this way, a technological revolution that pushed for horizontal forms of social organization also pushed, by reaction, for the most vertical systems of government that had ever existed.

For more than a hundred and fifty years, internal revolutions and external wars erupted in a pattern of violence that escalated into a thirty-year episode of collective madness, perhaps the worst in history: World War I, the establishment of communism in the Soviet Union, the Holocaust, and World War II.

～

The industrial and connectivity revolutions are quite different in substance. However, the ripple effects created by each are alike, leading to serious disruptions of the social order and to potential chaos and destructiveness. Since the turn of the twenty-first century, we have witnessed a progressive deterioration of our social order, with no new, competing order gaining ground except that of vertical, authoritarian regimes.

2

GHOSTS FROM THE PAST

And yet . . . the shadowy figures that look at us from the tarnished
mirror of history are—in the final analysis—ourselves.

Detlev J. K. Peukert

A DISTANT MIRROR

The core trends that Marx and Engels thought would destroy capitalism—that is, the concentration of income and wealth, economic instability, and low long-term rate of growth of income and employment—disappeared at the end of World War II. For several decades, these problems were forgotten except by historians, as if they were simply a temporary phase in the development of capitalism. Then, suddenly, at the turn of the twenty-first century, they returned, like ghosts coming back from a dead past, along with many other ghosts that had interacted with them in the 1930s.

As happened in the 1930s, these ghosts are political responses to Marx's core trends, even if some of them are economic in nature. They include the terrible divisiveness that is tearing apart the United States, and many other countries as well; the strong pressures to abandon free trade; the fragmentation of the world order, based in large measure on the idea that globalization is working against most people; a change of mood in the population, from great optimism in the second part of the twentieth century to one of deep pessimism today; a growing disenchantment with liberal democracy, which is being blamed for all of the above; the search for lost social unity by blaming problems on a specific group or subgroup and inciting the rest of the population against them; and the emergence of authoritarian leaders all over the world. In the 1930s, these ghosts were so interrelated that they led to a concatenation of events that resulted in the worst tragedies of the twentieth century. Now they are back, and they are the source of the idea that capitalism is no longer working.

The Three Economic Ghosts: Marx's Problems

Taking flight in our time are the beliefs that capitalism has failed, that the government is a puppet in the hands of the ultrarich, that the latter will become richer and richer while the rest of society will become poorer and poorer, that the growth of production and employment will be low even if that growth is high today, and that crises will become periodic. Few people realize that these ideas were all contained in the work of Karl Marx and Friedrich Engels.

The trend toward income concentration started at the end of the 1970s and has continued unabated into the 2020s. The other two apparitions, economic instability and unemployment, reappeared in the first decade of the twenty-first century. This instability, and particularly the instability that triggered the 2008 Great Recession, marked the point at which the great enthusiasm for capitalism that followed the fall of the Soviet Union turned into a deep disenchantment. There were other events contributing to it, also triggered by the Great Recession and by the idea that the rich had not suffered from, and indeed had profited from, the crisis. This was when many people came to believe that governments were at the service of the elites.

The instability and low rates of growth that accompanied the Great Recession seemed to have disappeared by January 2020. Then, an unrelated disaster, COVID-19, struck in early 2020, generating a new global economic crisis. Within months, Marx's three problems were well entrenched in a new normal.

Divisiveness

The fourth ghost is divisiveness. There were certainly divisive periods during the last part of the twentieth century—particularly the period around the 1960s, which was a period of turmoil regarding the Vietnam War and civil rights. But today's dissension is different; it is not over specific issues that can be overcome with particular changes in policy or institutional reform. The dissension in the 1960s did not question the social order. Nobody doubted that it should be based on liberal democracy. Today's divisiveness is more akin to that of the 1920s and 1930s, driven by different beliefs regarding the features of the structure that should frame the social order. As in the 1930s, this new dissension resembles something usually alien to US culture: ideological enmity.

Technological revolutions create political divisiveness just as they skew income distribution: they split societies between people who take immediate advantage of the change and those who lag behind in their adaptation to it. The latter tend to attribute the resulting difference in wealth and income to unfairness in the economic system. But these political divisions go well beyond the economic sphere. They are also marked by conflicting approaches to traditional mores, customs, and political views. The interaction between these conflicts in different dimensions tends to damage social cohesion and threaten the stability of institutions, which leads people to speculate about what new social order should prevail in the transformed society. Such speculation is the most divisive of all themes and is the fourth ghost.

American politics has been progressively dominated by what the philosopher John Rawls calls comprehensive doctrines—doctrines made up of overarching views of what should be done to improve society in all its dimensions. When such doctrines become "unreasonable," their believers have a predetermined answer to every question and demand that their ideas, and theirs alone, should determine the direction of social action in each and every dimension. Comprehensive doctrines, especially unreasonable ones, have not typically been part of American political thought and behavior.[8]

Such doctrines have a long tradition in Europe, however, where philosophers like Marx and Nietzsche provided an intellectually coherent basis for communism and Nazism, respectively. In the United States today, these doctrines have been based not on philosophical constructs but instead as agglomerations of single-issue movements, each of which demands total support for its ideas in exchange for its support of the ideas of all the other members of the same agglomeration. This tendency has made these comprehensive doctrines extremely rigid and thus unreasonable. Ideas that some of the constituent groups would have been willing to negotiate because they were not central to their welfare must be defended unyieldingly because they are central to the interests of other groups in the same coalition. Because nothing is negotiable, each party tries to impose its comprehensive order on the rest of the population. The result is a polarization in American culture to a degree unprecedented since the 1930s, possibly without any comparable precedent. And it is not just happening in the United States but in almost all of what is called the developed world.

Broadly speaking, there are two main comprehensive doctrines in the United States, one associated with conservative and the other with progressive attitudes. These two attitudes have always existed in the country, but they were not strictly defined in all dimensions of life so that generally conservative and generally progressive people could easily agree on many specific issues. Not all generally conservative people shared the same opinion on any conceivable issue. The same happened with progressives. Now, conservatives and progressives attach themselves to their respective comprehensive doctrines so closely that in almost all important issues, the country has been split in half.

I call this uniformity of general opinion self-profiling. People expect that if others disagree with them on the issue of, say, gun control, they would also disagree with them on health reform, abortion, immigration, and the confirmation of a specific nominee to a judicial position. Of course, the very people who profile themselves by adopting the positions that their conservative or progressive profile requires protest vigorously if someone profiles *them*. Self-profiling coincides with the profiling of political adversaries. If people say that they are against abortion, they are often accused of being racist, authoritarian, antifeminist, and antitransgender, and if they are pro-choice, then they are accused of many unconnected sins, including being antireligion and fiscally lax.

One of the results of this polarization is that large numbers of people on both sides of the ideological spectrum no longer want to elect middle-of-the-road, or centrist, politicians. Rather, they support determined fanatics. And they ask from them total ideological consistency. Even if the current comprehensive doctrines do not have an ideological basis as explicit as communism or Nazi-fascism, they have the same practical implications: it is expected that people will accept the ideas of these comprehensive doctrines in their entirety, without exception. And hatred is quite visible in people's attitudes, their language, and their actions. Predictions of civil war, something unheard of for almost a century in the United States, have become frequent. These predictions are wildly exaggerated, but their existence shows the temperature of the emotional exchange.[9]

Abandoning Free Trade

The fifth ghost is political support for the abandonment of free trade. This ghost is linked to a strong nostalgia for a faraway past that has taken over substantial portions of US society, captured in Donald Trump's slogan "Make America Great Again." This slogan has existed before, most prominently when Ronald Reagan used the slogan "Let's Make America Great Again" in his 1980 presidential campaign. Yet there is a big difference between these two slogans. Reagan's call was for a restoration of a simpler way of government and a leaner agenda for the federal government, which Reagan associated with the dynamism the American economy had shown in a vaguely defined postwar past. Trump's version refers to the restoration of concrete, low-value-added industries and activities that were taken out of the United States by the globalization of chains of production, a process that began precisely in the Reagan years.

With one major exception, the auto industry, the Reagan reforms were oriented toward the liberalization of trade and the integration of the American economy with that of the world. It was forward and outward oriented. The driving force of Trump's reforms has been toward trade protection as a means to force the low-value-added industries to come back so that these enterprises could work in the United States even if uncompetitive, and people who had been working in those enterprises could get their jobs back. That is, while Reagan's program was related to the simplification of government to make the economy more competitive in the future, Trump's program aimed at restoring the past in a very concrete fashion that is backward-oriented. If successful, it would result in the country producing things that it is, in reality, too rich to produce—such as low-value-added products like cheap appliances, or low-technology parts and components of more sophisticated goods.

Trump was not the only candidate in the 2016 elections promising to reverse the free-trade stance that the United States has maintained since the end of World War II. Hillary Clinton made the same promises, including stopping the Trans-Pacific Partnership (TPP) that Trump dismantled as soon as he assumed the presidency. Regarding this partnership, which would have unified the Pacific Rim within a single free market, she said, "I oppose it now, I'll oppose it after the election, and I'll oppose it as president."[10]

This stance against free trade has an ominous precedent. The United States adopted a similar approach in the late 1920s and 1930s, which helped trigger the Great Depression. International import tariffs were quite low or nonexistent during the great international trade expansion that accompanied the second stage of the industrial revolution at the turn of the twentieth century. During World War I, however, international trade collapsed and belligerent countries were forced to produce many goods that were part of industries in which they had no competitive advantage. At the end of the war, they introduced tariffs to support these uncompetitive industries, starting a creeping tariff war. This war negatively affected trade, which in turn threatened to affect economic growth. In the World Economic Conference held by the League of Nations in Geneva in 1927, member countries agreed to stop increasing tariffs. In the 1928 presidential election campaign, however, Herbert Hoover promised to introduce legislation to increase protection in the United States. The resulting Smoot-Hawley Tariff Act triggered retaliatory measures from other countries around the globe, and trade between the seventy-five largest countries fell by 70 percent from 1929 to 1932, contributing mightily to the Great Depression.[11]

Another precedent to this kind of resistance to change aimed at ensuring the survival of certain old activities by eliminating the competition of more efficient producers occurred during the Great Depression. It was the result of the policies associated with the National Recovery Administration (NRA) during the First New Deal, from 1933 to 1935, which I analyze in Chapter 8. Under the NRA, the competition to be eliminated was domestic, and the instrument to eliminate competition was not trade protection but a complex system of domestic regulations that put new and more efficient producers at a disadvantage relative to the larger, well-established enterprises.

Even if managed with different instruments, the objectives of the NRA, the trade restrictions of the 1930s, and the protectionist policies of Donald Trump, were the same: to stop change and thus stem the social, political, and economic effects of technological advance. Like other ghosts, this one disappeared in 1935 and came back in 2017. And its reappearance coincided with a technological revolution.

The Fragmentation of the World Order

The sixth ghost also comes from the past: international fragmentation. One hundred years ago, international circumstances were very similar to today. First, there were two new players among the world powers, Germany and the United States. The rise of the latter was no threat to Britain, but that of Germany was parallel to the rise of China today. Second, Britain, which had been the foundation of the international order in the nineteenth century in economic, monetary, and political terms, became unable to control the more complex world that emerged from World War 1. Today, the United States is seeing a similar decline in its power to steer world order. Third, right after World War I, which had witnessed the first major intervention of the United States as a dominant world power, the country became disgusted with international politics and opted for a policy of isolationism. This left the new mechanism that the victorious powers had dreamed would be the foundation of a new international order, the League of Nations, without coercive power. Today, the United Nations and other international institutions that have depended on US support for the last several decades are losing that support.

Today, the United States is not passively retreating from the international arena but instead actively dismantling the liberal international framework that it established after World War II—the network of alliances and international institutions that supported free trade and the defense of the liberal democracies. These institutions were based on a differentiation of the economic and political dimensions of international relations so that domestic politics would not contaminate the conduct of long-term trade and defensive arrangements. For four years, the Trump administration largely dismantled this system from within, breaking its institutional structures and using trade to further political objectives, and vice versa.

The circumstances are not exactly the same, but the results are similar: a dismantling of an order that protected international relations for almost a century. As happened a hundred years ago, this dismantling is taking place precisely when that order is urgently needed, when international problems are becoming increasingly critical. The disintegration of international order always points in an ominous direction. In the early decades of the twentieth century, it prefigured two world wars. Today, we cannot discount the possibility of war. Russia, China, Iran,

North Korea, and other countries are behaving aggressively without any concern for international law, often in pursuit of geographical expansion. As a result, there are many hot spots around the world.

The Trump administration's withdrawal from the network of democratic allies interacted perversely with this disorder. As the relative power of China and Iran grows, the defense of democracy and the preservation of peace require the strengthening of international democratic institutions. Yet the United States has been doing the opposite. In the pursuance of small objectives, the Trump administration cut the bonds of trust that traditionally unified the West. It has shown, to the most powerful and faithful of its allies, that it is willing to destroy a system of mutual trust for the sake of a tariff here and a tax there. Two new factors—which are not the subject of this book but which suffer hugely from global fragmentation—are climate change and the treatment of pandemics such as COVID-19. Addressing these issues requires a worldwide coordination capacity that is being lost because of international fragmentation. There is no doubt that the US government has had legitimate reasons to be discontent with some trade agreements and international organizations. But there is no reason to throw the baby out with the bathwater, destroying links that are more needed than ever.

While the Trump administration was weakening international institutions, national governments were being weakened from another flank. International networks created by connectivity are becoming more powerful by the day, and they may already be more powerful than the ability of domestic governments to regulate them. This is only natural because, as a result of the emergence of the global chains of knowledge and material supply, markets and enterprises can no longer be split in terms of geographical borders. New technologies are making possible the creation of worldwide networks running on smart and encrypted contracts, capable of managing businesses without personnel, headquarters, or even a physical address—that is, totally out of the control of government. In their book *Blockchain and the Law: The Rule of Code,* Primavera De Filippi, a legal expert at Harvard University, and Aaron Wright, a law professor at the Cardozo School of Law, describe how a new world is emerging where program code and algorithms are beyond the reach of the laws of any particular country.[12] National institutions cannot cope with what the new technologies have unleashed, particularly in the areas of taxation, the financial system, and trade.

Technology has weakened national governments in a deep and permanent way. Many people believe that governments can still avoid this weakening by isolating themselves from the rest of the world. But doing that separates them from the global chains of knowledge and supply. Such a separation also weakens government structures. That is, current structures of government are unavoidably weakened, one way or the other. Rather than ignoring this problem by hiding behind isolationist economic and political structures, what is needed is a new frame of international cooperation, built on the foundations that were so successful in the second half of the twentieth century.

More than a hundred years ago, ignoring these problems led not just to a depression but to two terrible world wars. We must heed this warning. As the historian Robert Kagan has written, World War II taught Americans that "their way of life could not be safe in a world where Europe and Asia were dominated by hostile autocratic powers."[13] In our new world, this means that the United States cannot be safe if it does not have properly organized alliances. Today, this lesson seems to have been forgotten.

The Change of Mood

The reappearance of these ghosts today is prompting a change similar to that which took place at the time of Lenin's dash from Switzerland to Russia in 1917. From a time of optimistic confidence in the future, the world has moved quite quickly toward one of uncertainty and fear. This is the seventh ghost. It is uncannily like one that occurred over a century ago.

Stefan Zweig, one of the most popular novelists of the early twentieth century, described what it felt like to grow up in Vienna, one of the most splendid cities in the Europe of those years, and then to discover that what seemed to be a growing stability actually concealed an incoming explosion:

> When I attempt to find a single formula for the period in which I grew up, prior to the First World War, I hope that I convey its fullness by calling it the Golden Age of Security. . . . This feeling of security was the most eagerly sought-after possession of millions, the common ideal of life. Only the possession of this security made life seem worth while, and constantly widening circles desired their share of this costly treasure. . . . Progress was also made in social matters; year after year

new rights were accorded to the individual, justice was administered more benignly and humanely, and even the problem of problems, the poverty of the great masses, no longer seemed insurmountable. . . . Today, now that the great storm has long since smashed it, we finally know that that world of security was naught but a castle of dreams.[14]

Something similar is taking place in our time. From a world that seemed increasingly secure, we have moved to one where almost nothing seems to be so. The events of 9/11 revealed a danger that had been looming from afar. The two decades following that tragedy revealed that the external dangers exposed in 9/11 were being confronted by societies that were fragmenting from the inside. Then these fragmented societies had to confront a terrible pandemic and its grave economic sequel. People perceive the increasingly worrying realities of these times as forerunners of worse things to come.

The year 2016 seems to have been the year of widespread realization that many changes taking place globally were cataclysmic and were occurring even in countries that had been bulwarks of stability and progress. By the summer of that year, Britain, for decades one of the centerpieces of the European Union (EU), was about to vote on whether to leave or stay with the EU; the presidential primary elections in the United States were closing a campaign that was characterized by bullying and insults; terrorist attacks were becoming increasingly common; a wave of refugees from the Middle East wars was inundating Europe; extreme nationalist parties were increasing their share of power in European elections; and the American federal government, which had been shut down for lack of funds in October 2015, faced the prospect of a new budget crisis in the fall of 2016. Bad behavior was common within political parties and across party lines. As Jonathan Rauch put it in the August 2016 issue of the *Atlantic*, "The political parties no longer have either intelligible boundaries or enforceable norms, and, as a result, renegade political behavior pays. . . . Chaos becomes the new normal."[15]

The political analyst Peggy Noonan has captured perfectly the anguish of this ghost, this premonition of a change from an inherently safe to an inherently unsafe world:

The Moment is that sliver of time in which you realize something epochal is happening in politics, that there has never been a presidential year like 2016, and suddenly you are aware of it in a new, true and personal way. It tends to involve a poignant sense of dislocation, a knowledge that our politics have changed and won't be going back.[16]

In the years since, not just in the United States but all over the world, this sense of doom has increased. There have been similar moments in history—although not in our immediate past. These problems are not a continuation of the problems we had in the second half of the twentieth century, what we would have expected in a linear world. They resemble that which existed almost one hundred years ago, at the turn of the twentieth century, when we were besieged by the same problems that surround us today, problems that we thought developed countries had overcome at least eighty years ago.

Here is Walter Lippmann, describing the environment that existed in 1933:

> The old relationships among the great masses of the people of the earth have disappeared, and there is not yet an ordered relationship among them. The certain landmarks are gone. The fixed points by which our fathers steered the ship of the state have vanished. . . . For the traditional moral codes are not easily applied to such new and intricate circumstances, and as a consequence there is widespread feeling today among the people that their codes, their rules of life and their ideas are without relevance, that they lack the power to guide action, to compose and fortify their souls. . . . Thus, underlying the disorder in the outer world, there is disorder in the spirit of man.[17]

Doesn't that sound familiar? As Lippmann rightly pointed out, the inner problem was a disorder in the human spirit—a disorder of values, a disorder that has returned.

Disenchantment with Liberal Democracy

In this context, the eighth ghost emerged. The feeling that something is fundamentally wrong with liberal democracy is creeping back all over the world, just a few years after it was hailed as the victor in its century-long struggle with communism.

The criticisms of liberal democracy are primarily focused on its economic component: capitalism. In *How Will Capitalism End?* Wolfgang Streeck summarizes these attacks, enumerating several "systemic disorders" that he thinks are likely to lead to the gradual fall of capitalism in our times. These disorders include those mentioned by Marx plus three more: the plundering of the public domain, corruption, and global anarchy. Marx's criticisms were aimed at capitalism as it developed during the industrial revolution, although they eventually proved to be temporary. Streeck's other three criticisms, however, have existed throughout history, well before capitalism. They also existed in the communist Soviet Union, which was not liberal democratic or capitalistic. In fact, it is difficult to think of a more corrupt country than the Soviet Union or one where the public domain was plundered more thoroughly. Many add greed, envy, and egoism to Streeck's list, sins that are part of human nature, of course, not sins invented by capitalism. As in the 1920s and 1930s, however, many are blaming these problems on capitalism and liberal democracy.[18]

In the same vein, other critics blame capitalism for everything that the Western powers have done in developing countries, from imperialism to genocide, forgetting that empires existed for thousands of years before capitalism emerged. The noncapitalist Soviet Union was an empire that imposed its command and its economic system on scores of countries, from Eastern Europe to the depths of Asia. These critics also forget that this same empire had existed (although in smaller form) in the times of the tsars, who commanded an economy that also was not capitalistic. They also blame capitalism for consumerism, as if the inhabitants of communist countries did not dream of having available all the goods and services of a capitalist economy.

This disenchantment is a very dangerous signal. It is the prologue for the demise of liberal democracy. It is similar to that which prevailed during the interwar period (from 1918 to 1939), when communism and Nazi-fascism emerged as substitutes for liberal democracy in crisis. As the Columbia University professor Mark Mazower has written of the similarities of our time with the 1930s:

> There is at least one other crucial respect in which the interwar years and ours mirror one another uncomfortably. What we should probably be thinking about is not so much who became a fascist as who lost faith in parliamentary government, in its checks and balances and basic freedoms. . . . Underpinning the rise of fascism was a profound crisis of liberal democracy. The real lesson waiting to be learned is from this interwar crisis of democratic institutions.[19]

With faith in liberal democracy lost, the witnesses of those interwar years spoke of how easily the populists of their time installed their tyrannies.

In this vein, the Spanish politician Francesc Cambó noted in the 1920s: "When one examines the contemporary problem of European dictatorships, one of the facts which immediately strikes one is the ease with which they have been established and the even greater ease with which they stay in power."[20] A contemporary historian, Emilio Gentile, described what happened when the fascist regime took over Italy in the early 1920s:

> The [fascist] regime met no serious opposition from established institutions or from traditional economic and social interests as it set about demolishing the liberal state. The monarchy, the armed forces, and the industrial and agrarian bourgeoisie accepted the demise of parliamentary government with little evident sign of regret, and seemed more impressed by the advantages that the new regime had brought them by restoring order and discipline in Italian society, and in particular over the workers.[21]

Very much like Cambó and Gentile, many people are astonished today at how easily the new populist leaders transgress previously respected democratic institutions, mores, customs, and old alliances, subverting the order that has framed the world's progress for the last two or three centuries. Such ease is ominous. It suggests that more fundamental institutions may be less solid than we think and would be easier to overturn when the time comes.

What Mazower warned us about is that those who rejected parliamentary democracy in the early twentieth century did not embrace moderate regimes. There is no such thing as a moderate illiberal regime. What should worry us is that we refuse to realize that when we hear that liberal democracy has failed, we are actually being pushed onto a slippery slope leading to tyranny.

Perhaps this is why most people who argue that we should dispose of liberal democracy do not mention what the replacement would be, preferring to leave the impression that in their new social order, people would keep on enjoying the rights that go with liberal democracy—only within a framework that would be more effective. But if liberal democracy were discarded, the replacement would be an illiberal regime—which, by definition, is tyranny.

Fortunately, we haven't seen any advanced society discarding its rights. Some, however, are moving in this direction, motivated by the urge to suppress their political enemies in the confrontation of comprehensive doctrines that dominate modern politics.

The Search for Unity through Divisiveness

One of the most alarming ghosts is the ninth one: the trend to form winning political coalitions by framing all the problems of society as the result of the perverse actions of a minority, thus injecting divisiveness into political discourse as a means of unifying the majority against the minority. In *Mein Kampf,* Adolf Hitler explained (years before he came to power) how to take political advantage of divisive circumstances to legitimize destructiveness and impose tyranny:

> The art of leadership, as displayed by really great popular leaders in all ages, consists in consolidating the attention of the people against a single adversary and taking care that nothing will split up that attention into sections. The more the militant energies of the people are directed towards one objective the more will new recruits join the movement, attracted by the magnetism of its unified action, and thus the striking power will be all the more enhanced. The leader of genius must have the ability to make different opponents appear as if they belonged to the one category; for weak and wavering natures among a leader's following may easily begin to be dubious about the justice of their own cause if they have to face different enemies. . . . Such uniformity intensifies their belief in the justice of their own cause and strengthens their feeling of hostility towards the opponent.[22]

This is exactly what Hitler, Mussolini, Lenin, Stalin, and Mao did to assume power. They identified an enemy, a minority in society, blamed all problems on them, and elicited hatred against them to form a political majority. Then they let loose the hatred of the majority against the minority and used the blood of the latter as a cementing social bond.

In the late 1920s and early 1930s, while Hitler was trying to blame the Jews and communists for all problems, the communists were blaming the bourgeoisie and Nazis. A similar range of finger-pointing exists today—some blame immigrants, others white males, and still others the Jews for our social problems or our inability to solve them. What happened in Germany, the Soviet Union, China, and elsewhere was that a single party eventually took power and proceeded to convert, through propaganda, its enemies into the enemies of the entire population. And we are foolish if we think the same can't happen here, today, if the social order collapses and people turn to a strong leader to reinstall order.

A process like this is difficult to stop. When people become convinced that a minority is guilty of destroying their lives, they fill themselves with hatred and demand action to stop and punish them. A leader trying to stop a raging mob loses credibility and is easily deemed a traitor. That is why the current climate of hatred is so dangerous. Hatred can turn populism into destructiveness.

This competition of hatreds is the perfect environment for chaos, which in turn conditions people to accept tyranny for the sake of a strong social order. This is what legitimized destructiveness in the twentieth century. It is what may legitimize destructiveness in our own time if we don't stop this sinister competition. Ironically, the more groups that hate each other, the higher the probability that one of them will win the competition because the generalized use of hatred legitimizes it and increases the possibility of chaos—and in a society in chaos, the possibility of grabbing power increases exponentially for anyone who decides to do it. The more hatred that is injected into our societies in the twenty-first century, the closer we are getting to the slippery slope into destruction.

Of course, leaders play a crucial role in unifying people around a destructive idea. But such leaders emerge in response to a demand from the people. Albert Speer, Hitler's minister of armaments during most of World War II, described the dynamics of hatred that filled Hitler's rallies:

> Certainly the masses roared to the beat set by Hitler's and Goebbels' baton; yet, they were not the true conductors. The mob determined the theme. . . . This was no ardent nationalism. Rather, for a few short hours the personal unhappiness caused by the breakdown of the economy was replaced by a frenzy that demanded victims. And Hitler and Goebbels threw them the victims. By lashing out at their opponents and vilifying the Jews they gave expression and direction at fierce, primal passions.[23]

That is, people are mistaken when they think that mad rulers imposed their madness on otherwise sensible societies. Mad societies *looked* for mad rulers to fulfill their own madness. Destructiveness became legitimate because people asked for it—not against themselves but against the people they perceived as their enemies.

It is easy to see how destructive leaders used the hatreds of a divisive society to impose their totalitarian rule. But this combination of leaders and disgruntled masses is driven primarily by the mood of masses. A leader like Hitler could not succeed in a liberal society. However, a divisive society will find its Hitler or its Lenin, who will lead it into tyranny. This is what is so worrying today, as US society splits rabidly on almost any political or social issue.

So this ghost may be described as a predisposition of the population to believe that there is someone to blame for all the disruptions brought about by an intrinsically impersonal process of change. Such a predisposition is different from individuals who are willing and able to provide the stories that the population is demanding. It is difficult to discuss this ghost, however, without discussing at the same time the apparition of the tenth ghost: the authoritarian leaders who appear at the right place and at the right time to provide what the population is demanding.

Authoritarian Populist Leaders

The toxic combination of these ghosts has radically changed the political scenarios of liberal democracies. During the second half of the twentieth century, the archetype of a good politician was someone willing and able to compromise and create consensus. People trusted the system and the politicians operating it. In less than twenty years, the archetype of the good politician has today become someone willing and able to break the system by refusing to compromise—someone ready to destroy their political enemies. To do this, the new politicians must be inherently authoritarian, must carry the force of the resentments and hatred that move their followers, and must be able to focus these feelings on a designated villain. Given their controlling character, they do not easily fit in liberal democratic frameworks. This resentful authoritarian leader is the tenth ghost.

Western culture has been here before. The heated environment of the 1920s and 1930s gave birth to brazenly authoritarian political leaders who thrived on the hatred they whipped up against a chosen minority. The process started a competition to blame, to find a scapegoat, as Nazi-fascists and communists fought for the support of the European population.

Today, we have a similar competition. Donald Trump launched his presidential campaign with a brutal attack on Mexicans, a target he eventually expanded to include all Latinos, and then all immigrants. On the other side of the political spectrum, there has been a sustained attack by some leftist extremists on conservatives (and, by extension, white males), who, in accordance with some comprehensive doctrines, are responsible for slavery, the cultural enslavement of the rest of the country, sexism, and authoritarianism. Alarmingly, anti-Semitism has also come back with unexpected vigor, although the white nationalists driving this hatred tend to deny that they have anything against Jews.

While these new authoritarians have chosen different targets, they have also focused on two common enemies: what they call politicians, and the liberal democratic system, which they claim the politicians have rigged. Along with their competition, these two institutions are the enemies that they believe they must destroy before they reach their common, but mutually incompatible, objective: grabbing total power.

It is remarkable how many politicians around the world attack other politicians for being politicians, accusing them of being despicable while excluding themselves from their set. And it is a worldwide phenomenon. In the United States, Donald Trump accused his rivals of corruption and promised to "drain the swamp." Politicians in France, Italy, Hungary, Poland, and other countries have used the same strategy in their attempts to capture and maintain power. This strategy is identical to that used by populist politicians in the 1920s and 1930s. Milton Mayer, an American University of Chicago academic who lived in Germany in the late 1940s, just a few years after the fall of Nazism, interviewed in depth a small group of German citizens in an attempt to understand the reasons for Hitler's popularity. One of the interviewees explained his popularity in this way:

> National socialism was a revulsion by my friends against parliamentary politics, parliamentary debate, parliamentary government. . . . It was the final fruit of the common man's repudiation of "the rascals." They wanted [Germany] purified of the politicians, of all the politicians. They wanted a representative leader in place of unrepresentative representatives. And Hitler, the pure man, the antipolitician, was the man, untainted by "politics," which was only a cloak for corruption.[24]

Replace Hitler's name with the name of any of the politicians who play the antipolitician game these days and the message sounds familiar. As in the 1930s, it is easy to see the implication of these antipolitician messages—that politicians have corrupted the liberal democratic system, and to fix the system, it is necessary to replace it with an authoritarian regime. Thus, in practice, populists are demolishing the institutional framework that has protected society against corruption. As happened in the 1920s and 1930s, these populists have been extremely successful in attracting votes. Afraid of what they see, voters demand a strong, authoritarian leader to take care of them. The authoritarian leaders prey on the population's fears. Their ultimate product is security, which they project with their self-assurance, their aggressiveness, and their authoritarianism. Such security, however, goes up in smoke once the essential liberties are surrendered to them.

This is not the first time that leaders of this kind have emerged in the United States. Senator Joseph McCarthy generated collective hysteria in the late 1940s and early 1950s by blaming all the country's problems on a communist conspiracy that he pretended to be uncovering. According to him, the conspirators had taken over strategic positions in the government, the media, the arts, and the private sector and were working to establish a communist government within a few years. He combined these accusations with a denunciation of supposed homosexuals, who he accused of being vulnerable to communist blackmail.

Of course, there had been a few cases of espionage discovered by the Federal Bureau of Investigation (FBI) in the years leading up to McCarthy's scourge—as happens in almost any year. He used these cases to give credence to the lists of people, which he drafted daily and presented to the media, who he claimed were part of a communist conspiracy. He inserted the names of important people in those lists, targeting, among others, perfectly patriotic people with social democratic convictions, such as the great composer Aaron Copland and actors like Orson Welles, Lena Horne, and Charlie Chaplin. None of the people he accused went to jail, but many saw their careers destroyed. While he lacked the political machinery to take advantage of the collective hysteria he created, McCarthy showed the power that generating fear can give to an unscrupulous individual.

McCarthy was an exception. Developed countries in the years between the end of World War II and the second decade of the twenty-first century were mostly free of authoritarianism. But many of today's political leaders share traits with those who appeared in Europe after World War I—with their vast egos, their attempts to unify fragmented societies by spurring hatred in the majority against a minority, their exploitation of xenophobia, their black-and-white worldview, their desire to create a utopia based on the past, and their disrespect for the rule of law and democratic institutions.

Many observers believe we are not using the right terms to refer to these so-called populists. In the words of Rob Riemen, a Dutch thinker:

> Wise men like Confucius and Socrates knew that to be able to understand something, you had to call it by its proper name. The term

populism, being the preferred description for a modern-day revolt of the masses, will not provide any meaningful understanding concerning that phenomenon. . . . The use of the term populist is only one more way to cultivate the denial that the ghost of fascism is haunting our societies again and to deny the fact that liberal democracies have turned into their opposite: mass democracies deprived of the spirit of democracy.[25]

Donald Trump, Vladimir Putin, the Le Pen family in France, Viktor Orbán of Hungary, Mateusz Morawiecki of Poland, Jair Bolsonaro of Brazil, and Narendra Modi of India—these leaders, all associated with the political right, practice this kind of populist rhetoric. Not all the dangers come from the right, however. The left has its share of those who propagate hatred for those they oppose. Adopting an antipolitical stance, they show the same disregard for institutions. As happened in the 1920s, populist resentment exists independent of ideology. David Frum describes it in this way:

The angriest and most pessimistic people in America are the people we used to call Middle Americans. . . . They aren't necessarily super-conservative. They often don't think in ideological terms at all. But they do strongly feel that life in this country used to be better for people like them—and they want that older country back.

You hear from people like them in many other democratic countries too. Across Europe, populist parties are delivering a message that combines defense of the welfare state with skepticism about immigration; that denounces the corruption of parliamentary democracy and also the risks of global capitalism. Some of these parties have a leftish flavor, like Italy's Five Star Movement. Some are rooted to the right of center, like the U.K. Independence Party. Some descend from neofascists, like France's National Front. Others trace their DNA to Communist parties, like Slovakia's governing Direction–Social Democracy.[26]

Der Spiegel, a prestigious German magazine, recently deemed that "societies appear to be radicalizing across the entire continent while the political center empties out."[27] As in the United States, the disappearance of the center is raising concerns about the feasibility of liberal democracies in Europe, too, in a spiral that recalls a long-gone past.

Wolfgang Storz, author of a study on right-wing populism published by the Otto Brenner Stiftung, a German foundation with ties to labor unions, has commented on the disconnection between traditional ideologies and emerging populist movements. He uses the term "cross-front" to refer to the latter, a term that was used in the 1920s to refer to the mixture of socialism and nationalism that eventually led to Nazism. Referring to this new cross-front, Storz has written:

> The division between traditionally leftist and traditionally rightist attitudes is disappearing. . . . The actors are increasingly positioning themselves outside the classic right-left schemata.[28]

The problem is deeper than individual leaders of the left or the right.[29] Certainly, as I mentioned before, these leaders do have an impact on the shape of the social order—the institutional setting, the direction of policy, the channeling of emotions. It is easy, however, to overstate their role. Ultimately, they respond to their constituencies. Ultimately, they—in the left as in the right—are the product of their times. What is worrying in the United States is that the authoritarian mode seems to be the voters' preferred one, independent of their political orientation. The country is in danger of succumbing to authoritarianism not because of politicians, populist or not; the population itself appears to *want* an authoritarian leader or regime.

The Catalyst

World War I was an event of such magnitude that it changed the world in all dimensions of life. Yet the ideas guiding those changes were not new. They had been around for many decades, and when the social order collapsed under the violence of the war, the unfeasible suddenly appeared feasible. The apparently invincible German, Austrian, and Russian autocracies, which had resisted the gradual emergence of democracy for a century, broke down, creating a huge political vacuum that was rapidly filled not with democratic ideas but with destructive ideologies that had originated in the previous century.

The war was a catalyst. It destroyed obstacles that had been preventing the most radical changes from taking place and caused them to become a very radical reality.

We still don't know how deeply the trauma of the pandemic will change our world, but we know that its effects will be drastic and will mark a watershed in our lives. State intervention in the behavior of society, for example, is increasing to unprecedented levels in liberal democracies, and justifiably so. Yet history has shown that mechanisms restricting freedom in times of crisis can be very difficult to roll back once they have been put in place and the population has become used to them. Also, fear has increased and people seem to be willing to exchange freedom for security.

After the crisis of World War I, the United States emerged with a profoundly isolationist attitude. A similar reaction to the COVID-19 crisis could increase government control of the economy and affect the direction of technological progress, not just in the United States but throughout the world. In fact, the ghosts we have identified in this chapter could all be strengthened by the pandemic—just as happened a hundred years ago. We can't see the future, but we know that the effects of these ghosts will become even more relevant in the years to come as economic, political, and social instability grow as dangerously as they did in the 1930s.

ON THE BRINK

Of course, none of the current populists has reached the level of destructiveness of the old tyrants. But this was true in the 1920s as well. The populist leaders of the early twentieth century chose their victims early. Hitler never hid his hatred for the Jews, but initially, when he was not in power, he only attacked them verbally. Many people thought his anti-Semitism was a political pose that would not affect his policies if he assumed power. Many Europeans and Americans actually admired Hitler and Mussolini, thinking that their aggressive verbosity was just a device to defeat communism, and nothing else. But, of course, Hitler's attacks on the Jews became nightmarishly real, as the Nazis destroyed Jewish homes and businesses, forced them into exile, escalated violence against them, and finally killed them in the death camps. Nazi leaders turned from apparently harmless populists into the terrible monsters they became in the persecution of the minority they had chosen to destroy.

But these leaders in fact never changed. Those today who abuse minorities do not intend to inflict actual violence, but the damage is done; such abuse dehumanizes the members of the minority, which in turn makes it easier for the majorities to commit crimes against them, or at least to see as normal their degradation—as has happened in the separation of Latino families asking for asylum and with enclosing children in cages and the other terrible conditions in which they are kept. Sadly, if people see others treated like animals, they start to think of them as "other."

Writing about the terrible bloodshed of the French Revolution, Simon Schama has said:

> Historians are also much given to distinguishing between "verbal" violence and the real thing. . . . But the history [of the Revolution] suggests in fact a direct connection between all that orchestrated or spontaneous screaming for blood and its copious shedding. It contributed greatly to the complete dehumanization of those who became victims. . . . Humiliation and abuse, then, were not just Jacobin fun and games; they were the prologues to killing.[30]

It is alarming that framing groups as criminals seems to be working; it was one of the main campaign themes of Trump's successful 2016 run for the presidency. Left-wing extremism is increasing, and Jews and other religious minorities are being hit with real violence. This ghost is real.

The return of these ghosts is part of a response to the strains of a technological transformation, not evidence of a failure of liberal democracy or capitalism. The fact that the similarities are all related to the period that preceded the worst tragedies of the twentieth century is an ominous warning that a period of extraordinary divisiveness like ours, some of it resulting from the natural effects of a technological transformation and some of it from the incitement of populist leaders, may evolve into devastating episodes. With growing doubts about liberal democracy, this would leave us exposed to unthinkable destructiveness.

Discarding liberal democracy in the belief that doing so will solve these problems would be a tragedy. The only solution to our structural problems, as I will argue in the chapters to come, is to increase the flexibility of our society, and liberal democracy is the most flexible of all social orders.

3

THE ECONOMIC
EFFECTS OF CHANGE

No single thing abides, but all things flow.
Figment to figment clings; the things thus grow
until we know and name them. By degrees
they melt, and are no more the things we know.

Lucretius

FAR FROM EQUILIBRIUM

Simply by being invented, new technologies prefigure new realities and define a new direction for progress, promising success to some and failure to others—as when the invention of tractors prefigured an economy in which many agricultural workers would be redundant years later and would have to migrate to the cities, or when the establishment of Amazon in 1994 prefigured a new world in which many retailers would find their markets dramatically diminished within a couple of decades. Thus, these inventions leave society far from equilibrium—with too many agricultural workers or too many traditional retailers. As societies rush toward the new equilibrium, they experience drastic structural transformations that strain and often break the fundamental elements of social order. This happened during the industrial revolution and is happening today with the connectivity revolution. The economist Joseph Schumpeter called this process of development one of "creative destruction," referring to how specific technologies or products alter the economic landscape. But the destruction also extends to the social order.[31]

The introduction of new technologies that will prove highly beneficial to society also causes serious problems of adjustment. The descendants of the agricultural workers who found no jobs in the new, industrialized agriculture of the nineteenth century and had to emigrate to urban areas or to foreign countries, learning new skills and customs, are, for the most part, now quite affluent. The countries that went through this transformation with so much pain are today much richer than they were when the changes started. The pains come from the transformation, from the change, not from capitalism and liberal democracy.

For most of the 2010s, we were economically far from equilibrium in the three dimensions that Marx mentioned as the killers of capitalism: inequality, instability, and the long-term rate of growth of employment and production. Two of these problems seemed to have been solved by the late winter of 2019–2020, just before the arrival of the pandemic. Income distribution remained as skewed as in the previous two decades, most probably worse. Yet the economy seemed stable, employment was at record highs, and production was satisfactory. Of course, with the arrival of the pandemic, the three problems returned with a vengeance.

INEQUALITY

Inequality and Poverty

The growing inequality of wealth and income has become a hot topic in the last few years in the United States, attracting both moral condemnation and radical recommendations aiming at reversing it. We frequently read how the top 1 percent of the US population controls 40 percent of the country's wealth and 25 percent of its income. Many people interpret these figures as proof that the 1 percent is exploiting the rest of society. For them, inequality results only from exploitation.

It can be argued that what matters is not how the pie is divided but the size of the pieces apportioned to each member of society. For example, one individual may have a thousandth of the income of his next-door neighbor but still be a very rich person if the neighbor's income is $1 billion a year. But the same ratio would reflect a social problem if the richest neighbor had an income of $100,000, which would leave the poorer neighbor with an income of just $1,000 a year. The problem would be the poverty, not the inequality.

In a 2011 *Vanity Fair* article and in his book *The Price of Inequality,* Nobel Prize winner Joseph Stiglitz argues that inequality is intrinsically bad for four reasons.[32] First, he says that growing inequality is the flip side of shrinking opportunity. Second, he adds that many of the distortions that lead to inequality—such as those associated with monopoly power and preferential tax treatment for special interests—undermine the efficiency of the economy. Third, he argues that inequality blocks the "collective actions" that are needed in a modern economy—meaning investment in infrastructure, education, and technology. Fourth, he thinks that, because of the increased concentration of income, the majority of the population is unable to afford an education, leading to their further impoverishment, which in turn makes it harder to get educated until, one can assume, the United States would fall into general misery.

Stiglitz's arguments are weak. In the first place, growing inequality is most frequently the flip side of growing, not shrinking, opportunity. In fact, inequality is the mechanism through which the market generates and spreads innovation, which in turn generates opportunities for millions of individuals. Every innovation initially generates inequality in income as its inventors exploit it commercially, becoming richer than the average. This inequality attracts new innovators, as well as imitators, rapidly spreading the initial innovation. In this way, inequality generates many new opportunities.

In fact, an increase in inequality is frequently the price you pay for the reduction of poverty. The creation of enterprises where none existed naturally leads to an increase in inequality as a result of the differentiation of incomes between owners, executives, and workers. But the creation of enterprises also increases the community's income and those of the poorest workers. The industrialization of China is a good example because we can track the increase in inequality as poverty fell at the turn of the twenty-first century (Figure 1).

Stiglitz's second argument, that many of the distortions that lead to inequality, such as monopoly power and tax privileges, undermine the efficiency of the economy, is not based on solid evidence. Differences in income as wide as those observed cannot be caused by differences in taxes. Regarding monopolistic lack of competition, the chain of causation goes in the opposite direction: inequality leads to more, not less, competition, and more competition leads to less inequality.

Many studies have come to this conclusion. In a paper presented at the Jackson Hole 2018 world meeting of central bank heads, John

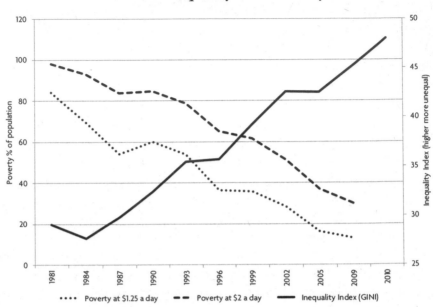

Figure 1
China: Inequality and Poverty

Source of basic data: World Databank, World Bank.

Van Reenen addressed the question of whether "the increasing gap between large and small firms reflects an increase in market power due to a reduction in competition arising (for example) from weakened anti-trust enforcement." He concluded the opposite:

> Although such arguments over rising market power from lax anti-trust enforcement should be taken seriously, I suggest a more nuanced view. There are other explanations of the increasing differences that do not rest on a generalized fall in product market competition. Indeed, an equally strong case could be made that the forces of globalization and new technologies have changed the nature of competition without necessarily diminishing it across the board.[33]

Stiglitz's third argument, connecting lack of investment in infrastructure, education, and technology with income inequality, is far-fetched. The economic influence of the so-called robber barons of the Gilded Age (J. P. Morgan, Andrew Carnegie, John D. Rockefeller, and others) was unparalleled. This period certainly created enormous wealth for a small number of barons, but it was also a time of unprecedented technological, social, and economic progress, much of it funded by this small wealthy class. The improvements in education and health during this era helped propel the United States to become a leading world power.

The fourth argument, the sinking hole of inequality leading to less education and more inequality, touches on a real problem. The growing volume of debt that young Americans are taking on to attend college sometimes does not translate into enhanced capacity to generate income. Although very important, this problem is not attributable to the overall distribution of income in the United States, and resolving it does not require carrying out a general redistribution of income at the national level. It requires giving it priority and forming a specialized task force with well-defined terms of reference.

Inequality and Technology

The widening inequality of income distribution in the nineteenth century convinced Marx that capitalism inherently increased income inequality indefinitely. History proved him wrong. In the twentieth century, income inequality did not increase uniformly. It increased, then declined, then increased again. This is not the behavior of a system that intrinsically tends to inequality; it is evidence of a system that is experiencing great change and reacting to it.

This variability attracted the attention of Nobel Prize winner Simon Kuznets. In his 1955 paper "Economic Growth and Income Distribution," he noted that the distribution of income in industrializing societies became more concentrated during the peak years of the industrial revolution and then became less concentrated so that inequality first increased and then decreased. He thought this was the logical result of the different speeds at which different groups in society adjusted to a profitable innovation.[34]

If everyone took advantage of the innovation at the same time, income distribution would not change because everybody's income would increase simultaneously. If some individuals took advantage of it first while the others lagged behind them, the income distribution would become skewed because, for a while, the pioneers would earn more than those left behind. At the end of the process, however, everyone would have increased their income, and the distribution would be as similar to what it was before the innovation was introduced. Plotting this trend on a graph creates an inverted U, which is called the Kuznets curve. Kuznets built and validated this curve with data from the previous century and a half.

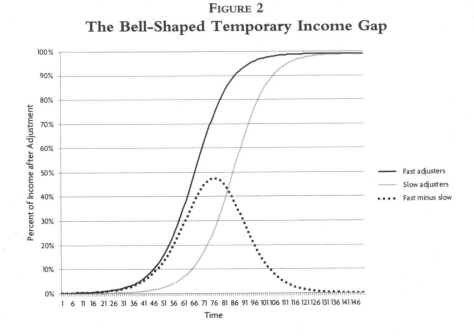

Figure 2
The Bell-Shaped Temporary Income Gap

Figure 2 depicts the adjustment of two individuals to an innovation. The horizontal axis measures time, and the vertical axis measures income. The evolution of the income of each individual is represented by a curve with the shape of elongated letters S in the upper part of the graph. This curve, called the logistic curve, is widely used to illustrate what happens through time when a system, any system, goes from one state to another.

At point zero in time, a radical innovation is invented. The invention is so radical that it allows each of the individuals to double their income if each has taken full advantage of the new technology. Initially nothing happens because people do not immediately realize the presence of the new opportunities. Then, one of the individuals, Alice, begins to master the new technology, and, as she does so, her income starts to increase. Her income increases slowly at first, but as Alice improves her mastery, her income grows ever faster until she reaches a point at which improvements in her ability result in slower increases in her income because she already knows almost everything that can be known about the new technology. Alice doubles her income around the 60 point of the horizontal axis. Her colleague, Bob, however, is much slower. He starts the adjustment later and he takes longer to master the technology, so he doesn't double his income until he hits 100.

The dotted curve at the bottom of the figure represents the difference between the incomes of Alice and Bob. Such difference generates a gap that will initially increase quickly, then will level off and finally decline as the slow adjusters catch up with the opportunities opened up by the new technologies. This is the Kuznets curve.

The Adjustment to International Inequality

How close to reality is Kuznets's idea? The reversal of trends that Kuznets noted can be observed in the evolution of both the international and the domestic distributions of income of industrializing countries during the industrial revolution.

We can start with the international dimension. Britain was the first industrial country, and it was the only one that could be classified in that category for several decades. As a result, British income per capita leaped ahead of those of other countries. Eventually, almost a century later, these other countries caught up with Britain, equaling or exceeding its income per capita.

Figure 3 displays the advantage of income per capita that Britain had over France, the Netherlands, Sweden, and Germany from 1800 to 1980. For instance, the British advantage over Germany increased from 421 international dollars per year in 1820 to 1,646 in 1910. It then declined to 909 in 1930 as Germany industrialized, and it declined to negative figures from 1980 on, which means that the German income per capita became greater than Britain's in those years. The curves have the same inverted-U shape of the Kuznets curve for all the countries. As predicted by Kuznets, inequality went up and then down as the technological advantage of Britain first increased and then decreased.

Seeing this effect in a European context is very useful because it puts in perspective the claims that the inequalities in income distribution are automatically a symptom of economic exploitation. The fact that the incomes of Britain increased well over those of Germany, France, Sweden, and the Netherlands during the nineteenth century cannot seriously be taken as a proof that Britain exploited those countries. It was not a failure of capitalism, either. It was not the result of the uncontrollable greed of the British. It was just the natural effect of innovation on the distribution of income.

This effect was also the cause of what is called the great divergence—the differentiation of the incomes of industrialized and developing

Catching Up with Britain: Income Per Capita Advantages of Britain over France, Germany, the Netherlands, and Sweden[35]

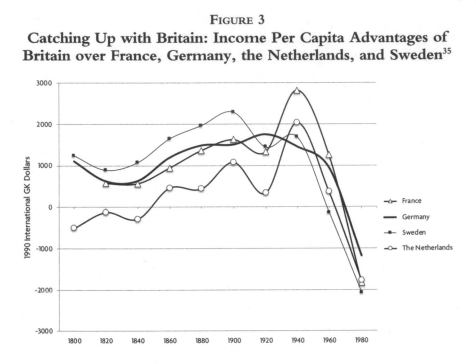

Source: Author with data from Maddison Project, http://www.ggdc.net/maddison/maddison-project/home.htm.

countries—which became more permanent than it did when comparing European countries. Figure 4 shows how the worldwide cycle of adjustment to the industrial revolution created the great divergence as the West's share of global income went up from 20 percent in 1800 to just below 60 percent in 1950. It then declined as developing countries began to learn how to take advantage of industrial technologies. This equalization, the reversal of the great divergence, is what now is called the great convergence.[36] Divergence and convergence together form another Kuznets curve.

The graph in Figure 4 suggests the opposite of what many people think is the failure of capitalism. The current trend is not toward a skewing of global income distribution but instead toward its equalization. The shifts in income distribution at this level are closing a two-centuries-long period of adjustment. From the point of view of the workers in developed countries now being displaced by this equalizing trend, what they see is that their advantage over their counterparts in the developing countries is narrowing and that the difference

Figure 4

Going Back to Normal: Western Developed Countries Gaining an Advantage over the Rest of the World and Then Losing It

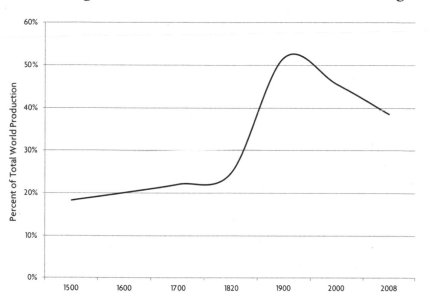

Source: Author with data from Maddison Project, http://www.ggdc.net/maddison/maddison-project/home.htm.

between their wages and those of the more educated workers in their countries is widening.

This disruption, the introduction of inequalities that did not exist just a few years before, creates real political problems. The people left behind see an increase in inequality in their own countries that for them is a disruption of what they think is the natural order of things. For them, the competition of the newly industrializing countries is eroding their lifestyles. And they are right. Of course, they did not perceive the movement of income and jobs in the opposite direction that took place during the upswing of the Kuznets curve in the early stages of the industrial revolution. Also, they do not realize that the average wage of their countries has increased way beyond the level that allows for profitable operations in the activities that are migrating toward the developing countries. In these circumstances, it is very easy to think that somehow the system is not working and that the government and politicians are not protecting the interests of American citizens.

Domestic Inequality

The different speeds of adjustment to the industrial revolution also affected the domestic income distribution of individual countries. Figure 5 shows how the income shares of the top 1 percent of income earners in the United States first increased from 1910 to 1928 and then declined to a nadir in the 1970s, delineating an inverted U— that is, a Kuznets curve. The first ascending portion of the curve coincides with the innovations of the second stage of the industrial revolution, while the decline leads to the end of the revolution at the end of World War II, when the advanced countries settled into the midcentury industrial age and the entire population had adjusted to the industrial economy. This neatly fit Kuznets's hypothesis up to the mid-twentieth century.[37]

Figure 5 also shows that, after falling from the early 1930s to the late 1970s, the share of income for the richest people in the United States began to increase again, along with the beginning of the connectivity revolution. As in Marx's time, many people are seeing this increase as a symptom that capitalism has an inherent trend to skew income distribution indefinitely. However, it seems to be the first part of the Kuznets curve of a new period of adjustment to a new cycle of innovations.

The fact that these fluctuations are linked to innovation is confirmed by another fact exposed in the figure. The lower curve in the figure shows the share of total income of the top 1 percent that remains after subtracting capital gains. That is, this lower curve represents income that is attributable to labor activities exclusively. As is evident in the graph, the labor income of the top 1 percent of the population makes for most of the total income of the group.

Thus, in the United States, the share of the top 1 percent is not determined primarily by the rents of their capital but instead by the returns on their work. The same is true of the top 0.1 and the top 10 percent.[38] And as shown in the figure, this is true not just for one point in time. It has been true for the last one hundred years, throughout the wavelike fluctuations first associated with the industrial revolution and then with the connectivity revolution.

The correlation of the two lines is such that Thomas Piketty, the creator of these graphs, wrote the following about the United States:

> One might also call this a "society of superstars" (or perhaps "super-managers," a somewhat different characterization). In other words,

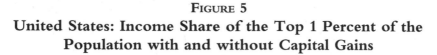

FIGURE 5

United States: Income Share of the Top 1 Percent of the Population with and without Capital Gains

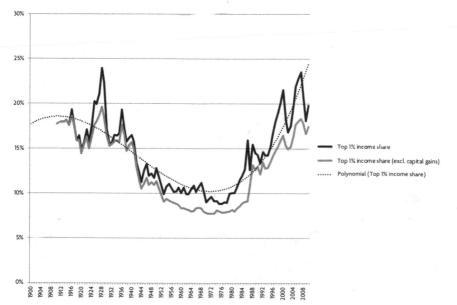

Source: Thomas Piketty, *Capital in the Twenty-First Century,* Cambridge, MA: Harvard University Press, 2014, p. 300, piketty.pse.ens.fr/capital21c.

this is a very inegalitarian society, but one in which the peak of the income hierarchy is dominated by very high incomes from labor rather than by inherited wealth.[39]

Piketty wrote his book as a scathing critic of capitalism. Remunerating the wages of creativity, however, could hardly be called a defect of capitalism.

Innovation and the Income Share of the Products of the Mind

A few examples illustrate how labor income has turned into wealth in our times. In 2012, Facebook bought Instagram for a whopping $1 billion. The latter, launched in 2010, had thirteen employees at the time it was sold. That equates to about $76 million per worker. Then in February 2014, Facebook bought WhatsApp for $19 billion. This company, founded in 2009, had fifty-five employees. That makes for $345 million per worker. The purchasing company, Facebook, created in 2004, has a market value of $153 billion with 6,818 employees.

That makes for $22 million per employee. Apple has $14 million per worker; Google, $10 million.

All these companies share a common feature: their market value is the result of pure thinking—a product of human capital. The value of the conventional capital goods owned by Instagram and WhatsApp at the time of their sale (computers, desks, cement, and bricks) was immaterial. What Facebook was purchasing was invisible software and access to the human capital that created it. Certainly, the people who produced this invisible wealth earned very good salaries and became extremely rich. But they became so rich because of their creativity.

These and many other companies have created a very large number of billionaires, a group that seems to be very fluid. According to *Forbes*, there were 1,810 billionaires in the world in 2016, with a net worth of $6.48 trillion, down from 7.05 in 2015. Of these, 198 were newcomers, while 221 had dropped out of the rankings. At this rate, the whole group could be replaced in ten years.[40] That is, as expected in a system that rewards creativity, the top of the heap is not a fixed group.

A similar process has been taking place in Britain. In the first Rich List published in 1989 by the *Sunday Times*, containing the thousand richest people in the country, just 43 percent of the entries had made their money themselves. The rest of them had inherited their wealth, and many of them were titled. In 2018, 94 percent had built their own fortunes. For the first time in history, the richest person in Britain was a self-made entrepreneur—Jim Ratcliffe, the founder of the chemical giant Ineos. He was raised in public housing. Tony Pidgley, an orphan who lived his early years in an abandoned railway carriage, is also among the richest, with a net worth of 310 million pounds. There are 141 women in the list, compared to just nine in 1989, and 86 on the list were from ethnic minorities, compared to 25 in 1989. Overall, only 5.7 percent of the 2018 list represents wealth passed from one generation to the next. According to the *Sunday Times*, "perhaps the most striking force blowing through the Rich List is technology."[41] Britain has also become a society of superstars in the midst of the new technological revolution.

As Massachusetts Institute of Technology (MIT) professor David Autor has concluded, "Rising inequality is mostly (not entirely) about skills. [There is] still a meritocracy rather than a pure plutocracy. . . . Rising skill returns largely due to two forces: slowing supply of new college grads after 1980 [and] secularly rising demand for human expertise, creativity, adaptability."[42] Our age is not one of privilege and shrinking opportunity but of equalization of opportunity. The disruptions caused by new technologies are permitting highly talented individuals to emerge and show their aptitude in an environment that was previously dominated by heavy business structures. The problem is not that opportunities are diminishing among the unskilled but that there are unskilled people in the most sophisticated economy in the world. The solution is to invest in their education, not try to reward the lack of skills.

Inequality and Political Power

Inequality is a complex phenomenon that cannot be attributed to exploitation, at least not in developed countries. It is frequently the result of progress, and in these cases, it becomes a mechanism to transmit creativity and efficient practices. Inequality works to eliminate itself by motivating emulation and competition. This is an essential fact in the dynamics of adjustment to change. However, there is one potentially damaging effect of the skewed income distribution that critics rarely mention, at least explicitly: beyond a certain limit, the economic power of the very rich can be transformed into political control, eroding the separation of economic and political powers that is essential for the functioning of liberal democracy. Such control may be exerted in many ways, from intensive lobbying to other unethical practices.

This is a grave problem. There is an important precedent to it. The Gilded Age had a distribution of income as skewed as that of today, which is why Teddy Roosevelt intervened to reduce the economic power of the great enterprises of the time. His intervention, which was quite effective, was not directed at killing capitalism but at keeping economic and political power separate in the United States. This is a classic example of how government intervention, which many free-market advocates suggest is always a bad thing, can be necessary and good.

THE GROWTH OF PRODUCTION AND EMPLOYMENT

Technological transformations also tend to create dips in the rate of growth of production and employment as a result of the "creative destruction" that comes along with technological change. When a new product is invented, it displaces an old one that played the same role, as when the automobile replaced the horse carriage. When this change happened, the economy both grew because it was producing autos and declined because it was producing lower numbers of horse carriages. In the same way, parts of the economy decline while others grow when new production techniques replace old ones, turning old production facilities and the people who worked them obsolete.

As I already noted, Joseph Schumpeter coined the expression "creative destruction" to describe this process. He thought it was an exclusive characteristic of capitalism. It is, in fact, a feature of any creative process. If a better method of production is discovered in a socialist economy and the government decides to implement it, the same process of creative destruction would take place as when the person deciding the replacement is the owner of a firm in a capitalist economy.[43]

Eventually, industrialized economies were able to absorb working forces much larger than those that existed during the first decades of the industrial revolution. The new jobs produced higher value and, as a result, they paid higher wages. But the generation of new jobs tended to be slower than the elimination of the old, preindustrial ones. The creation of new jobs depended on the emergence of new activities, which took much longer than the destruction of the old ones. For instance, the fall in agricultural jobs was compensated for not just by emerging industries but also by new services, which took a long time to be developed. This lag created a natural drag on overall job creation. The same happened with the growth of production, which was the net of the new one and the replaced old one.

Through this process, change has an impact on employment creation and destruction. The innovations that gave birth to the connectivity revolution are naturally leading to the creation of an economy where knowledge and the ability to coordinate complex tasks at a distance are the main sources of wealth. This will in time transform society, eliminating grueling industrial jobs while opening the opportunity for everybody to work and create value in healthy environments that resemble university campuses. The transition will be painful. It may take the form of a recession or a series of recessions. In fact, the Great Recession was in part an adjustment of the labor market to a more knowledge-based economy, as shown in Figure 6. Most likely, the effects of the COVID-19 in the economic structure will be similar in its direction—employment shifting toward more knowledge—but stronger in their impact.

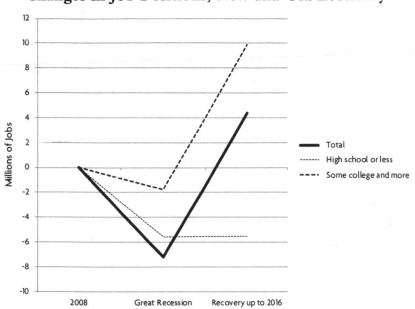

FIGURE 6
Changes in Job Positions, New and Old Economy

Source: Anthony P. Carnevale, Tamara Jayasundera, and Artem Gulish, *America's Divided Recovery: College Haves and Have-Nots,* Washington, DC: Georgetown University, 2016. https://cew.georgetown.edu/wp-content/uploads/Americas-Divided-Recovery-web.pdf.

From 2008 to 2016, people with at least some college education moved into 9.9 million jobs, while there was a loss of 5.5 million positions for people with a high school education or less. As a result, while the net job creation increase was 4.4 million, the total for the college-educated workforce was much larger. Thus, the Great Recession revealed a drastic adjustment of the economy: an increase in the demand for educated workers and an equally drastic contraction for unskilled workers.

The restructuring of the labor market that took place during the Great Recession was a continuation of a trend that had started well before. Data produced by the Hamilton Project shows how income in the United States changed for different educational groups from 1990 to 2013 in direct relationship to education. The two extremes of the distribution were men with no high school diploma, who lost 20 percent of their salaries over the period, and women with higher education, who gained 21 percent.[44] All other categories are in between these numbers, improving in proportion to education. In the member countries of the

Organisation for Economic Co-operation and Development (OECD), the share of workers with higher education increased from 22 percent in 2000 to 40 percent today.[45]

The adjustment that took place during the Great Recession seemed to have ended in early 2020. The unemployment rate had fallen to record lows, not just in the United States (3.6 percent) but also throughout the developed world. A 2019 article in the *Economist* described the situation in this way:

> "Unemployment numbers best in 51 years. Wow!" tweeted Donald Trump, America's president, last month. Theresa May, the British prime minister, bragged in February that "employment is at a near-record high and unemployment at a near-record low." The month before, Scott Morrison, Australia's prime minister, crowed that "more than 730 jobs were created every day last year under our government." Around the same time his Japanese counterpart, Shinzo Abe, let it be known that "the employment rate for young people is at a level surpassing all previous records." . . . Across the OECD a jobs bonanza is under way. In the past five years the group has added 43m jobs . . . in 2018, the employment rate among people of working age was the highest ever in Britain, Canada, Germany, Australia and 22 other OECD countries.[46]

In most of these countries, the jobs boom has included high- and low-skilled jobs, giving credence to the expression that a rising tide lifts all boats. As expected of the technological transformation, however, the boom has been much bigger for the highly skilled. Furthermore, the benefits of technological transformation were already kicking in. In the ten years to 2016, the cost of filling a vacancy fell by 80 percent in real terms as a result of the use of the internet.[47]

Of course, the 2008 crisis had several immediate causes, mainly excessively expansionary fiscal and monetary policies, a drastic relaxation of financial markets supervision, and a politically motivated drive to give homes to the poor that were being left behind in the transformation. But it is also clear that what we saw in the first two decades of the twenty-first century was a huge adjustment of the American economy to powerful pressures that the new technological revolution had been building up in the previous decades. But then, as the supply of more educated workers went up, the labor market began to grow again, and quite solidly. This is what Kuznets would have predicted. Plotting what happened in the labor market would produce a Kuznets curve. In fact, Figure 6 is an inverted Kuznets curve.

In *The Great Depression: Delayed Recovery and Economic Change in America, 1929–1939,* Michael A. Bernstein, now the provost of Stony Brook University, shows how the United States would have experienced very high rates of unemployment, even if no macroeconomic problems existed, during the 1930s, because of the same process we see in Figure 6—some sectors losing jobs while others increasing them, but not at the same time, separated at times by an entire decade. His findings confirm the idea that the Great Depression was part of the adjustment to the industrial revolution, very much like the Great Recession has been part of ours.[48] The same is going to happen with the COVID-19 pandemic.

INSTABILITY

Financial crises were known before the industrial revolution, but they were rare. They were caused by swindles and by the deflation of hysterical bubbles (as when people in Holland thought that the price of tulips would increase forever in the seventeenth century and paid a fortune for a single tulip plant). As shown in Figure 7, during the industrial revolution, crises became very common when change became part of daily life. Throughout this period, they occurred approximately every ten years. Like the other problems associated with change, however, they disappeared after the 1930s, and reappeared only eighty years later, when the connectivity revolution was emerging.

Technological change creates financial crisis and instability because it renders obsolete physical and human capital. Without income, owners of superseded physical capital and workers with obsolete skills cannot service their obligations, thus weakening the financial institutions supporting them. Often, people in these circumstances borrow even more to make their payments, worsening their finances until something happens that exposes their overborrowing and brings down the financial system. This happened periodically during the industrial revolution. The economic crisis that accompanied the COVID-19 pandemic was not started via such a mechanism, but the fact that, in response to it, the economy moved more quickly toward modern means of production—the increased use of electronic connectivity for work and commerce, for example— shows that, as in the classical crises, this one has served to accelerate technological change.

FIGURE 7

The United States: Financial Crises and Gross Domestic Product (GDP) Growth Rates, 1790–2016

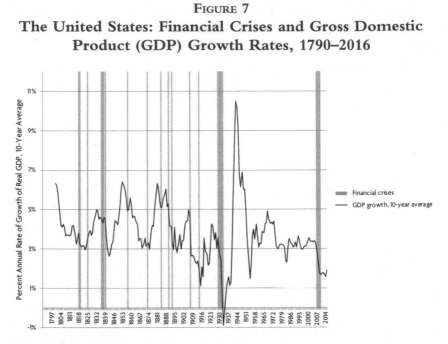

Source: Reinhart, Camen M., and Kenneth S. Rogoff, *From Financial Crash to Debt Crisis,* NBER Working Paper 15795, March 2010.

Note: The graph does not include the savings and loan crisis that occurred from 1984 to 1990 because it did not affect the banking system and the rate of growth of the economy.

Like the worsening of income distribution, the tendency to insta-bility is part of a process of change, not a feature of capitalism. Of course, crises can be triggered by other causes, including actions taken by governments and central banks to provide artificial stimuli for the growth of the economy.

POVERTY

Contrary to the suggestion, made by many, that globalization has increased poverty in the last few decades, the poverty rate (the number of poor people divided by total population) had not increased in the United States prior to the arrival of the pandemic. In the United States, this index fluctuated with economic cycles since the early 1990s. However, it didn't show a trend to increase from cycle to cycle. Data on European countries did not show any worsening of the poverty rate either.[49] And poverty in the developing countries had diminished.[50]

Thus, prior to COVID-19, globalization was accompanied by a decline in poverty in the world as a whole. As has been widely documented, up to the beginning of 2020 we were living through the best period in history in terms of the population's economic well-being. All indicators of welfare improved spectacularly in the last two centuries and have kept on improving in the first two decades of the twenty-first century.[51] Of course, the pandemic has undone much of that improvement, and it remains to be seen how liberal democracies will recover.

LEFT BEHIND

Even if the connectivity revolution is completely different from the industrial revolution in the direction of its progress, it is generating disturbances very much like those triggered by the latter. This is because these disturbances are not caused by the technologies themselves; they are the consequences of the waves of change that the two revolutions triggered.

Of course, the fact that the Marx problems are not inherent to capitalism does not mean that these problems and their political consequences may not be deadly. The new technological transformation is concentrating its negative impact on a single group: the less educated and more vulnerable. This is a very serious problem. Most other groups are threatened by one of the effects of the transformation but get benefits from the others. This group, however, is threatened by all of them. Their prospects are limited in this emerging knowledge society. Their incomes are being diminished by the transition to more skill-intensive methods of production, and in many cases robots are taking their jobs. Unemployment is hitting them savagely, and financial crises can only reduce the number of jobs available to them. Their fate has been so sharply defined that they have acquired a collective name in the literature: those left behind. They include people in both the developed and developing countries.

The concentration of the cost of the adjustment in this particular group bodes ill for the social and political stability of the world at large for several reasons. First, the group that is losing its income includes many millions of people. Second, this group's loss of income is adding to the social and political divisiveness now overtaking the developed countries. Third, the magnitude of its problems is spurring strong political pressures that, if not addressed properly, will play in favor of populist remedies. As the history of the industrial revolution clearly shows, these remedies may lead to results much worse than the infirmities themselves, as well as to more divisiveness and discontent. Fourth, the lack of adjustment for those left behind creates a serious economic problem for the rest of the population because knowledge embedded in the population is becoming the most important factor of production in the new connected economy.

So leaving people behind is not a matter of lack of solidarity. It is negligence, a failure to invest in the creation of productive capacity. In fact, the long period of high unemployment that accompanied the Great Recession witnessed a dearth of skilled workers, which, if available, would have reduced the rate of unemployment and increased the rate of growth of the economy, benefiting all businesses. Looking at this from a different point of view, unskilled workers can only work in low-value-added activities. The lack of an educated workforce can become a bottleneck in the creation of more wealth in high-value-added production, as is happening in the market for software programmers and other professionals all over the world. Keeping the country competitive requires investing in the education of those left behind.

FAR AWAY

The structural problems that Marx thought were the nemesis of capitalism are actually the result of being far away from equilibrium in the process of transformation. Coming back to equilibrium will be a very long process. The technology needed to establish Amazon was invented a long time ago. When Amazon was established in the 1990s, the enormous changes that its operation brought about in the commercialization of goods and services were still far in the future, although already written on the wall. So were the social implications of these changes.

Changes similar to those that led to the creation of Amazon have been taking place over the last several decades. This makes it reasonable to believe that other changes, as momentous as the founding of Amazon, have also been taking place, just waiting to grow and to create more disruptions than those we have contemplated in the last few years. The process is likely to accelerate because these disruptions escalate in exponential ways. We can reasonably suggest that the changes we have seen are just the tip of the iceberg. In fact, we will most probably never reach anything like what we could call equilibrium. The changes that we and the generations to follow will see will be astonishing and will require enormous capacity to adapt.

These changes demand flexibility, and liberal democracy is the most flexible social order. It is not an ideology or a specific set of policies to follow in all circumstances, but it is a set of rules to confront the inscrutable future, design the policies that seem to be the best, and correct them when they prove wrong while maintaining democracy and the rule of rights. To keep these rules operative, we must open ourselves to new ideas and be ready to use them and the new technologies in the attainment of these objectives—including a thorough revision of the role of government in society. We must look at our problems dynamically, taking into account the long-term nature of these problems.

THE RED LINE

The best strategy to resolve the Marx problems and exorcise the ghosts they have awakened is to accelerate the process of adjustment by helping those left behind to take advantage of new technologies. We must make society flexible, which in turn requires intense and targeted education. Such a strategy would help close the income gap. In graphical terms, we should flatten the Kuznets curve and make it shorter. This would reduce instability as well as the damage done to employment by the obsolescence of human capital.

Such a strategy must be effected in the context of liberal democracy. Discarding liberal democracy would worsen the problem because it would increase the rigidity of the economy and thus the height and length of the Kuznets curves. But the costs of abandoning liberal democracy would be much worse than economic. The costs could include being sucked down the road of destructiveness that bled the twentieth century.

Such an assertion may seem exaggerated to people who think that there must be some middle point between liberal democracy and destructive tyranny. But a red line separates liberal democracy from tyranny: the priority given to democracy and the rule of rights. When this red line is crossed, the result is not a moderate hybrid of liberal democracy with a vertical regime but a slippery slope that eventually leads to destructiveness. And the main reason societies are led into this trap is resistance to change.

4

THE LEGITIMATION
OF DESTRUCTIVENESS

*I should like merely to understand how it happens that so many men,
so many villages, so many cities, so many nations, sometimes suffer
under a single tyrant who has no other power than the power they give
him; who is able to harm them only to the extent to which they have the
willingness to bear with him; who could do them absolutely no injury
unless they preferred to put up with him rather than contradict him.*

Étienne de la Boétie

PLAYING WITH FIRE

Donald Trump started his presidential campaign in June 2015 with a
speech in which he identified the culprits for what he thought was the
disastrous condition of the United States: Mexicans, Latinos, and immigrants in general. He asked:

> When do we beat Mexico at the border? They're laughing at us, at
> our stupidity. And now they are beating us economically. They are
> not our friend, believe me. But they're killing us economically. The
> U.S. has become a dumping ground for everybody else's problems.
> . . . When Mexico sends its people, they're not sending their best.
> They're not sending you. They're not sending you. They're sending
> people that have lots of problems, and they're bringing those prob-
> lems with us [*sic*]. They're bringing drugs. They're bringing crime.
> They're rapists. And some, I assume, are good people.[52]

The last sentence, the bland assertion that he assumed that some of the
Mexicans were good people, did not ameliorate the impact of the attack.

Up to that moment, immigration had been a source of concern, but it was not at the center of American politics. Even though racist and cultural discrimination had existed before, allocating moral features along with the color of the skin was considered a bad, divisive practice that privileged prejudice over reality. This speech, Trump's subsequent utterances, and many of his presidential actions changed that. Immigration and the presence in the country of previous immigrants of non-European stock became, in the perception of many Americans, the source of their problems.

Trump's actions have triggered reactions across the political spectrum, including extreme views on the left (which have been around for some time) that blame white, Eurocentric culture for exploiting the rest of the country economically, politically, and culturally. In many US universities, for example, students and professors have petitioned for the exclusion of works and even entire subjects produced by white men. Views on the left have often grown inflexible, fueling the culture wars that can sow hatred and vitriol. Such hatred reaches even the highest levels of partisan politics, as evidenced by the acrimonious battles between Democrats and Republicans over, for example, presidential nominations to the Supreme Court.

At the same time, attacks on Jews, which for decades after the end of World War II had been received with general opprobrium, have reappeared. These attacks have taken on an ominous trend and materialized into physical attacks, resulting in the death of many American Jews. Singling out one group as the culprit of all or most of our fundamental social problems is a political device aimed at gathering support within a confused society, one looking for someone to blame for the problems elicited by a fundamental transformation.

COLD-BLOODED DESTRUCTIVENESS

We know from history that countries that cannot control divisiveness and hatred can descend into a terrible destructiveness. Nazi and communist destructiveness was special in four respects. First, its magnitude was extraordinary by any standard of measure. A new word, *genocide*, had to be invented to describe the enormity of their crimes. Second, most of their victims were killed not in the spur of the moment but in sustained efforts aimed at wiping out entire races or social classes. These regimes had an institutional approach to murder that resulted in a chillingly efficient organization of destruction. Third, for their supporters, genocide was a legitimate step in their pursuit of a state of social perfection, the communist paradise or the Thousand-Year Reich of Nazism. Fourth, the victims had no possible escape. They were accused not of having done something but of being something—either Jews in the case of Nazism or bourgeois in the case of communism.

There was no precedent for this kind of destructiveness. It was an original contribution of the twentieth century to the annals of humankind. We must examine these tragedies to understand why they happened and to help ourselves avoid them in the future. As F. A. Hayek said in the 1940s of the Nazis:

> The problem is not why the Germans as such are vicious, which congenitally they are probably no more than other peoples, but to determine the circumstances which during the last seventy years have made possible the progressive growth and the ultimate victory of a particular set of ideas, and why in the end this victory has brought the most vicious elements among them to the top.[53]

Even if the destructiveness of Nazism was acknowledged almost from its inception, that of communism was ignored until very recently. The progression of violence that led to its formalization in the Soviet Union was glorified in many history books as the heroic struggle of the masses to liberate themselves from the poverty and political oppression that ruling minorities had imposed on them in the preindustrial age. Even people who think communism was a destructive ideology can believe that the waves of violence that culminated with the creation of the Soviet Union were aimed at liberation.

Many theories have been advanced to explain the inconvenient fact that these glorified struggles, like those of Nazism, ended with terrible explosions of destructiveness. According to these theories, communist destructiveness was:

- the unfortunate result of the chance appointment of serial killers as the leaders of the destructive regimes.
- natural in the bloody battles that the revolutionaries had to fight against the old regime, both to take over power and to defend it once they had succeeded.
- the consequence of the generalized poverty, or impoverishment, of the revolutionary society.
- a manifestation of resentment about wide income differences.
- the only course available to open the road for progress against the obstacles posed by the old regime.

I believe the destructiveness of the communists was similar to that of the Nazis and that, as in the case of the Nazis, it was not exercised by a mad dictator acting alone but by the entire society. Such violence was not necessary; was not aimed at bringing about freedom from poverty and political oppression; and, of course, did not attain these pretended aims. Contrary to what the above theories say, like Nazi-fascist violence, communist revolutionary violence was aimed at *stopping* the autonomous change that was moving society in the direction of progress and freedom. This violence was supported by the majority of the population, in processes that resembled the ancient art of witch hunting. The exorcised devils were precisely the social forces pressing for progress in trade, finance, and democracy. The similarity of Nazi and communist violence is such that their two kinds of destructiveness can be discussed as a single perversion.

The idea that communism and Nazi-fascism are expressions of the same destructiveness is by no means original to this book. Among the many authors who have noticed the similarity are Hannah Arendt, who analyzed both of them in her classic *The Origins of Totalitarianism,* and Friedrich Hayek, who has a chapter called "The Socialist Roots of Nazism" in his classic *The Road to Serfdom.* In a speech she gave in 1982 about the acts of communist repression in Poland, Susan Sontag said: "I would contend that what they illustrate is a truth that we should have understood a very long time ago: that Communism is Fascism—successful Fascism, if you will . . . I repeat, not only is Fascism (and overt military rule) the probable destiny of all Communist societies—especially when their populations are moved to revolt—but Communism is in itself a variant, the most successful variant, of Fascism."[54]

THE PRETEXTS

Pathological Leaders?

The idea that communist and Nazi destructiveness was attributable to certain mad individuals exclusively is quite popular. Socialists dismiss the genocide perpetrated in the 1920s and 1930s in Russia as the action of one single madman, Stalin. The Chinese blame their genocide on Mao. Many people blame Nazism on Hitler. And so on. These ideas have become conventional wisdom. But the view that the terrible destructiveness of the twentieth century was the result of the chance emergence of psychopaths as the leaders of the Soviet Union, Germany, China, and so many other countries is hard to accept.

There is no doubt that sinister characters like Lenin, Stalin, Hitler, and Mao played a crucial role in the establishment of a reign of terror in their respective countries and abroad. It is also true that the application of terror cannot be explained without reference to the personalities exercising it and that, by definition, a psychologically healthy person cannot apply terror. Pathological killers exist in all countries, but they do not become the national leaders. One person alone cannot kill millions of individuals. He needs the cooperation of the population. The terrible truth is that Lenin, Stalin, Hitler, Mao, and others like them were able to dominate their countries because their terror was consistent with what their compatriots wanted. There is no doubt that these societies suffered terrible pains in the rampages of destructiveness they engaged in. Yet they brought it upon themselves.

As expressed so well by the popular saying, all countries have the government they deserve. This includes not just the countries that elect their leaders democratically but also those that are governed by tyrants. This is so because the power of a government depends on people *believing* that it has power, which ultimately depends on its legitimacy. Legitimacy is best understood in the sense that, to be obeyed, commands must seem reasonable to the people, and they must be in harmony with their conception of how the world is and how it should be. Only when commands are in harmony with this conception will people obey them. This may happen in two ways. People living in societies where the social order is based on principles obey because the commands are consistent with the prevailing social values. In societies where social order is based on the savage logic of power, people obey because they think that everybody else will find the command reasonable and will obey; if they rebel, they will be easily caught and punished.

The mechanism also works in reverse, that is, when the commands are not legitimate in the minds of the population. The power of previously redoubtable governments can collapse in a moment—as in the case in the fall of the French Capetos, the Russian tsars, the crowned heads of Central Europe at the end of World War I, and the communist tyrannies in the Soviet Union and Eastern Europe in the early 1990s. In all these cases, regimes collapsed when people stopped believing that the government was legitimate and therefore powerful. There was no army, or police, or KGB large or strong enough to stop the collapse. In fact, as a manifestation of the dissolution of the power of the government, in all cases these repressive institutions stopped defending the regime, even to the point of joining those calling for its demise.

One of the most successful absolute rulers in history, Catherine the Great, empress of Russia from 1762 to 1796, expressed the same idea when somebody told her that she had the advantage of enjoying blind obedience from her subjects:

> It is not as easy as you think. In the first place, my orders would not be carried out unless they were the kind of orders which can be carried out; you know with what prudence and circumspection I act in the promulgation of my laws. I examine the circumstances, I take advice, I consult the enlightened part of the people, and in this way I find out what sort of effect my law will have. And when I am already convinced of general approval, then I issue my orders, and have the pleasure of observing what you call blind obedience. But believe me, they would not obey blindly when orders are not adapted to the customs, to the opinion of the people, and if I were to follow only my own wishes not thinking of the consequences.[55]

Legitimacy is essential for the workings of government in both societies based on principle and those based on naked power. If a government stops being legitimate in the minds of the population, it falls. And if tyranny remains legitimate even after the tyrant dies, other tyrants will take his place. The source of tyranny is not inside the tyrants or their thugs but inside the population. As G. A. Borgese wrote, commenting on the end of the Roman Republic:

> Yet Caesar died, and tyranny lived on. For the seat of tyranny was not in the heart of Caesar; it was in the heart of the Romans.[56]

Heinrich Jaenecke, a German military officer who fought in the Eastern and the Western fronts during World War II, expressed this idea in a different way:

> What was it actually that drove us to follow [Hitler] into the abyss like the children in the story of the Pied Piper? The puzzle is not Adolf Hitler. We are the puzzle.[57]

Alan Bullock, a distinguished historian of Nazi Germany, explained Hitler's success along similar lines:

> It is wrong to lay stress only on the element of coercion, and to ignore the degree to which Hitler commanded a genuine popular support in Germany. To suppose that the huge votes which he secured in his

plebiscites were solely, or even principally, due to the Gestapo and the concentration camps is to miss what Hitler knew so well, the immense attraction to the masses of force plus success.[58]

The roots of destructiveness are much deeper than the characters of Lenin, Hitler, Stalin, and Mao. The terrible events that characterized the communist and Nazi societies were possible only because destructiveness was legitimate in those societies.

So what happened in communist and Nazi-fascist countries to make destructiveness legitimate?

Revolutionary Fervor or Poverty?

The most common answer to this question is that destructiveness was natural to the bloody battles that the revolutionaries had to fight against the regimes that had kept them in poverty, both to take power and to defend it once they had succeeded. That is, destructiveness was necessary to open the road for progress against the obstacles posed by the remnants of the old regimes that resisted the revolution from the inside.

But the idea that massive violence erupted in the course of these bloody battles does not fit with the facts. Such violence was staged by the revolutionaries once in power, not by the old regimes or the revolutionary mobs during the struggle for power. Such mobs, acting on the spur of the moment, cause and suffer surprisingly low numbers of casualties.

The idea that cold-blooded destructiveness was prompted by generalized poverty does not fit with the facts either. In Europe, the worst manifestations of destructiveness took place in two completely different countries, Russia and Germany. While the former was one of the poorest countries, the latter was among the richest and most prosperous.

Most important, destructiveness was not needed to open the road to progress, as the myth of the French Revolution contends. The French revolutionaries portrayed the French Revolution as a breakthrough that accelerated progress throughout the world. Extending this myth to the Russian Revolution, communists succeeded in portraying Marxism as a "progressive" ideology, labeling "reactionary" any tendency opposing it.

The measure of progress is the extent to which societies become able to manage themselves in freedom. The industrial revolution tended to create a horizontal structure of social order, a new society that relied on networks of millions of free people spontaneously coordinating their economic and political activities rather than resting on the old vertical tyrannies of the preindustrial order. This new horizontal social order was and still is the road to progress, both because freedom is the only social objective that makes sense from the individual point of view and because it brings about creativity, the mother of material development.

The democratic regimes that met this criterion did not emerge from the kind of rampant destructiveness that characterized the French, Russian, and German processes. In fact, the American Revolution and the evolution of the British constitution, the midwives of modern democracy, were born out of remarkably peaceful processes. Many British historians mark the beginning of English democracy with the peaceful Glorious Revolution of 1689. The war of independence in the United States was not the result of domestic conflicts; rather, it was the result of the new country's desire to become independent from Britain. No domestic war was needed to write the US Constitution. There was little violence during the industrial revolution in Switzerland, the Nordic countries, Holland, Belgium, Australia, Canada, or New Zealand, all societies that, along with the United States and Britain, helped create the model of the modern industrial state.

Of course, the history of British social order includes not just the Glorious Revolution but also the civil wars that ended with the beheading of Charles I and the aspirational theocracy under Oliver Cromwell. It is equally impossible to detach the US Civil War from the development of US democracy. It cannot be denied that these wars were quite bloody or that they left long-lasting grudges among the population, particularly in the case of the United States.

What these cases have in common, however, is that their episodes of violence did not break the institutional setting that kept the social order in place, either physically or in terms of legitimacy. Cromwell fought against Parliament and established a military tyranny, but when he died his successors recognized the legitimacy of the old order.

In the United States, the institutions of both sides kept working throughout the Civil War, and each side maintained a remarkable level of internal social cohesion. Mobs carrying heads on pikes, à la the French Revolution, did not run through the streets. There were no reigns of terror.

The idea that mobs running amok are the source of democracy is a truly dangerous lie. They actually reinstall the conditions for the opposite. The French Revolution, which dethroned a king, resulted in the enthronement of an emperor a few years later. The social order built by

Napoleon was similar to that established in the seventeenth century by Louis XIV. It took France almost a hundred years to install the democracy that the revolution was supposed to have created. Before its arrival, the country went through the Restoration of Louis XVIII in 1814; a second revolution that put Philippe, duke of Orléans, on the throne in 1832; and a third revolution that established a republic in 1848, only to be converted into a second Napoleonic empire in 1851. It was only when Napoleon III fell in 1870 and Paris went under the terrible mob rule of the Commune that a sustainable democracy was established from outside Paris by a legitimate national government. This was almost a century after the original French Revolution. By this time, Britain, which had had no internal violence since the mid-seventeenth century and no revolutionary chaos since time immemorial, had become the world's most advanced industrial country and a much more democratic country than France.

The German Revolution that dislodged the kaiser in 1918 ended in 1933 with the elevation of a superkaiser, Adolf Hitler, who was much worse than the absolutist kaiser of the Second Reich. The Russian Revolution, which ended the autocratic Romanov dynasty in February 1917, established a new and more autocratic Bolshevik dynasty eight months later. In all these cases, the new regimes reasserted authoritarianism that had been the basis of the regimes they dethroned, only worse. That is, the revolutions returned to the past.

Seen from this perspective, it is clear that these revolutions dislodged the kings not because they were tyrants but because they were *incompetent* tyrants. People replaced them with more authoritarian ones—Napoleon, Lenin, Mussolini, Hitler, Mao, and many others. They were more efficient and bloodier tyrants than those they replaced.

Consistent with their focus on the past, communists and Nazi-fascists established economic structures like those that existed in the preindustrial era. To control the German economy, the Nazis went back to feudalism in agriculture and to guilds in industry. The Soviet communists established a state-controlled industrial system that resembled that created by Peter the Great in the early eighteenth century. Their state farms turned peasants into serfs who worked for almost nothing and left them a small plot on which to subsist—exactly as feudalism had.

The backwardness of the regimes that emerged from these revolutions was so catastrophic that one must recall Edmund Burke's words about the French Revolution:

By following those false lights, France has bought undisguised calamities at a higher price than any nation has purchased the most unequivocal blessings! France has bought poverty by crime! France has not sacrificed her virtue to her interest, but she has abandoned her interest, that she might prostitute her virtue![59]

Can we say, however, that the authoritarian regimes that emerged from these revolutions were manifestations of the will of the people? Certainly. They elicited strong popular support. Napoleon was the most popular of all French rulers. When Stalin died, Russians cried as if they were left orphan. Hitler was immensely popular in Nazi Germany. Germans fought for him fanatically and cooperated enthusiastically with his macabre racial policies. Six million people cannot be vilified, humiliated, dispossessed, deported, and killed without the knowledge and approval of many more millions of people who were their neighbors, workmates, acquaintances, friends, or soldiers watching the executions. The leaders of Napoleonic France, Soviet Russia, and Nazi Germany embodied what the population wanted. People revealed their preferences through them.

This postrevolutionary preference for the past is evidence of how the aim of each population was not opening the road for the new but filling a more urgent social need: reestablishing order in the midst of chaos. They did that by following leaders promising a return to an idealized past in the midst of a vortex of a social transformation caused by a technological revolution. Rather than bringing back harmony, this reaction created additional vortices that became increasingly chaotic and eventually led to a violent reassertion of order in a vertical way. Rather than accelerating the creation of a new social order, revolutions marked the collapse of the institutional settings of the old order. They were part of the past, not of the future.

This is how revolutions and destructiveness became legitimate: they provided a road out of chaos, a road that reestablished the vertical social order that had prevailed in prerevolutionary times. They provided a road out of divisiveness in societies that had become divisive as a result of the uncontrollable social and political changes elicited by a technological revolution.

FROM DIVISIVENESS TO DESTRUCTIVENESS

As perverse as it may seem, destructiveness was a socially unifying force in societies that had fallen into chaos; it renewed the social bonds that the industrial revolution had dissolved. Destructive ideologies provided a unifying force by splitting the world between "we"—the majority of destroyers—and "them"—the minority to be destroyed. To motivate the majority to attack the minority, the members of the majority invented narratives showing that the minority perversely blocked the majority's access to a paradise on earth. In this way, Hitler unified Aryan Germans by giving them a common objective of hatred: the Jews. The communists did exactly the same with the bourgeoisie.

These societies did not legitimize destructiveness because of the chance emergence of a pathological killer as their leader or as a result of poverty and oppression. Rather, they did so because destructiveness became an instrument to unify a society that was divisive because it was unable to manage change. To put it another way, the tendency to revolutionary violence, the dogmatism that accompanied it, and the destructiveness of subsequent regimes, emerged as a perverse cure for the social dissolution caused by rapid and uncontrollable change in societies too rigid to handle it in a harmonious way.

Nazi-fascist and communist countries got their revolutions and their subsequent periods of destructiveness not because their preindustrial societies were poor and oppressed but because they were divisive and therefore rigid. This is a sobering lesson for our times, when voters are turning toward vertical, authoritarian leaders who will increase the rigidity of their societies and who should make us ask ourselves: Why are some societies more divisive than others?

5

THE MAGNETIC FIELDS

[The] power of vested interests is vastly exaggerated compared with the gradual encroachment of ideas . . . soon or late, it is ideas, not vested interests, which are dangerous for good or evil.

John Maynard Keynes

THE FUNDAMENTAL CONTRADICTION OF SOCIETIES

What is the source of a culture's and a country's rigidity or flexibility? What does liberal democracy have that countries that fell into destructiveness don't have?

The answers to these questions are intimately related to the way different societies deal with the problem of harmonizing the potentially chaotic diversity of their citizens with the need for a uniform social order. They are related to the set of ideas that keep society functioning as a unified body while accommodating social change.

Societies are like magnetic fields, directing their individual members toward the achievement of a common goal. The features of this field—the nature of the magnetic ideas, their strength, and their direction—give societies their identity and character. A given society's basic ideas are not necessarily spelled out in their entirety; they may even be vague. Nevertheless, they produce what is called national character and very precise behavioral expectations. This is what is implied in statements like "This would never happen in England," "Everything works in Germany," or "This is the American way." Such statements are the result of comparing a potential course of action or an event with the collective mind's concept of itself.

As the famous Austrian psychologist Alfred Adler noted, collective ideas and the character they generate are ultimately rooted in the psychological needs of individuals, who define themselves in terms of their goals and their success in meeting them in lifelong pursuit. People see their lives as a unified act of performance, and the unity is provided by the pursuance of their ultimate goals. Self-respect comes from the level of our success in approaching these goals, and societies are fields attempting to establish common ground for the virtual infinity of individual goals.

Nations are so large and so diverse that societies are inherently unstable. They can attain equilibrium only dynamically. The goals of individuals can be known only after they have become manifest in actions, so social life is bound to be chaotic. At any given moment, millions of people are taking actions that will produce results only after some time, in some cases minutes, in some cases years or even decades. There is no certainty that the outcomes of those millions of actions will be even remotely consistent with one another when they come to being. And often, of course, the success of some people leads to the frustration of others.

Society can work only when the dispersion of these results, including the reactions of those who are frustrated or disgruntled, is reduced to acceptable levels, that is, when there is a minimum level of predictability that allows people to believe they will be able to reap the benefits of their actions. Institutions, which embody the complex systems of rules of behavior that frame societies, provide this minimum level of social predictability.

A social order needs permanent elements, characteristics that do not change even if everything else does. This set of permanent elements gives identity to a society and, more important, lends an essential predictability to its behavior. Growth and change need those permanent elements to flourish. Stable connections between the past and the future are essential to calculate if it is worth investing today to get benefits in the future. This is true not just in economic terms but in every other aspect of life. To build on top of an existing infrastructure makes sense only if such infrastructure is to last. What is the use of a social order if it is not stable, if one cannot be sure that it will last?

So we have a fundamental contradiction. To introduce predict-ability, institutions have to restrict individual behavior. At the same time, they have to allow for individual freedom to satisfy people's craving for growth. Resolving this contradiction is the key to creating a stable society.

Examining the solutions that different societies have found to this conflict between predictability and social change allows us to determine the difference between healthy absorption of rapid change and fields of behavior that produce an equilibrium that is unstable and destructive.

THE TWO RESPONSES

Societies can take one of two basic positions in their search for pre-dictability. The first gives governments the power to create a reality defined in material and concrete terms—everybody will have a house, everybody will have a job, nobody will be richer than you are, the company where you work will never fold—regardless of what you do. Such governments tell the population, *Your circumstances will be those we are promising you.* In this case, the stability that society needs to function in the long run is defined in a primary, objective material way. People in these societies derive their sense of stability from the attainment and permanence of the promised state of affairs. They consider their gov-ernment legitimate only to the extent to which it promises to keep this state of things in place and honor that promise. In these societies, the government defines outcomes, indicating to its citizens what they have to do, in what quantities, and using what technologies. In this way, the government provides the stability of outcomes that people demand.

The second position is less concerned with the outcomes of social behavior than with the rules of the game—that is, it aims to provide certainty in regard to individual rights. In these societies, change is accepted as long as these rights are preserved. They tell individuals, *Your circumstances may change, but your rights will always be preserved.* People in these societies derive their security from the certainty that their integrity as individuals will always be protected. For them, stability is defined as the protection of these rights.

In the first response, citizens demand entitlements; in the second, they demand rights. These two words are sometimes used synony-mously, but they are not synonyms. They are both promises by a gov-ernment. But there are three fundamental differences between them.

First, rights empower people to enjoy a certain measure of freedom, while entitlements establish a claim to *have* something. A right, for instance, promises the freedom to speak freely, while an entitlement is the claim on a government's promise to receive, for example, a house.

Second, rights are free of material costs, so granting them does not require transfers of money from one individual to another. In contrast, any entitlement, such as free medical care, can be turned into reality only if some resources are taken from those who have and given to those who do not have.

Third, as a consequence, rights protect individuals from government interference while entitlements require government interference to be delivered.

At their extreme, countries taking the first position are ready to sacrifice everything in the pursuit of their concrete objective. Individual rights take second priority when colliding with this objective. Conversely, prioritizing individual rights in case of conflict is also an exclusive proposition. If such a priority has been established, there is no given status, social dream, or ideal that can have more importance than those rights. The first position focuses on keeping stable the outcomes, while the second one focuses on keeping stable the processes; the first looks at the ends, the second at the means.

In practice, most societies are a blend of these two positions, with emphasis on one or the other. Of these two positions in the extreme, only communism has existed in reality. Under communist governments, citizens do not have rights, and what they receive materially from their government is a result of a *theoretical* entitlement because there is no relationship (again, theoretically) between what citizens receive from the state and what they contribute to society through their work. In Nazi-fascist regimes, citizens also depended on the will of the leader to receive anything material, and they had no rights.

Most modern societies have both rights and entitlements, and having the second does not necessarily make a society rigid or prone to fall victim to destructive regimes. In fact, a society with entitlements may be more flexible than one without them. As we discussed in Chapter 3, the basic economic source of a society's rigidity in regard to the disruptions of innovations is the different speeds of adjustments of different citizens—a difference that is largely attributable to differences in education. So a society with universal education can be more flexible than one without it. The crucial point in differentiating between the two kinds of society is how rights and entitlements are prioritized. What creates rigid societies is not the addition of entitlements to individual rights but the violation of rights. As we'll see, societies that demand outcomes over individual rights set in motion a logic that inevitably leads to the establishment of authoritarian governments and, in extreme cases, tyrannical ones.

The One-Dimensional Society

To honor their promises of specific outcomes, governments have to assume the control not just of political but also of economic matters—fusing economic and political power into a single vehicle of control. This fusion is essential to this kind of society because governments must restrict the economic and political freedoms of their citizens to prevent them from straying into creating activities or relationships that could disrupt the circumstances the population wants to keep in place. All powers in society must be subservient to this objective. We will call these societies one-dimensional because in them everything is reduced to a single dimension, the political one. All other dimensions of life are surrendered to the commands of political power.

All governments and all politicians make promises of specific outcomes, and, to honor them, they use the power of the state. There is ample room in liberal democracy to do that without violating individual rights. Yet there is always the risk of getting onto a slippery slope and becoming vertical, especially in the midst of a period of rapid change. In this way, for example, a government that has received the mandate to keep financially unproductive coal mines in operation to benefit the mine owners or the miners, or both, cannot attain this objective if it does not force the population to use coal for energy, even if there are more efficient and cleaner sources. To do that, the government would have to protect the coal industry, with tariffs, for example, from the competition of firms using more efficient energy sources. Protectionism leads to other problems, requiring further government intervention, which in turn creates still more problems and more government intervention, and so on.

As such promises accumulate, a government must assume a stiff command of the economy to be able to honor them. Three things can happen in these circumstances. First, the economy would be subjugated to the political power. Second, as a result of this subjugation, attaining economic success means shifting from producing efficiently to having connections with the government. Everything becomes political. As the government assumes more economic power, it has to restrict political freedoms to remain in place. Third, with its hands tied in so many ways, the private economy becomes extremely rigid. This is the origin of the one-dimensional state, which fuses economic and political power into a single composite dimension—so that the same group controls both the government and the economy. Government control of the economy becomes a route to political tyranny.

Dealing with the short-term political symptoms rather than the multifaceted realities of complex transformations means that the problems are never resolved. They are swept under the carpet. Eventually, however, the pressure to resolve them becomes too strong, and the whole structure collapses.

The feudal and mercantilist societies of preindustrial continental Europe were of this resistance-to-change type. As the industrial revolution progressed and disrupted all sectors of production and employment, societies demanded more stability in the outcomes, which meant keeping in place the social and economic conditions of the preindustrial economies. This was impossible in an environment where industrialization was changing everything. Societies can survive when a few of their institutions are obsolete but not when all of them have become so. Then change becomes the enemy.

Some societies did not accept the changing conditions of work and the uncertainty about the future that came with the industrial revolution, and they demanded guarantees of security that could be assured only by increasing the rigidity of society. But the string stopping change eventually snaps. When it did, these societies slid into chaos and from there to destructive regimes. As we will see later in the book, this was the case in prerevolutionary France, precommunist Russia, and pre-Nazi Germany. In two of these cases (communism and Nazism-fascism), extreme forms of the one-dimensional societies resulted in unprecedented destruction. They were even more rigid than their predecessors. They told their citizens, *We will take you to paradise and then you will not have to deal with change again.* To get to paradise, the governments needed totalitarian control.

One-dimensional societies may survive without totalitarianism for a long time if they are not subject to profound change. Within such a society, however, the definition of the desired state of things rapidly converges with a strong resistance to change. The slope becomes slippery and those societies can easily become totalitarian.

The Multidimensional Society

In a multidimensional society, government does not promise a utopia or ideal state. Instead, it promises to defend individual rights, which gives society economic and political freedom. Nobody is restricted by a goal established by the government. Economic and political powers remain separate and independent from each other, and with these dimensions separate, the society develops a politically critical flexibility.

Multidimensional societies create an environment of natural checks and balances, an economic and political umbrella under which other dimensions of life—art, academic pursuits, civil society—tend to flourish. This natural flexibility is the basis of what we know as liberal democracy.

The Competition of Systems

In the long run, over periods of both steady and turbulent technological progress, countries giving priority to individual rights not only protect those rights but also create better objective conditions for their citizens than one-dimensional societies. Multidimensional societies are more amenable to change and progress, for several reasons.

First, the one-dimensional society, dealing with outcomes, tends to be more divisive and therefore more rigid. To give something concrete to one citizen, the government has to take from other citizens the resources to produce it. The government distributes. On the other hand, in a multidimensional society, an impersonal institution, the market, directs the distribution. Taking away from someone to give to another one is naturally divisive, especially because the mechanism to do it is naturally political. In the multidimensional society the mechanism is economic.

Second, the social order of countries that aim to preserve a specific set of historical conditions or circumstances is fragile and prone to collapse into chaos because it is based on something that is naturally ephemeral. The shape of society changes rapidly in periods of rapid technological progress. The social order of societies giving priority to individual rights is resilient to change because it is based on something that can always be preserved.

Third, the rule of individual rights neatly reconciles the need for a social order with the possibility of change. Multidimensional societies do not see change as a threat but as the normal manifestation of the freedom of the individual. In contrast, the population wanting to maintain the status quo naturally develops a negative attitude to change. Anything that disturbs the social and political equilibrium is seen as immoral and illegitimate.

Fourth, in the long term, societies basing their stability on individual rights tend to develop self-reliant individuals. For this reason, the overall adjustment of horizontal societies takes place day by day, through the infinite adjustments that individuals make in their daily activities. In contrast, societies based on the maintenance of a status quo tend to develop individuals who think that the government has to resolve their problems. Economic success comes to depend on political power because governments can grant subsidies and protection to some individuals and not to others.

Fifth, when economic power becomes a manifestation of political power, one-dimensional societies, where the state controls the economy, are prone to catastrophic revolutions. One-dimensional governments have the power to vanquish opponents not only politically but also economically. This turns political conflicts into all-or-nothing affairs, in which the winners take all, politically and economically, and losers lose everything. Within such an environment, political violence becomes rational for all parties, creating a fertile field for cold-blooded destructiveness.

Sixth, because multidimensional societies are free from these all-or-nothing incentives, they are also free from the propensity to violence. That is, multidimensional societies are not just more conducive to change; they are also less likely to fall into destructive infighting because losses in one dimension of life can be compensated with gains in another. This happens not just because people can move from politics to economics, or the other way around, but also because they can move from national to local politics, or from any starting point to independent institutions, such as universities or civil society organizations. This cannot happen in vertical societies where all power, national and local, political and economic, has to be concentrated to ensure the unity of society.

Seventh, the multidimensionality of life also facilitates political compromise enormously because politicians can give advantage to their opponents in one dimension in exchange for gaining an advantage in another. Compromise is easier when there are many issues at hand rather than one; also, it is easier when there are many layers of power than when there is only one, overwhelming central power.

These features of multidimensional societies make them much more amenable to change. They also make the social order much more resilient to change. We know for sure that change is going to take place in the long run, so we can be sure that the horizontal, multidimensional order is by far the best, not just because it is compatible with freedom but also because it tends to be more successful in terms of material and humane progress.

Multidimensional Societies and Social Cohesion

If flexible societies have the advantage in the long run, why do so many societies choose vertical, rigid forms of organization? Vertical order is the most common because it is the easiest to obtain. Vertical order subordinates the diversity of a conglomerate to the will of a central decision maker. It uses coercion to create uniformity out of diversity. Horizontal order is much more difficult to achieve because it does not create uniformity. Rather, it harmonizes the strains of diversity to produce a collective will, leaving diversity in place. Reducing the dispersion of the results of diversity to an acceptable range requires a very strong basis of self-control on the part of the individuals—ultimately rooted in shared values of respect for the *individual* rights of everyone else. To have this self-control, individuals need social interest.

Verticality is the only way to create social order when such self-control does not exist. That is, vertical societies depend on authoritarian structures, while horizontal ones depend on *social cohesion*. To be multidimensional, a society needs to include social cohesion among its values. Social cohesion, in turn, is interconnected with the rule of rights.

THE RULES OF THE GAME

The Tyranny of the Majority

What kind of rules create and sustain a multidimensional society? It is a common mistake to presuppose that the protection against verticality is embedded in democracy. It is not. A society ruled by a majority can be as vertical and one-dimensional as any absolutist monarchy. There is nothing in democracy that would protect a society from tyrannical machineries if the majority of the population agrees or at least acquiesces to what these machineries are doing.

In fact, *all* the destructive tyrannies of the twentieth century rested on the mobilization of the majority against a minority. The only safeguard that can stop this monster, the tyranny of the majority, is the existence of a set of individual rights that cannot be violated by anyone, not even by the majority of the population. Everybody must respect this fundamental rule.

The existence of these rights is so crucial that democracy is not sustainable without individual rights. Democracy has lasted only in those countries where these rights have been respected. The essential element of a multidimensional society is the rule of rights.

The Rule of Law and the Rule of Rights

I use the expression "rule of rights" rather than the more common "rule of law" to refer to the essential judicial element in a multidimensional society because the expression "rule of law" can be confusing at best and misleading at worst. The rule of law can be beneficial or malevolent depending upon the nature of the law it refers to.

Consider the Nuremberg Laws, created by the Nazis in 1935. These laws established clear criteria for the classification of the population as Jews and Aryans and specified the rights that should be taken away from the former depending on the percentage of Jewish blood in their veins. Courts scrupulously applied these laws, providing a perverse example of how the rule of law can be used for nefarious purposes.

The Nazis also issued laws legalizing the sequestration of freedom and other individual rights from the general German population. Less than two months after Hitler came to power, the Reichstag changed the existing constitution with what was called the Enabling Laws. These laws transferred legislative authority to the chancellor, consolidating all formal powers in the hands of Hitler. The Enabling Laws met all the formal requirements needed for a valid modification of the constitution, including the approval by a two-thirds majority. From then on, the rule of law consisted of obeying Hitler's arbitrary wishes.

According to many prominent legal experts of the Nazi era, including the famous constitutional authority Carl Schmitt, the laws issued by Hitler on his own authority were legitimate. In June 1934, just a few days after Hitler assassinated many of his political rivals in the Night of the Long Knives, Schmitt wrote a piece in a legal journal with the title "The Fuhrer Protects the Rule of Law."[60] Theodor Maunz, another constitutional expert, stated in 1943, "The command of the Fuhrer . . . is the absolute center of the present legal order."[61] Thus, the Nazis took good care of ruling in the name of the law. The Soviets also pretended to rule in the same legalistic way.

They even enacted secret laws so that people would violate the law without knowing it.

Values and Social Cohesion

Of course, this sense of the law is a perversion of the classic Western concept of the rule of law. Most people would think that the Enabling and the Nuremberg Laws contradict our innate sense of right and wrong. That sense, as applied to different circumstances in life, is what we call natural law. The belief in natural law as the legitimate guide of all legislation, and the belief that law is whatever a body with authority to legislate enacts, give life to two completely different conceptions of law.

Sophocles contrasted these two conceptions of the law in his tragedy *Antigone*. Creon, the ruler of Thebes, issues an edict commanding that the body of Polyneices, a rebel who had died in battle, should remain unburied. This meant that his soul could not proceed to his final resting place in the underworld. Polyneices's sister, Antigone, defies the law by burying the body so that his soul could rest. Creon confronts Antigone, and the following conversation takes place:

> CREON: Now, tell me thou—not in many words, but briefly— knewest thou that an edict had forbidden this?
> ANTIGONE: I knew it: could I help it? It was public.
> CREON: And thou didst indeed dare to transgress that law?
> ANTIGONE: Yes; for it was not Zeus that had published me that edict; not such are the laws set among men by the justice who dwells with the gods below; nor deemed I that thy decrees were of such force, that a mortal could override the unwritten and unfailing statutes of heaven. For their life is not of today or yesterday, but from all time, and no man knows when they were first put forth.[62]

The difference between Creon's and Antigone's conceptions of the law gives birth to the two kinds of society: Creon, who believes that laws are laws because they carry the will of the ruler, embodies the vertical principle; and Antigone, who believes that laws are legitimate only to the extent that they are based on the natural rights of the individual, embodies the horizontal.

A long line of philosophers and legal experts understand the rule of law in Creon's way. They argue that the law is the law as long as it is enacted in accordance with established procedures, and should be applied and respected independently of its alignment with the people's principles. Even if not using the same revolting example of the Nuremberg Laws, they justify their application in all cases.

This school is based on the Scottish philosopher David Hume's concept of positivism. He claimed that there are no "self-evident truths" except in mathematics, and there only because they are tautological. Two plus two is always true because the number *two plus two* and the number *four* are one and the same thing differently expressed. Therefore, Hume argued, reason in itself cannot dictate a way of acting.

Under this line of reasoning, there cannot be a natural law. Because Hume believed that propositions about the self and society are simply equivalent to propositions about one's own experience, expressions such as "We hold these truths to be self-evident" cannot be demonstrated to be true. (Hume wrote his *Treatise on Human Nature* in 1739 and 1740, decades before American independence, so that he could not have used this example, but he clearly disqualified its line of reasoning.) Following Hume's logic, we cannot say that a certain kind of morality is superior to the next; thus, he demolished the idea of the "natural law."[63]

In one sense, Hume was right. We cannot assume that all people in all cultures uphold the same values and cherish the same concept of rights. In some countries, the values embedded in the culture do not support individual rights but legitimize the killing of minorities if the majority believes that they are obstacles for progress. In other societies, people think that human sacrifice is fair and legitimate, and others believe women do not have equal rights. Surely, you can find certain categories like "justice" in the minds and hearts of all human beings, but the specific definition of what is just or unjust may vary widely.[64]

This uncertainty regarding what is good and what is bad has resulted in the elimination of values from the academic discussion of economic, social, and political issues because, as many social scientists ask, who can guarantee that Western values, which have been at the core of the creation of the modern industrial, democratic state, are "better" than the values of other societies? What is better? The fact that other societies have different values shows that they prefer them and therefore that they think that they are better for them. True enough.

The elimination of values from the academic discussion of economic, social, and political issues has been a tragedy, however, because, even if it is true that values may be relative, they play a fundamental role in shaping societies. Different sets of values produce different outcomes.

If you believe that certain races and social classes should be eliminated and that doing so is fair, you get Nazi and communist regimes. If you believe that the only legitimate law is the sharia, you get a fundamentalist Muslim society. If you believe that even the people you hate have the same rights that you have and therefore cannot be deprived of life, liberty, and many other rights, then you get a liberal, horizontal society.

That is as true today as yesterday, and across different societies, in the sense that if unrestricted, the growth of racism in today's America would logically lead to a society like that which existed in Germany in the 1930s, in the same way as China's appalling repression of its Muslim minority is beginning a process that could lead to genocide. Values, or the absence of them, shape societies, independent of a person's skin color, background, or geographical location. And values are the only standard that can be used to make absolute judgments about human behavior. And the only set of values that respond at a global level to the Golden Rule—do onto others as you would have them do unto you—is what we call natural law.

Natural law was the only argument that could be used to condemn Nazi war criminals. Adolf Eichmann defended himself by arguing that he had simply obeyed orders when sending millions of people to their deaths in the concentration camps. According to German law at the time, the orders were valid. According to natural law, they were not.

What really distinguished the societies that succumbed to destructive regimes and those that did not were their sets of values. The set of values that gave priority to the rule of rights produced multidimensional societies, which adjusted better to the transformations of the industrial revolution, while those that gave priority to the attainment and maintenance of a given outcome fell under the sway of destructive regimes. The former got their social cohesion from social interest; the latter got it from the coercion of a tyrant. Societies have a choice between social interest and tyranny.

Social Interest and Development

Not all societies are either vertical or horizontal. Developing countries have not reached the point of organizational proficiency that allows them to handle the basic social and economic problems in the either–or matrix of one-dimensional and multidimensional societies that I have been describing. Many developing societies are indeed vertical, but full development consists in getting to the point of social interest that makes becoming multidimensional possible.

There are many examples of the lack of social interest in developing societies. The American sociologist Edward Banfield spent time in the 1950s trying to understand why a small village of 3,400 inhabitants in southern Italy was so poor and backward. He found that, even if most of the inhabitants were scarcely educated, they knew what their main problems were: the badly managed school, the even worse health system, and the indifference of their elected functionaries to the needs of the population. He noted that most of these problems could be solved if only people cooperated with each other. But they could not organize themselves for collective action even if these problems were keeping them poor. There was only one association in the village—that of twenty-five better-off men who met to chat and play cards. They had never undertaken a project for any purpose. There was not enough food for the children, but no peasant or landed proprietor had even given a young pig to the orphanage.

Banfield compared the communal negligence of the Italian village with the normal life of a small village in Utah, which was full of interactions and activities.[65]

> Americans are used to a buzz of activity having as its purpose, at least in part, the advancement of community welfare. For example, a single issue of the weekly newspaper published in St. George, Utah (population 4,562), reports a variety of public-spirited undertakings. The Red Cross is conducting a membership drive. The Business and Professional Women's Club is raising funds to build an additional dormitory for the local junior college by putting on a circus in which the members will be both clowns and "animals." The Future Farmers of America (whose purpose is "to develop agricultural leadership, cooperation, and citizenship through individual and group leadership") are holding a father-son banquet. A local business firm has given an encyclopedia to the school district. The Chamber of Commerce is discussing the feasibility of building an all-weather road between two nearby towns. "Skywatch" volunteers are being signed up. A local church has collected $1,393.11 in pennies for a children's hospital 350 miles away. The Country Farm Bureau is flying one of its members to Washington, 2,000 miles away, to participate in discussions of farm policy. Meetings of the Parent Teachers Associations are being held in the schools. "As a responsible citizen of our community," the notice says, "you belong in the PTA."[66]

In the last quarter of the twentieth century, American academic Robert D. Putnam studied the difference between the developed northern part of Italy and its much poorer south and confirmed that those places with more social interest had attained a higher level of development:

> For at least ten centuries, the North and the South have followed contrasting approaches to the dilemmas of collective action that afflict societies. In the North, norms of reciprocity and networks of civic engagement have been embodied in tower societies, guilds, mutual aid societies, cooperatives, unions, and even soccer clubs and literary societies. These horizontal civic bonds have undergirded levels of economic and institutional performance generally much higher than in the South, where social and political relations have been vertically structured. Although we are accustomed to thinking of the state and the market as alternative mechanisms for solving social problems, this history suggests that both states and markets operate more efficiently in civic settings.[67]

This problem is common to all developing countries. Societies develop when they learn to cooperate among themselves to solve the increasingly complex problems of shared life. Social bonds are much stronger in developed societies—in fact, this is why they are developed, as many studies have shown.

The relationship between the ability to coordinate complex collective tasks and a society's degree of development helps explain why in almost all cases totalitarian regimes have taken hold of poor societies—the exceptions being Nazi Germany, prefascist Italy, and some Eastern European and Southern European societies. In general, we can say that the poor societies are unable to establish the minimum coordination that is needed for the efficient functioning of the state and the economy, even in the common cases in which the government is vertical and tyrannical. Destructive societies can develop this coordination, but it is based on coercion; creative societies generate such coordination voluntarily.

Public Good and the Role of the State

This argument, of course, does not mean that the government should not exist or must be very weak. There is no society that has survived without a government. The state is needed in a free society for two main reasons: (1) because, as expressed by Karl Popper, freedom cannot subsist without a state controlled by the citizens; (2) because of the problem of the public good, which is such that all people can equally enjoy it, whether or not they have paid for it. For instance, national defense provides security for both those who pay for it and those who don't. Those who pay could complain and refuse to contribute so that the service would not be provided. But then everyone would be worse off. In some cases, especially when the number of individuals is small, these problems can be solved with voluntary cooperation. More frequently, it is necessary to create a government to force all the beneficiaries of the public good to pay for them through taxation.

The definition of the public good is not black and white. Many people reduce it to national defense, policing, and indispensable physical infrastructure. Many others consider the dire consequences that living among sick and ignorant populations produce for everybody and include general investment in human capital. This is a very important point in times of a rapid technological revolution, when many are left behind. Certainly, investing in their education and health is very expensive; however, it is much cheaper than not investing in them. We return to this point in Part 3.

SOCIAL INTEREST AND LIBERAL DEMOCRACY

So the essence of, and the precondition for, liberal democracy is the existence of social interest. When it is present and manifest in the rule of rights, the exercise of self-interest becomes a boon for society. In its absence, people allow groups with stronger self-interest to take tyrannical control because, without the balance of social interest, self-interest becomes divisive and then destructive. But how can a multidimensional order be created?

In the following chapters, I shift gears to look at the historic processes that created one- and multidimensional societies and their responses to change during the industrial revolution. The countries I analyze are France, Britain, the United States, Germany, Sweden, and the Soviet Union. We will see quite clearly that countries that were able to adjust harmoniously to the radical transformations caused by the industrial revolution were the multidimensional ones—that is, those that were driven by a combination of self- and social interest. It is not a matter of degree. There is a clear line dividing creative and destructive societies. But we also see that there are no perfect cases. Even in the creative cases, you can see a very serious problem: while many have been able to create full multidimensional societies for what they define as their population, all of them have failed in the application of their democracy and their rule of rights to people outside those groups. For example, while Britain was developing its admirable liberal democracy, it was also trampling the rights of millions of people in their colonies. The same is true in the United States, which turned broad sections of the country into an internal empire where Native Americans enjoyed no rights and African Americans were first enslaved and then deprived of theirs.

History is complex. But the fact still remains that these countries, the liberal democracies, were the ones that came closest to humane treatment of minorities while creating a model that was not just flexible but also more fair than all others, a model that can be extended to all races and nationalities. They also avoided destructiveness in times where so many other nations could not.

PART II

The past is never dead. It's not even past.
William Faulkner

6

THE BIRTH OF THE
TWO ORDERS

*Liberalism and state-interference are not opposed to each other. On the
contrary, any kind of freedom is clearly impossible unless it is guaranteed
by the state . . . only a state which is controlled by free citizens can offer
them any reasonable security at all.*

Karl Popper

THE DOUBLE-HEADED EAGLE

In late June 1991, I was in Kiel, the port city on Germany's Baltic
coast, attending a seminar on the disintegration of the social order in the
Soviet Union. I was frequently invited to the Kiel Institute, a famous
institution of learning that had been put in charge of following up the
events taking place in Eastern Europe, and for several years I had been
visiting the region, including the Soviet Union, on behalf of a large
international financial institution.

That morning, I watched a beautiful three-mast sailing ship from
Leningrad enter Kiel Harbor. A magnificent double-headed eagle
adorned its foremost sail. This eagle, with one head looking west and the
other looking east, is a well-known symbol used by empires spanning
Western and Eastern cultures. It is the emblem of both the Byzantine and
Hapsburgs empires. However, the fact that it was displayed on a Russian
ship left no doubt about its significance. Ever since 1472, when Ivan the
Great married Sophia Paleologus, a niece of the Byzantine emperor, it
had also been the emblem of Russia's tsars.

The display of this symbol on a Russian ship was a sign of change, a manifestation of the speed of the transformation then taking place in the Soviet Union. Only a year or two before, it would have been unthinkable for a Soviet ship to display an emblem of the tsars. The presence of that eagle signaled that the old nationalism associated with the tsars had survived communism.

The two heads of the eagle were also the sign of the permanence of the deep schism that has marked the whole history of Russia: the painful indecision about who Russians are and what they want. Meant to represent two perspectives enriching the views of a country exposed to two different cultures, the double-headed eagle had in fact become a symbol of two forces pulling in opposite directions. For centuries, the country has fluctuated between wanting to be European, uniquely Russian, or a blend of its European and Asian heritages. The glaring difference between the planned city of St. Petersburg—built by Peter the Great in a magnificent European style—and the wonderfully Asiatic spires of Russian churches—foremost among them Saint Basil's in Moscow—is a symbol of the inner division of the soul of the Russian people.

The roots of Russia were in Europe. Historically, its population shared its origins with the Western branches of the Indo-European tree of peoples, and its cultural and commercial links that emerged in the last centuries of the first millennium were predominantly Europe-facing. In those centuries, Russians became Christian and were integrated in the trade that developed around the Baltic Sea. Like the Germans, Russians never shared the Roman domination experienced by most of Europe, yet by the beginning of the second millennium, they seemed to have joined the mainstream of European history.

Then three events took place that isolated Russia from the rest of the continent. The first was the 1054 schism of the Western and the Orthodox branches of Christianity. As a result of this schism, Russians came to see Westerners as uniformly heretical and barbaric, and avoided contact with them as they would avoid contact with the devil. The second event was the invasion of Russia by the Golden Horde, the Mongols, who dominated the country from the thirteenth to the fifteenth centuries. Under the Mongols, Russia turned away from Europe and toward the cities of Karatoram and Sarai, the Mongol capitals located in the depths of Asia.

The Golden Horde collapsed in the fifteenth century as a result of internecine fighting, and Russia again became independent. However, a third event prolonged Russia's isolation when Swedes and Poles, traditional enemies of the Russians, took over the eastern shore of the Baltic, sealing off Russia's sea access to Europe. For nearly another hundred years, Russia remained isolated from the West. This long period of isolation, up to five hundred years altogether, made Russian society radically different from those of Western Europe, a difference that has persisted ever since.

Russia tried to change its course several times in the centuries that followed. Under several reforming tsars or leaders, from Mikhail Romanov in the early seventeenth century to Mikhail Gorbachev in the twentieth—the country launched several attempts to recover its European roots and to modernize itself along the lines of its Western neighbors. These attempts were all "revolutions from above"—that is, they were aimed at forcing the population to progress in the direction and within limits established by the rulers. And they all failed because of a persistent misidentification of objectives. In all cases but Catherine the Great, Russian reformers aimed at securing the material and intellectual benefits of a free society rather than the freedom that unleashes the creativity that leads to those benefits. This misplaced objective repeatedly led Russian leaders to believe that society could be transformed quickly and that the best way to carry out the transformation was by commanding the changes to take place. A true transformation requires time, and the authoritarian approach contradicted the ends that were pursued—it killed the spirit of individual initiative and responsibility that has been the secret of progress in Europe.

The tragic saga of Russia—its centuries-long search for the elusive secret of humane progress and the terrible episodes of destructiveness that have accompanied the search—is a manifestation of the vicious circle that is the curse of vertical societies. For Russia, freedom has meant chaos, and rule has always been based on the assumption that the state is inherently superior to the individual. Thus, Russia's population has never developed the self-restraint that is the basis of social order in a free society. Restraint has always been the task of the state.

So as I watched that magnificent ship sail into Kiel that morning, I thought of the deeper significance of the double-headed eagle: the schizoid search for progress by the Russian people. For many centuries, they longed for the prosperity of free societies, but they looked for it in the social order of slavery. They have done so because their social order has been based not on principles of social interest, which unify, but on those of naked self-interest, which create chaos, a state also implied by the double-headed eagle.

Russia became a country through the unrestricted application of property rights. In a fierce competition to acquire more land, one person eventually became the owner of everything and, through sheer economic power, became the tsar of a large dominion. The authority of the tsar, which had this economic origin, created the political reality of Russia. This newly formed society was so one-dimensional that it resembled a private estate more than a country.

Eventually, the tsars determined that, to increase their military prowess, they needed a state like those that existed in Western Europe—a professional state separated from the sovereign. In the early eighteenth century, Peter the Great claimed to have created such a state, but under Peter, Russia remained an autocracy, no different from the estate that had existed before. This new estate survived until the Russian Revolution of 1917, which resulted in a transfer of the old estate to a new set of owners, the Communist Party.

The history of Russia shows that tyrannical, one-dimensional societies are not necessarily the result of the extension of the power of government. They can also emerge from the extension of the power of private interests.

THE PRIVATE STATE OF THE EAST[68]

Russia's history and development were strongly affected by the domination between the thirteenth and the fifteenth centuries of the Mongols, who were not interested in governing Russia but only in extracting revenues from it. They ruled that each locality could keep its own form of government provided it paid its tribute. They warned that they would destroy any community that failed to deliver its contribution on time and established some exemplary precedents. Furthermore, all the inhabitants of a community were jointly and severally responsible for the payment of the communal taxes, so that if one of the inhabitants did not pay his due, the others had to pay for him.

Because this system turned people into oppressors of their neighbors, Mongol rule introduced strongly divisive forces inside Russian communities. It eliminated the possibility of a direct relationship between the individual and the central state; for the Mongol leadership, the individual did not matter, only the taxpaying collectives. Furthermore, the system broke any link between taxes and benefit—the state provided no benefits to its subjects except the negative one of not being destroyed. The central state had only rights, and the subject had only obligations.

These features of the Russian political landscape have survived to this day. They became the basis of the power of the tsars once the Mongols left and also that of the communist state. They underpin the tyranny that Vladimir Putin is imposing today. Ironically, these state-dominated systems emerged from a regime that negated the existence of the state: the patrimonial regime of the tsars.

Ivan of Muscovy, a Russian prince during Mongol rule, gained the confidence of the rulers to the point that they entrusted him with the collection of the tribute of other Russian princes, which he carried out while charging a commission for the service. Ivan was an entrepreneur. He assumed responsibility for the delivery of all tribute, even the parts of the tribute that he failed to collect. In return, he was given a monopoly over the business of collections and access to the khan. His success led to his nickname Ivan Moneybags.

Ivan was a clever man with a long-term perspective. When dealing with principalities that could not pay their tribute in any particular year—a common occurrence given the stiffness of the taxes—he financed the deficit against a loan to the defaulting prince. In return, he took the land of the principality as collateral. Because the responsibility for the payment of the taxes lay with the community as a whole, the collateral was all the land in the principality. As many communities defaulted on their borrowings, Ivan expanded his dominions greatly by foreclosing on the collateral. At the end of his life, he controlled a territory several times bigger than the one he had inherited from his father, a control not only as ruler but as owner. Like the Mongols, he had no obligation to the people living on his land. On the contrary, they were obliged to him because they lived on his property.[69]

One of Ivan Moneybags's successors, Ivan the Great, defeated the Mongols in 1480 and proclaimed himself tsar and autocrat of all Russia. By the end of the fifteenth century, the core of what is Russia today was the private property of the tsars, including land, buildings, productive assets, even the people themselves. In addition to extracting rents in the same way that the Mongols had, the tsars also controlled whatever profitable businesses they could identify—including the fur trade, salt production, all exports and imports, and even the buying and selling of Persian rugs. No one could engage in business without the tsar's permission or participation. To keep their countrywide business enterprise going, the tsars used the same system of oppression as the Mongols, with dispossessed nobles as instruments to exploit the mass of the population.

Also like the Mongols, the tsars left local government to local inhabitants, which developed into a system of government centered on village councils elected democratically by the peasants. "Democracy" in this case, however, mainly meant ensuring that tsarist exploitation was spread equally among everyone in the village. In addition to its tax-collecting responsibility, the village council controlled permission to use the land, which, of course, was all owned by the tsar. Because such permission could only be obtained by political means, and because families that progressed more than their neighbors were cut down to size to prevent or give satisfaction to envy, the social order of the village, supposedly a horizontal, democratic one, in reality was one-dimensional. The road to economic success was political and ran through the village council.

Also like the Mongols, the councils tied the people to their villages so that they could not escape the council's control. This created a one-dimensional world at the local level. People gaining access to political power through the village council also got control of the allocation of land and therefore of the village's economic power. It also legitimized envy, which became Russia's characteristic sin. The concept that land and subsequently everything that could produce wealth should be owned by the central power—be it the tsar or the communist state—became ingrained in the Russian mentality as a way of ensuring that no neighbor could become richer than oneself. Village democracy did not result in freedom but in the imposition of restrictions on the freedom of one's neighbors. It created and maintained divisiveness.

In this world of negative incentives, where the interests of everyone were opposed to those of everybody else, Russians came to believe that economic activity is exploitative by nature and that the role of the central power—whether the tsars or the communist state—was to defend people against the exploitation of everybody else. Central power was a fact of life. It was the price they had to pay for the social order they wanted to keep in place, one that kept their neighbors from becoming richer than they were.

This divisiveness opened the door to tyranny. Divisiveness became the root of Russia's long-standing rigidity and destructiveness. Through the centuries, Russians have had few opportunities to express their will. When they have done so, it has been to curtail the progress of their fellow Russians rather than to foster the progress of all.

THE PUBLIC STATE OF THE EAST

In the early 1700s, Peter the Great started a long process of reform for military reasons. In the sixteenth and seventeenth centuries, the Russian army, while strong enough to defeat the armies of the Asiatic nations gradually being folded into the Russian empire, proved to be no match for modern European armies. The Swedes and the Poles inflicted countless defeats on the Russians, even at times when they were also fighting each other. Economic factors explained their superiority over the Russians. First, as a result of the technological strength of their weapons suppliers, they had better hardware. Second, they relied on professional soldiers, who remained mobilized during peacetime and were continually being trained. Russia could afford neither.

In the seventeenth century, under tsars Mikhail and Feodor, Russia imported Western military experts to introduce the new warfare techniques, but because the country couldn't afford to keep its soldiers mobilized, these new techniques did not stop a string of defeats to European armies. In 1697 and 1698, Peter traveled throughout Western Europe to discover the source of its military success. He was impressed by Europe's differentiation between state and sovereign. Also, he was impressed by the orderly way in which a professional bureaucracy managed the affairs of the impersonal state. He became convinced that Russia would trail behind the West as long as it remained a patrimonial state, without any regard for the progress of the country. Peter set out to replicate the impersonal state in Russia as soon as he returned.

The public state that Peter created, however, was unlike those existing in the West. He did not consider replicating the political structures that gave life to the impersonal state or even creating the right environment to nurture its emergence. Instead, he simply substituted the "state," embodied in the tsar, for the person of the tsar as the owner of Russia. He proudly proclaimed that he had become the first slave of Russia. Then, to make sure that a professional bureaucracy would run his new public state, he formally enslaved the nobles and forced them to become bureaucrats and managers of state-owned industrial and agricultural enterprises.

Peter also decided to copy the primitive industrial operations that he saw in the West. However, the industries he imported from Europe extended serfdom from the agricultural to the industrial sector and did not help Russia modernize. The new industrial enterprises were called private. They were not. They were owned by the state, given in concession to private individuals for their management. Peter chose the managers and, when they refused to take their positions, sent the army to force them. He formally turned the captured managers into serfs of their factories to ensure that they would not escape.

These enterprises sold their products primarily to the government—they were intended to supply the army—at low prices fixed by Peter. He took two actions to ensure that the new enterprises would have costs low enough to sell profitably. First, to reduce the cost of labor, he gave the industrial enterprises entire villages in what was called serfdom but in fact was slavery. The populations of these villages worked for free for the enterprise and fed themselves with the product of land plots given to them by the village—exactly as in feudal times. Second, he fixed the prices of the agricultural inputs. Then he enslaved those villages not given over to industry and gave them to the rural nobles in administration so that they could produce low-priced raw materials on the state-owned lands they managed. Of course, the nobles could not allow people to leave their villages so, by the end of Peter's reign, slavery was worse than before. The elements of modernization he brought to Russia actually made the country more archaic. This perversion of change established a pattern that would repeat itself over the next two centuries.

Russian society did change under the sway of new technologies and radical political thinking. These changes, however, were deformed by the rigidity of the social order. It happened under Peter the Great and it happened later. The solution that Peter had provided to establish a creative economy, by creating serfs of the population, became Russia's worst problem for centuries to come, forcing most of his successors to enact reforms to counteract his reforms.

Half a century after Peter's death, Catherine the Great liberated the nobles from the serfdom that Peter had imposed on them. To do it, however, she gave them full ownership of the lands they had been managing on her behalf—defining full ownership in the Russian sense. The peasants, who had begun as slaves of the tsar and then become slaves of the state, now became slaves of the nobles. The rigidity of the social order did not allow for progress.

A hundred years later, in 1861, Alexander II liberated the peasants from serfdom and forced landlords to sell land to them on credit provided by the government. However, he gave the land to the villages, not to individuals, making all villagers liable for paying the debt to the government, even if their activities were not related to land. Thus, he established the same set of incentives that the Mongols had introduced in the villages 650 years earlier. To prevent the peasants from escaping from these payments, the government kept in place its ban on internal migration. Thus, the peasants were liberated from their serfdom to the nobles only to become the slaves of their village communities in yet another turn of the screw.

By the first decade of the twentieth century, however, it appeared that Russia was finally on a path to true modernization. Prompted by the social turmoil that accompanied the disastrous defeat of Russia by the Japanese in the 1904–1905 War of the Pacific, Tsar Nicholas II reluctantly created a parliament and liberated the peasants from the village. While the new parliament was a consultative body, it gave new life to politics in Russia. Elections took place; political debate became a fixture of the system.

Then World War I came. Facing increasingly catastrophic defeats, Nicholas abdicated in early 1917. Parliament took over, and an elected prime minister became the country's leader. Russia had its first democratic regime in history. The new regime was doomed, however. It never ruled. It just presided over a chaotic process of disintegration of the social order. A parallel government, the Petrograd Soviet, which claimed to represent the workers and soldiers of Russia, challenged the power of parliament and made decisions and issued orders alongside the official government. Soldiers in the field were defecting and walking back to their homes to take over land from landlords and other soldiers. At this point, Lenin traveled by train from Switzerland to Russia to prepare the revolution that put the Bolsheviks in power. Chaos culminated with the October communist uprising, which put Lenin in power.

In this way, the vertical mentality of Russia perverted the modernizing trends of the industrial revolution. The source of these perversions was the country's inability to manage itself in freedom. To remain stable, its population had to be enslaved to somebody else in a chain that led to the absolutist ruler.

THE PUBLIC STATE OF THE WEST

The path of Western Europe shifted away from that of Russia by the end of the fifteenth century. It diverged even more in subsequent centuries. Seen from a certain perspective, Russia was living through an era that Western Europe had experienced almost a millennium earlier. Just as Russia was emerging from the domination of a foreign empire, the Golden Horde,

Western Europe had emerged from the domination of the Roman Empire between the third and the sixth centuries. But the two processes of disengagement from foreign empires were different in three crucial respects.

First, in Russia, a new empire emerged to substitute for the dying Mongol empire; in Western Europe, the remains of the old Roman Empire became a collection of small states warring with each other. Second, in Russia, the emperor managed the country as his private property, and it was therefore one-dimensional; the Western principalities developed a public sector, which did not exist in Russia. Third, the new Russia remained absolutist; in Western Europe, most of the small states evolved into primitive democracies. This duality created the basis for the multidimensional society.

These differences were unintended. The Western princes were as ambitious as the Muscovite princes, and they fought continuously to impose their rule on their neighbors. However, no Western prince accumulated as much relative power as the successors of Ivan Moneybags had done in Russia. The Merovingian and Carolingian empires, which tried to inherit the power of the Roman Empire, collapsed within a generation as their territories were divided and subdivided among the descendants of the emperors. Eventually, Western Europe became a collection of small states fighting with each other in a perpetual stalemate. Because the contenders were roughly similar in economic and military power, the fight for absolute power became more protracted and more sophisticated—both militarily and economically—than in the East.

In this truly competitive environment, European princes soon discovered that economic restrictions and insecurity in individual ownership depressed economic activity and weakened the principality as a whole. The most successful princes tended to be those who allowed their subjects to thrive economically. A rich state provided more taxes and better soldiers than a poor one. Wise princes understood that they had to allow for freedom in the pursuit of wealth and that it was in their interest to protect such wealth once it was obtained. In this way, the princes developed an interest in protecting the ownership rights of their subjects. Furthermore, they discovered the power of free trade, particularly in northern Italy and northern Germany, where cities attained tremendous progress through trading alliances with other cities, within Italy and Germany and abroad.

While successful in strengthening the principalities, the liberal strategies of the most enlightened princes also set in motion a new dynamic that produced an unintended result: reduction of the power of the princes themselves. By protecting the economic rights of their subjects, they created the conditions for the emergence of an independent source of power: the bourgeoisie, which had created the new wealth. The stronger the bourgeoisie, the greater their capacity to impose limitations on the power of the princes. Eventually, the local magnates, angry at the instability that princely fights caused in their lives, used their economic power to limit the political power of the princes and imposed on them the concept of state as an entity separate from the sovereign. *With this invention, they moved from a one-dimensional to a multidimensional society.*

This concept of state was very different from that which the tsar had imposed on Russians. The capitalists and merchants of the West wanted a state that would protect the rights of citizens in an unstable world created by the dynastic fights of princes. Throughout Western Europe, as the princes asked for more taxes with increasing frequency, the leading merchants negotiated with princes the conditions under which they would provide the required funds. Their conditions included keeping a state's territory undivided, regardless of princely marriages, inheritances, and wars; refraining from imposing taxes and entering in new alliances or new wars without the consent of the population; and establishing councils of representatives of the estates, which would then regulate the relations between the prince and the community. In many cases, the princes also promised to solve their dynastic problems before these councils rather than through war. Most strikingly, in most principalities, the possibility of conflicts between the prince—or the state—and individual citizens was spelled out, and a procedure to solve them established in the councils.

Through this process, Western princes lost absolute power inside their own communities. The community councils became the true sovereigns in their dominions. The state was separated from the person of the prince, and political and economic power was separated as well. The state became the representative of the will of the population. It was not fully democratic, for only the members of the most important families had the right to a seat on the councils, but the democratic principle was established. Eventually, even if there were discontinuities in the process, the concept of self-determination was extended to the rest of the population. The importance attached to the community was the birth of social interest in Western societies.

This process was more than an assertion of a different sort of power, however. The legal revolution that limited the power of the princes also opened the door to new institutions for *any* legitimate purpose, to be regulated by their members, not by the prince.

The Emergence of the Multidimensional Society

Imposing domestic restraint on the holders of economic and political power created a safe environment for a third kind of people: those who were not overly interested in wealth or politics. In this safe environment, these citizens could live and prosper pursuing their own interests, discovering new dimensions in life beyond economics and politics. These included the arts but also philosophy and science. While Russia lived in one dimension, the separation of powers allowed Western societies to develop infinite dimensions of progress.

This multiplicity was evident in the creation of great centers of learning throughout Western Europe—including Oxford, Cambridge, the Sorbonne, Heidelberg, Salamanca, and Bologna—which did not have a counterpart in the East. The life of the common citizen was much richer as a result of this diversity, and the results were evident in terms of creativity in all the dimensions of human activity. Very subtly, the existence of these activities resulted in an increase in the political and economic power of the entire society. In the interstices of this equilibrium of power, people became free to be inconsistent with each other, to think and create. European societies became varied and creative, and thus multidimensional.

As Toby E. Huff wrote in his *The Rise of Early Modern Science: Islam, China and the West,*

> Europe in the twelfth and thirteenth centuries experienced a profound social and intellectual revolution that placed social life on an entirely new footing. At the center of this revolution was a legal transformation that redefined the nature of social organization in all its realms—political, social, economic, and religious. As a result of the legal reforms a variety of new, legally autonomous collectivities emerged. These included residential communities, cities and towns, universities, economic interest groups, and professional guilds, such as the surgeons and other medical specialists. As a result, each of these collectivities was granted a degree of legal autonomy to make its own internal laws and regulations, to own property, to sue and be sued, and to have legal representation before the king's court. In effect, the first vestiges of neutral space, a relatively independent space free from the interference of religious and political

censors, began to emerge. This social and intellectual revolution opened the doors, above all, to intellectual freedom, which was created by the establishment of autonomous universities with their own intellectual agendas and internally established rules and regulations.[70]

What Huff calls "the neutral space" is the mark of what I call the multidimensional society. The separation of political and economic power did not create the rule of rights and the glorious explosion of intellectual creativity of the West, but it allowed the emergence of people who devoted their lives to do it—judges, philosophers, artists, writers, scientists.

In this way, the Western European localities (kingdoms, principalities, dukedoms, city-states) developed two long-lasting features. One was a furious resistance to unification, which resulted in uncountable wars. The other was a diversity that was not matched in any other region in the world. This diversity and the competition in all dimensions that it permitted propelled Western Europe to an amazing burst of creativity that started with the Renaissance and has not ended to this day. This creativity, nothing else, turned Europe into the most developed region in the world.

By contrast, Russia, a unified state for most of its history, acquired the opposite features. Subject to a single will, the empire of the tsars was always more peaceful internally than Western Europe, but it lacked the creativity that comes from diversity. The tsar commanded the sources of both economic and political power, and politics and economics remained tied together in a symbiosis in which the former had preeminence over the latter. The unified state was built from the bottom up in Western Europe and from the top down in Russia.

RETROGRESSION

But then Europe learned a nasty lesson: historical progress is not linear. After the fifteenth century, most of continental Europe reverted to tyrannical regimes. City-states lost their freedoms when their primitively democratic political systems failed to keep pace with the tensions created by the unprecedented economic and political changes over two centuries. Feudalism was not so easily dispensed with, and there was tension everywhere—both between the countryside and the cities and within each of these parts. As would later happen during the industrial revolution, the city-states were not able to manage their newly acquired freedoms and power in a sustainable way. Without a tyrant controlling the vested interests of everyone, the factions that developed inside these incipient democracies fought with each other for power and privileges until the system collapsed and a new tyrant asserted his authority to reestablish the old vertical order, with the consent of the population.

The process was different in each city. In all, however, there was divisiveness. Societies split into groups differentiated by economic interests. Each of these groups sought economic privilege through political means so that the gain of one group had to be the loss of another. At the end of this process, many medieval individual rights and democratic traditions, and the institutions that supported them, were lost. With the demise of these institutions, societies lost the local mechanisms that generated a daily contact between the princes, the nobles, and the commons.

What emerged in the sixteenth and seventeenth centuries, pioneered by the Catholic kings in Spain and by Louis XIV in France, was the political consolidation of the principalities within national units. This created absolutism at the national level, suspending for a long period the horizontal principles of the late Middle Ages and Renaissance.

Fortunately, there were exceptions to this renewed vertical social order. The power of the church remained largely independent from that of the local princes, leaving in place an umbrella that created space for legal, institutional dissent. Many autonomous institutions (residential communities, cities and towns, universities, economic interest groups, and professional guilds) that had become free in the previous centuries remained so throughout Europe even as absolutism increased.

Europe remained a haven for independent thinking, independent not just from the political authorities but also from each other. Eventually, these centers interacted with each other to launch the great scientific revolution that preceded the industrial revolution. This freedom of thought was reinforced by the Reformation, which opened the minds of people not just to Luther's ideas but also to those of innumerable religious reformers, adding further dimensions to the already multidimensional European scene.

A few countries, like Switzerland, retained their freedoms, or they retained their will to be free even if outsiders conquered them at some point in their history, as in the case of the Netherlands. The largest country among those that kept their freedoms was Britain, which would lead to the industrial revolution.

7

FRANCE AND ENGLAND

*In fact it might even be argued that the [French] Revolution drew much
of its power from the (ultimately hopeless) attempt to arrest, rather than
hasten, the process of modernization. And in many respects
it was all too successful.*

Simon Schama

*We will sell to no man, we will not deny or defer to any man
either Justice or Right.*

Magna Carta

THE MYTHICAL REVOLUTION

The history of the French Revolution is surrounded by the myth that
the terrible events of 1789 to 1792 were prompted by the people's strong
commitment to freedom and that their success set France—and the rest
of the world—firmly on the path of democracy and economic modernity. None of this is true. The revolution was started by the nobles to
perpetuate the privileges they were losing as a result of the modernization
of French society. The success of the revolution brought about a reign of
terror, worse than any absolute monarchy, and resulted in the rule of an
emperor that reestablished the main features of the regime the revolution
had toppled. For a century, France lagged behind Britain economically
and politically and behind Germany economically.

The nobles were not the only unhappy group in prerevolutionary
France. Most of the population, discontent with the instability brought
about by the transition to modernity, opposed modernization. Compared to his subjects, Louis XVI actually looked progressive. Contrary
to what is normally asserted, he made many efforts to remove the

obstacles to progress that were ingrained in the old order, although his actions made him increasingly unpopular and brought him closer to his downfall. The rigidity of France was more ingrained in the minds and hearts of its people than its rulers.

In fact, French society of the late seventeenth century is a classic example of a vertical society that has become so rigid in its resistance to change that it is embedded not just in the sovereign or the nobility but in the people at large. It is also an example of how such societies resist change strenuously until it breaks the social order, leaving the people in chaos, vulnerable to destructiveness and the inevitable reassertion of vertical authority to recover a semblance of order. Britain, on the other hand, remained a creative, multidimensional society. The grandeur of France from the sixteenth to the early nineteenth century was based on the vertical power of its sovereigns, that of Britain on the freedoms of its citizens.

The Central Bureaucracy of Louis XIV

Ironically, France's rigidity came from what was considered at the time to be a claim to modernity: the new political and economic structure that Louis XIV had put in place during his long reign, from 1643 to 1715. Even today, the Sun King is deemed a great statesman for his efforts to unify France and create the first centralized state in Europe administered by professional bureaucrats who relied on their capacity—rather than on right of birth—for their advance up the ladder of administrative power.

To accomplish this feat, which required the neutralization of the feudal nobility, Louis relied on brute force and enticement. He resolved his conflicts with the most elevated nobles by separating them from their fiefdoms and bringing them to a life of ease and luxury at Versailles. Others he bribed with increased privileges, which allowed them to live in splendid idleness. In the economic field, he substituted the tight control of feudal institutions on local producers with even tighter controls imposed by the central government. Unlike British nobility, French nobles did nothing to unify their country.

This process weakened the intermediate stratum between the central power and the population, an event that would have momentous consequences. But even more important, the process eliminated the only credible domestic counterbalancing power that could oppose the absolute authority of the king. Certainly, France never reached Russian levels of one-dimensionality. Even at his most tyrannical, Louis XIV never wielded the total, absolute power that the Russian tsars commanded. But the verticality of the central-ized regime introduced a fatal rigidity into French society that led not just to the bloody French Revolution but also to the century of revolutions and instability that followed.

The Interventionist State

Jean-Baptiste Colbert, Louis XIV's first minister of state, began the reform of the bureaucracy by focusing on the basics. As Peter the Great would do several decades later in Russia, Colbert decided that cheap food was needed to sustain large armies, and he established a thorough system of controls on the price of grain. To ensure enforcement, he ruled that only people with government-issued licenses could trade grain, and he gave monopoly privileges to license holders over certain regions. He also promoted the creation of new industries by granting them monopolies until they were well established and by creating a system of licenses in the industrial sector as well. He also granted tax exemptions and state financing to industrial firms at interest rates lower than those prevailing in the market.

To ensure the harmonious functioning of this system, Louis XIV cre-ated an all-encompassing corporate state. For each industry, the govern-ment regulated product design, quality of output, production methods, sales volume, prices, finances, wages, and recruitment and promotion practices. Colbert made work obligatory, granting thirty-eight days of rest per year in addition to Sundays. To set the standards for private industry, Colbert nationalized the famous Gobelin factory in Paris and turned it into a model of efficiency and quality. He absorbed several of the feudal guilds, which controlled production at the local level, into a national system of guilds that enforced his production controls.[71]

While Colbert's strategies allowed Louis XIV to be more absolutist than his royal colleagues in neighboring nations, they also introduced a fatal rigidity. His economic regulations, while initially successful in pro-moting the creation of incipient industries, choked economic growth and retarded industrialization.[72] Price controls on agricultural products and the high rents the government guaranteed to the intermediaries discouraged production to the point that large extensions of fertile land were left idle. The system of licensed monopolies encouraged complacency in the few individuals fortunate enough to get a license and discouraged the eco-nomic creativity of the rest of the population. Altogether, Louis XIV's one-dimensionality killed the entrepreneurial spirit of France.

The Attempted Modernization

Looking across the English Channel, French statesmen of the eighteenth century could see that France was trailing liberal England economically, even before the industrial revolution began in earnest. Britain was the main exception to the rigid social order of continental Europe, which largely resembled that of France. In Britain, state intervention in the economy was practically nonexistent; new enterprises were not funded by the government but by private investors, directly or through the stock exchange, and people did not need government permission to engage in productive activity.[73] French visitors—including Voltaire— were surprised at the ease with which individuals could move up and down the social ladder in Britain. They also admired the absence of privilege. They noted that aristocrats paid the same turnpike tolls as common people. The peers had the right to be tried by the House of Lords but, if condemned, they were publicly executed like any other criminal. In 1760, the Earl Ferrers was hanged for murdering his servant, something unheard of in continental Europe.

It is also important to note that trade and finance were not looked down on in England. Business success competed with nobility of origin as a source of social respect. Unlike the continental European powers, which legitimized government control of the economy, the British had a long tradition of economic freedom. These trading traditions were the source of their progress.

The Ancien Régime statesmen of the mid- and late eighteenth century did recognize the problems caused by Colbert's interventionist economic policies and devoted substantial energy to trying to solve them. The most thorough efforts of modernization were carried out by a series of comptrollers-general who served under both Louis XV and his grandson Louis XVI. These functionaries were members of a group called the *physiocrats;* they believed that the progress of France was being hindered by the pervasive intervention of the state in the economy introduced by Colbert and Louis XIV. History proved them right.

The physiocrats realized that the commercial and industrial development of the country was blocked by price controls established by the national and local governments; by restrictions to trade that the local governments imposed on goods produced in other French localities; by state-sponsored monopolies and oligopolies that controlled production, commerce, and finance; by the myriad of regulations that regimented practically all economic activities; and by the large fiscal deficits that the government continuously ran, mainly as a result of wars. They prescribed fiscal prudence, economic liberalization, and policies aimed at developing an independent private sector. The opposition to their ideas came not from the king but from the population, which wanted to keep in place the ineffective policies of Colbert and Louis XIV.

In 1774, Louis XV died and his grandson became Louis XVI. The new king revamped the government. He appointed as comptroller-general the most determined of all the physiocrats, Anne-Robert Jacques Turgot, Baron de l'Aulne. The comptroller-general obtained the new sovereign's approval for a thorough reform of the economy of France, which, had it been implemented, would have turned France into a liberal economy similar to Britain. Turgot wanted free trade, free labor, free capital, no government intervention. He emphasized the importance of educating the population with the latest industrial techniques—which the government supported with the publication of wonderfully illustrated manuals. He also sent deputations to study British industries. He appointed his friends Condorcet and d'Alembert to a committee aimed at improving river navigation and, in an additional touch of extraordinary modernity, reducing pollution. He wanted to decentralize power to local assemblies. It is impossible to think of a more progressive program, even today.[74]

The Rejection of Modernity

Turgot failed, however, to put his reforms in place. His program faced tremendous opposition from the nobility but also from the population at large. The people did not want modernization. Although they protested against the effects of feudalism, such as the inefficient supply of goods, they still wanted the security that feudal structures granted them, with its restrictions on economic freedom. So the French people embodied both change *and* opposition in their beliefs—a contradiction that was self-defeating.

This contradiction made the economic problems insoluble. People protested against the scarcity of grain, yet they wanted to keep in place the controls that depressed their supply. They denounced hoarding, yet they wanted to hoard regionally by forbidding sales to other localities. They wanted more job opportunities but also wanted to preserve the guild system, which prevented the expansion of those opportunities.

Following the example of the physiocrats, Turgot liberalized the price of grain and its derivatives, including bread, in all parts of France except Paris. Knowing this measure would lead to pricing uncertainty and thus encourage hoarding and excessive prices, he arranged beforehand the importation of grain from abroad. He also removed the local tolls on the product, abolished the monopolies, and disbanded the administrative bodies that granted them. Pierre Samuel du Pont de Nemours, a physiocrat who eventually established the famous American firm bearing his name, wrote an introduction to the edict. Voltaire was elated and sent Turgot a letter of congratulation.

But the people revolted. They burned farms, emptied granaries and threw their contents to the Seine, and blocked the transport of imported grain from Le Havre to Paris. More ominously, a mob of five thousand marched on Versailles and would have stormed it had not Louis restored price controls on the spot. Turgot protested and prevailed. Louis restored controls when the mob was gone, the imported grain arrived, grain prices fell, hoarders were forced to sell, and the crisis ended.

Turgot took advantage of this victory. He abolished the monopolies of chandlers, merchants, and porters. He deregulated the meat and fish markets, disbanding the powerful Bourse of Sceaux and Poissy, which set the prices of these products, and he abolished the regulations that forced the sale of certain parts of animals through special guilds.

Encouraged by the speed of his reforms, he then proposed to finish off feudalism altogether. He wanted to abolish all trade guilds and their monopolies as well as the restrictions they imposed on nonmembers. Finally, he wanted to eliminate the *corvée,* the forced labor that the state imposed on the commoners to build roads, and proposed financing public works with a tax on property, paid equally by all sectors of the population, including the nobility.[75]

This was too much. The new measures encountered a solid wall of opposition. They caused, or threatened to cause, the same kind of public response as the liberalization of grain prices. Most local authorities—themselves posed to lose from the reforms—chose not to enforce them. Turgot reacted by sending opponents and procrastinators to the Bastille. When Louis hesitated, Turgot told him unceremoniously that he (the king) was not only a bad judge of men but also a weakling. This was another mistake. Louis dismissed him and restored the guilds and other restrictions on free enterprise, to the great relief of the nobility and the population at large.[76]

Then the king involved the country in one of the most popular wars of pre-Napoleonic France: the war against Britain in support of the revolting American colonies. It was also one of the most expensive. The fiscal deficit increased enormously, to the point where it created the political crisis that ushered in the French Revolution. In this crisis, Louis found that no group would stand behind him, partly because his antecessor, Louis XIV, had weakened the natural allies of monarchy, the nobles.

The Missing Link

The nobility had lost touch with the people either because they lived in Versailles or because, even if living in their own localities, they had withdrawn from any economic activity apart from collecting rents. Their political functions were largely superseded by the bureaucracy, so they had no clear reason to exist. While many nobles participated in the creation of modern businesses and increased their wealth in the second half of the eighteenth century, most of them looked for bureaucratic positions in the centralized government and the sinecures that would afford them a living. Not being part of the centralized apparatus of government, they lacked the credibility to mediate solutions between the king and the population. The French nobility became a weak anachronism, and France lost the intermediate stratum that could have helped stabilize society.[77]

Many of the nobles tried to prop up their declining economic status by demanding additional economic privileges from the crown—such as increased tax exemptions and the exclusive right to occupy lucrative positions in the national bureaucracy. In the late 1780s, as France was falling under the weight of unsustainable fiscal deficits, the nobles forced Louis XVI to call the Estates General, believing that they would be able to negotiate these new privileges against some immediate taxes and contributions. Instead, as we all know, the convocation of the Estates General was the beginning of the end.

The nobles lost control of the process to the supporters of a more egalitarian society, and both were eventually eclipsed by extremists on both sides. The collapse of the moderates created a vacuum that was filled with violence and terror. The king—himself deluded by the idea of a return to absolutism—was alone against these terrible forces. Society slipped into chaos and, from there, to terror.

The Revolution

The explosion of violence was a clear sign of the rigidity of French society. Because of the politicization of economic life, the spirit of compromise that enlightened British political processes was absent in France. In the asphyxiating economic system of the epoch, everybody's economic success or failure depended on political decisions: most entrepreneurs became rich or poor on the basis of their ability to get licenses or concessions, and the acquisitive power of workers depended on the salaries and prices dictated by the government at different levels. The most lucrative business of the time was tax farming—advancing money to the state in exchange for the right to collect taxes (like Ivan Moneybags).

In this environment, all economic issues were transferred to the political arena, which was already overloaded by the conflict between democratic and autocratic ideas. Conflict in French society became an all-or-nothing affair.

Unable or unwilling to understand their own contradictions, the French revolted in frustration, killing the king, murdering thousands of others, and abolishing religion, only to discover that living without a king or Catholicism was not what they wanted. They did not want freedom but an emperor who would tell them what to do and reestablish predictability to their lives.

But they took the wrong path. Nothing in those years anticipated the democracy and the rule of rights that would become the foundation of the modern, free, liberal democratic state that would evolve during the nineteenth century. On the contrary, what the French Revolution produced was wholesale savagery that would characterize the communist revolutions and regimes that would rise 120 years later to defy liberal democracy.

The political system broke, not because most of the people wanted to change and a minority wanted to keep things as they were but because *most of the people did not want to change,* and things were changing by themselves.

THE FIRST INDUSTRIAL NATION

The Three Legacies

England and those countries that directly followed its example have bequeathed three great inventions to humankind: the rule of rights, modern democracy, and the industrial revolution. These three legacies are not unrelated: the rule of rights made possible sustainable democracy, and democracy and rights created the conditions for the emergence of the industrial revolution.

The historical process that delivered this outcome was complex. It started with the gradual establishment of the rule of rights, which had existed for centuries in England, not just among the aristocrats but across the entire population. Across this span of time, the concept of equal rights encouraged a belief in political equality in the minds of British citizens, which was firmly rooted by the early eighteenth century, along with the parallel belief that the king's power should be limited. By then, a kind of democracy already existed, although the political equals were all aristocrats, called peers. The quiet revolution that began at that time, about a century before the industrial revolution, consisted in extending the democratic rights of the peers to all subjects of the kingdom. In Britain, rights came first, and democracy, based on those rights, came later.

The Birth of Rights

The process that led to the British concept of rights had three distinctive features. First, consistent with British pragmatism, rights developed organically, not as part of a general academic theory but as a response to specific problems. The rights themselves, as well as the order in which they appeared, cannot be understood without reference to the circumstances in which they were first recognized. The word *recognized* is warranted because, throughout the process, the attitude of the population was that these rights existed as part of the human condition; they were not invented but recognized by society.

Second, the rights were acknowledged in two ways, by the courts and by the legislature. Usually, the latter gave shape to rights in statutes only after the judges had recognized them for centuries.

Third, progress was not linear. Kings often recognized rights only to renege on them soon afterward. The rights came back again and again, however, until they were part of the blood and bones of British society and had to be accepted definitively.

The most famous event in this long process is the Magna Carta of 1215, which enumerated the rights of an Englishman. Its contents were taken largely from a previous charter of liberties, which had been issued by King Henry I more than a century earlier, and from the coronation oaths of preceding kings.[78]

Many people believe that these rights referred only to the aristocracy. Yet most of the rights it included referred to the entire English population. As expressed by Sir James Clarke Holt, an expert on the Magna Carta:

> Magna was not a sudden intrusion into English society and politics. On the contrary, it grew out of them. . . . Laymen had been assuming, discussing and applying the principles of Magna Carta long before 1215. They could grasp it well enough.[79]

The rights included in the Magna Carta have survived the test of time. They have become part of the law in many countries. Three of its articles have retained even their original wording. The most important, Article 39, still reads:

> No Freeman shall be taken or imprisoned, or be disseised of his Freehold, or Liberties, or free Customs, or be outlawed, or exiled, or any other wise destroyed; nor will We not pass upon him, nor condemn him, but by lawful judgment of his Peers, or by the Law of the land. We will sell to no man, we will not deny or defer to any man either Justice or Right.[80]

Most of the rights listed in the Magna Carta do not refer to the petty interests of nobles, and all of them go much beyond what could be called economic legislation. Prohibiting the selling of justice, for example, goes against the interests of the very wealthy nobility. The document makes it clear that the aristocracy recognized dimensions that monetary power should not control. Because they held that power, this article eliminated any advantage that their money could give them in the management of justice.

King John signed the Magna Carta but repented immediately and asked for the pope's support to repudiate his signature. When the pope excommunicated the rebel barons who had drafted the Magna Carta, the First Barons' War exploded. Within a few months, John fell ill and died, leaving his nine-year-old son, Henry III, as heir to the throne. To secure the crown against the rebel barons, the new Henry pledged to comply with the Magna Carta.

The Magna Carta would be rejected by other kings, readopted by them, modified several times, and pledged to many more times. It became the basis for a king's oath of office. According to Sir Edward Coke, whose allegations against King Charles I in the sixteenth century, based on the Magna Carta, led to Charles's beheading, the Magna Carta was reconfirmed at least thirty-two times and as many as forty-five times between the thirteenth and the fifteenth centuries.[81]

By the early thirteenth century, common law judges were using writs of habeas corpus to ensure that no person was detained without legal cause. These writs required the accused, together with details of the date and cause of his detention, to be present before a court so that it might examine and determine whether such cause was legal. In the fifteenth century, trial by jury was established and torture was abolished.[82]

Judicial independence was affirmed in 1601, in a case involving the queen. In 1598, Queen Elizabeth granted a twelve-year monopoly to Edward Darcy for the manufacturing, import, and sale of playing cards. In 1601, he sued Thomas Allen for infringement of this monopoly. The court favored the infringer, holding that the queen could grant privileges and charters but only to promote the commonweal. They saw no benefit for the public in the monopoly of playing cards. To save face for the queen, the decision asserted that she had been deceived into approving something that she could not approve. The court set a clear limit to what the queen could do, and the queen obeyed.[83]

In 1610, the principle that "the king has not prerogative but that which the law of the land allows him" was established in a case involving James I. [84] Then, after the Glorious Revolution of 1689, the English Bill of Rights was passed into law, establishing rules to which the crown would be subject. Lord Bingham summarized those as follows:

> No monarch could again rely on divine authority to override the law. The authority and independence of Parliament were proclaimed; the integrity of its procedures were protected; and there could be no standing army in time of peace without its sanction. The power to suspend laws without the consent of Parliament was condemned as illegal. So was the power of dispensing with laws or the execution of laws "as it hath been assumed and exercised of late," a provision which later legislation was intended to clarify but never did. Personal liberty and security were protected by prohibiting the requirement of excessive fines, the imposition of excessive bail, and the infliction of "cruel and unusual punishments."[85]

As in the case of the Magna Carta, the Bill of Rights was not a late-hour invention. It reasserted in legal form what had been considered rights of English subjects for centuries. All these important laws and proclamations were critical steps in Britain's emergence as a multi-dimensional society.

THE QUIET REVOLUTION

The history of how these new social forces were absorbed into this already multidimensional society is a fascinating one because it is the chronicle of a powerful and haughty old elite presiding over the gradual dismantling of its own economic and political power. Democracy already existed, and political equality was cherished, but only for the aristocracy. The quiet revolution that took place in the nineteenth century consisted in extending those rights to all the subjects of the kingdom. The process turned everyone into a political peer. The fundamental principle that gave legitimacy to the British regime—that the power emanated from the people—was maintained throughout. The change was the definition of the people: from aristocrats only, to aristocrats and bourgeois, to all males, and then to everyone. The process was one of downward extension of a horizontal web of relations that had prevailed in British peerage, a process consistent with the requirements of the industrial revolution. The past and the future were harmonious and so was the adjustment.

At the beginning of the industrial revolution, England certainly had a precedent for violent change of government: the three civil wars that led to the beheading of Charles I and the establishment of a republic that lasted eleven years in the mid-seventeenth century. This experience, which in Britain was generally considered traumatic, may have influenced the attitude of the British people toward both violent change and pure societies, conditioning their response to the challenges posed by the industrial revolution.

Along with those civil wars and the peaceful Glorious Revolution, the seventeenth century witnessed a very important phenomenon: the unification of the country into a single economic and political space. Unlike France, the unification was not led by the central state but by the aristocracy, which kept its local functions while connecting its localities with the British Parliament. Throughout the process, the aristocracy provided a counterbalance to the power of the king, creating the space needed for a multidimensional society. The aristocracy also led the transition of power to the people.

Why no revolutions and no tyranny, even though the aristocracy had the upper hand, politically and economically? The aristocracy was a multidimensional group within a multidimensional society. Its members may have shared a common social origin, but they were not a uniform group and did not act in concert politically. On the contrary, they had substantial differences of opinion and acted in accordance with them. Independence of mind was a basic tenet of their education. Also, they were individualistic in their business interests.

In fact, the only truly unifying feature they shared was their respect for the rights of the Englishman and for the institutions they had inherited from their forefathers. They shared those principles with the entire British population. They knew that tyranny was unacceptable to their peers and to the rest of the people.

The process through which the British aristocrats relinquished their power during the nineteenth century was led by the Whig Party, which later became the Liberal Party. They could not be distinguished from their opposition—the Tories—in terms of wealth, distinction, or lineage. These formidable aristocrats dominated British politics from the end of the seventeenth century to the end of World War I by the force of their ideas, which pushed the country in the direction of classical liberalism.

The demolition of their own authority started in 1832 with the Reform Act.[86] This act initiated the expansion of enfranchisement, which would culminate in 1918 with the approval of universal suffrage. Their liberal ideas also convinced them to abolish the Corn Laws, which reduced their own income by establishing free trade. These laws had protected domestic agricultural producers since 1815, and although many aristocrats had expanded their economic base to mining and manufacturing, most of their income came from agriculture. With the abolition of the Corn Laws, the price of agricultural goods declined sharply and so did the income and land value of peers. Expanding the franchise also reduced their political power. Gradually, the House of Lords became the only place where the aristocracy still enjoyed exclusive access to power, although over time even this power declined in favor of the House of Commons.

The Lubricants

This relatively peaceful transfer of power was helped by four channels that established a multidimensional communication between the old and new elites, and between them and the rest of the population. One was business. The aristocracy invested heavily in industrial and commercial activities and joined the economic wave that was sweeping away their privileges. The second was the merging of the aristocracy with the bourgeoisie, which allowed aristocratic structures of social status and prestige to remain untouched. The aristocracy enabled this change by allowing their sons and daughters, whose wealth was declining, to marry the offspring of the wealthy bourgeoisie; allowing the sons of the bourgeoisie to attend their elite schools, where the values and attitudes of the aristocracy were asserted; selling at handsome prices old manors to the new millionaires; and even doing things as simple as inviting the bourgeoisie to their exclusive parties.

Third, the plutocrats of industry and finance entered en masse into the aristocracy through their participation in politics. Most of them did not participate directly in the electoral process but sponsored politicians who reciprocated by ennobling their patrons. The fourth channel enveloped the entire citizenry. It was the shared conceptions of society and justice. For centuries, aristocrats had used these conceptions to push kings into becoming subject to the rule of law. In the nineteenth century, the aristocracy could not abjure those principles and rights. They had to go on and apply throughout society what they had maintained in their conflicts with the kings.

All these mechanisms were possible only in a multidimensional society, where the sources of economic success, political power, prestige, and distinction were disseminated among many different groups so that no individual could control all the levers that moved society. This process was the opposite of that taking place in vertical societies like Germany, where the *Junkers*, the feudal lords of German agriculture, coopted industrialists to defy democracy and workers.

The End of Harmony

The seemingly harmonious world that prevailed domestically in Britain for most of the nineteenth century came to an end in the early 1900s, when, like today, everything that seemed to be in order suddenly fell into disorder. Politics, which had been courteous throughout the nineteenth century, suddenly became so rough that for a few months it seemed the country would fall into a civil war over the issue of Ireland's home rule. The relationship between the House of Commons and the House of Lords turned into an open battle over social expenditure and the relative powers of the two houses. The civilized relationship that had existed for many decades between workers and employers also went sour, and for the first time Britain suffered from large and angry strikes. Suffragettes, then campaigning for women's right to vote, resorted to arson and other terrorist actions to push for their objectives. To make things worse, Germany, a formidable enemy just across the North Sea, was becoming increasingly aggressive. Its economy had become bigger than Britain's, and it was posing the first credible threat to the Royal Navy's domination of the seas. Everything was coming apart.

Of these crises, only the Irish problem proved lasting. When World War I ended, Ireland got its independence, although a piece of the island, Ulster, remained part of the United Kingdom. Catholics and Protestants would continue to fight throughout the twentieth century. The other crises were settled, some of them immediately, some of them decades later. Women got the vote, the country became a full-fledged welfare state, the empire was dissolved, and labor unrest calmed as the country found new ways to deal with labor conflicts in a peaceful way.

The solutions to these problems were part of a deep process of transformation that changed the country radically in four main dimensions. One was the change in the composition of production. The kind of goods and services that Britain produced in the late nineteenth century were different from the ones that would characterize its economy during the midyears of the twentieth. The second dimension was the change from being the most powerful country in the world to becoming a distant third by the end of World War II and to a more relegated position in the ensuing decades. The third was the completion of a transformation to full democracy. The fourth was the government shifting to meet the new role that citizens demanded from a welfare state.

These transformations were so far-reaching that they would be enough to break any social structure. Pressures like these destroyed Germany's institutional framework. But the British structure not only resisted; its core, the rule of rights, remained untouched.

The twentieth century took Britain from the right to the left and back. It went from being the utmost exponent of liberal capitalism to being one of the most socialistic economies in the world through the nationalization of many large industries, and it went back to being one of the most capitalistic societies after these nationalized industries were privatized. And all this happened with typical British ease. Through its long experiment with socialism, the British kept in place the most important features of their society: their love of freedom, their social cohesion, and the rule of rights. This protected them against the imposition of tyranny and allowed the country to engage in political and social experiments that did not limit their freedom or their ability to come back from what they thought was wrong.

The Empire

There was another side to the history of Britain. For many years during the nineteenth century, the supply of labor grew faster than domestic demand, and many people became permanently unemployed, prompting an enormous wave of emigration to the United States, Canada, Australia, New Zealand, and to a lesser extent some parts of Latin America. From 1853 to 1910, emigration from Britain totaled 2.2 million people, or about 12 percent of the total population.[87]

Britain's growing empire helped resolve the unemployment problem not just through migration but also through the creation of an imperial bureaucracy and army, as well as through the sale of British industrial products to the colonized societies. It also provided a national goal. Yet this change was not a positive one for the country. And it did not fit the nation's multidimensionality.

India was a case in point. Around 1757, the East India Company, a joint-stock company chartered in 1600 by Queen Elizabeth to trade with the East, got involved with Indian domestic conflicts and took possession of growing portions of the disintegrating Moghul Empire. The company developed a bureaucracy to govern India and recruited young graduates from British universities to run it. It appointed a governor to head this government and created an Indian army with Indian soldiers and British officers.

In this way, India became a private empire supported by the British government, which sent British battalions to serve alongside the Indian army. The Royal Navy also patrolled the seas around India and their navigation lanes. So economic and political power in India was fused. This one-dimensional imperialism contrasted with Britain's core multidimensionality. The consequences of such one-dimensionality were harmful for both Britain and India.

The negative consequences for India were obvious. Prior to 1757, when the relationship between the East India Company and India was still purely commercial, the British paid for Indian goods. Indian demand for British wares was almost nonexistent (Indians were too poor), and during the seventeenth and eighteenth centuries, the company could not pay for what they bought in India by selling British goods. So the cotton and silk shipped from India were paid for with gold. After the company conquered Bengal, it stopped sending gold. The Indian products were paid with taxes that the company imposed on the Bengalis. That is, the company obtained for free the products of Bengal, courtesy of the Bengalis themselves, who paid high taxes even if they were very poor. The result was a series of famines that marked the early years of the Indian Empire. The worst of them, in 1770, killed millions of Bengalis.[88] Whig politician Horace Walpole wrote the following in a 1772 letter:

> We have murdered, deposed, plundered, usurped—nay, what think you of the famine in Bengal, in which three million perished, caused by a monopoly of the provisions by the servants of the East India Company.[89]

The power of the East India Company went well beyond India. In the late 1830s, the Chinese emperor decided to put an end to opium consumption in China, which was fed from British India, mainly by the East India Company and other British companies. A few months after the emperor's decision, a formidable British naval force, which included the rocket-launching iron steamer *Nemesis,* destroyed the weak Chinese navy. The East India Company had commissioned the *Nemesis* a few years before, but most other ships sailed under the flag of the Royal Navy. As in India, private companies and the government were difficult to differentiate. The British companies regained the right to sell opium in China, and the British crown took over Hong Kong. China also opened five ports to trade: Canton, Amoy, Fuzhou, Ningpo, and Shanghai.[90]

Although the most barbarous episodes of exploitation came to an end in the ensuing decades, mostly as a result of public opinion in Britain, imperialism continued to be a blot on a country that otherwise led the world in liberalism and multidimensionality. And the violence associated with vertical control continued. In 1857, certain units of the Indian army rebelled and committed terrible atrocities against the British. The British responded with equally terrible atrocities against the rebels. The rebellion was so traumatic that the British government decided that India could not be left to the management of a private company and appointed Queen Victoria empress of India.

In Africa, the British government conquered territories rich in minerals, conquests that required the frequent use of military force. The bloodiest of these wars, against the Boers, was fought at the close of the nineteenth century for control of the Witwatersrand gold mines. During that war, the British implemented a scorched earth policy to prevent the Boers from getting their supplies locally. They poisoned wells; slaughtered livestock; destroyed crops; salted the fields; burned down homesteads and farms; and forcibly interned women and children in concentration camps, where they lived in appalling conditions. By the end of the war, 27,000 Boers (mainly children, about 14.5 percent of the entire Boer population) had died in those camps. A further 14,000 black Africans died in separate camps.[91] Most of them died of starvation or infectious diseases.

The negative effects of this one-dimensional exploitation were not limited to the colonies. Imperialism was a corrupting force. The one-dimensionality of imperialism filtered into Britain in many ways. The men coming back from the colonies purchased not just mansions but also political representation. They became a source of corruption and pressed for imperialistic policies. Prime Minister William Pitt the Elder wrote in the eighteenth century:

> The riches of Asia have been poured upon us and have brought with them not only Asiatic luxury, but Asiatic principles of government.[92]

The reality of the empire, however, was more complex than any one-dimensional description could render. The South African concentration camps were barbaric. Almost a sixth of the Boer population found their death there. A British woman, Emily Hobhouse, got access to the camps and strongly denounced their terrible conditions. Back in England, she convinced the government to appoint a commission to investigate her claims, and conditions in the camps improved immediately.[93] The British people did not forget the camps, and their revulsion for this episode was an important factor in the catastrophic defeat of the government in the 1906 elections (although this was no consolation, of course, for the Boers who suffered in the camps).

This was not the only case in which public opinion was instrumental in controlling the excesses of empire. There were many defenders of the rights of oppressed peoples. It is impossible to imagine a German woman visiting a Nazi extermination camp in the 1940s, denouncing them in Berlin, and obtaining immediate improvement in the conditions or the liberation of the prisoners. It would be just as impossible to imagine the same happening in the gulags in the Soviet Union.

In the end, the British discharged a good portion of their imperial burden, with varying degrees of application and success. Proof is in their material and intellectual legacies in their ex-colonies, and in the cultural linkages and special relationships that have remained between the old imperial center and its colonies. But history cannot be changed, and the justification of aggression based on the notion of superiority was there. For this reason, Hannah Arendt, in *The Origins of Totalitarianism,* included imperialism among the three totalitarian systems of the last two centuries, along with communism and Nazism.[94]

This discrimination between local and foreign populations is, of course, not a result of capitalism or liberal democracy. It has happened throughout history in all places and societies under all kinds of social orders. It has existed even in the most civilized countries. Many societies that have been victims of imperialism practiced by liberal democracies have been, at the same time, victimizers of weaker societies. If anything, it has been in liberal democracies where voices have been raised to apply the rights that they grant to their citizens to everybody living under the power of their government, locally or abroad.

THE LESSONS OF BRITAIN AND FRANCE

The British experience was radically different from the French. France looked for a government-managed industrial revolution; immersed itself in a bloody political revolution; and trailed well behind Britain in the development of democracy, the rule of rights, and capitalism. The fact that France had the most impressive bureaucracy in the world did not help its economic, social, and political development. On the contrary, the rigidity of the bureaucracy was a major factor in France's lagging response to industrialization. French rigidity, of which the bureaucracy was just one symptom, was a contributing factor to its collapse in chaos during the revolution and to its subsequent instability.

The Count of Mirabeau, a moderate leader in the initial stages of the French Revolution, wrote a secret letter to Louis XVI analyzing the proclamation of equality by the revolutionaries, which eliminated the privileged classes and the nobility. He suggested that the proclamation was good news for the king as it eliminated the effectiveness of the aristocracy and thus the checks and balances that prevented the king from exercising absolute power. If everybody was reduced to the same level, the country would have one very powerful magnate, the king, and millions of individuals incapable of organizing an opposition.[95] That was the secret of the power of the tsars, communist leaders, Hitler, Mao, and their colleagues in absolute power.

Ian Kershaw explained the same point when discussing Hitler's ability to drag Germany into a suicidal war:

> The dominant elites, divided as they were, possessed neither the collective will nor the mechanisms of power to prevent Hitler taking Germany to total destruction. *That* was decisive.[96]

Elites may lack the power to oppose a potential tyrant because they are divided or have been weakened. The secret of the multidimensional society is the existence of equilibrium between very powerful groups, not their debilitation. Equally damaging is a weakening of the government. Of course, Mirabeau did not foresee that totally eliminating the intermediate stratum that Louis XIV had weakened would help impose a different tyranny. As we will see when looking at the United States during the Great Depression, some important checks and balances, arguably the most important of them all, are embedded not in government procedures but in the way that power is distributed in the society at large.

8

THE GILDED AGE:
THE UNITED STATES
AND GERMANY

*We can return to the beasts. But if we wish to remain human, then
there is only one way, the way into the open society.*

Karl Popper

THE APPARENT TWINS

The responses of autocratic France and liberal Britain to the ideas of
the Enlightenment are a good measure of the differences in behavior
between one- and multidimensional societies. It would take France a
century to catch up with Britain. A comparable difference separated the
behavior of Germany and the United States at the turn of the twentieth
century. The second stage of the industrial revolution introduced several disrupting trends in both countries: increasing returns to scale, the
monopolies and large combines that resulted, and conflicts between the
new industrialists and their workers. These trends took place in Britain
as well, but Germany and the United States experienced almost identical development.

These two countries were the emerging markets of the time. They
competed against each other and against the first industrial country,
Britain. Unlike Britain, they closed their domestic markets to foreign
competition and exploited their economies of scale with enormous
monopolies and trusts. In both Germany and the United States, new

industrial entrepreneurs accumulated fortunes that gave them great political power, threatening to turn their countries into one-dimensional industrial societies. But only Germany became one-dimensional. In fact, it had turned one-dimensional in the previous centuries, and the industrial revolution only reinforced its verticality.

Why did the same stimuli that reinforced Germany's one-dimensionality help the United States confirm its multidimensionality? Answering this question is challenging because the United States started from a much more vertical situation than Germany. Germany had a vertical government, but the United States had slavery and a policy of killing or exiling Native Americans. At the end of the period, Germany had become more vertical, while the United States, even if still stained by wholesale discrimination and even clearly imperialistic, had nevertheless become more horizontal.

THE UNITED STATES

Slavery

By the time the United States gained its independence from Britain, its thirteen new states had evolved into two different societies, so different that they could have been separate countries. While the North had remained democratic and egalitarian, in the South an aristocratic, unequal society rooted in slavery had developed. Gradually, this immoral institution had turned the South into a profoundly vertical society that threatened to pull the entire United States into destructiveness.

In the early 1830s, the French writer Alexis de Tocqueville observed the difference between North and South and the horrible effects slavery had on both slaves and the people who owned them. He noted that "the influence of slavery affected the character of the masters, and imparted a peculiar tendency to their ideas and tastes."[97] He described his experiences when floating down the Ohio River, looking at the free state of Ohio on his right and the slave state of Kentucky on his left:

> Upon the left bank of the Ohio labor is confounded with the idea of slavery, upon the right bank it is identified with that of prosperity and improvement; on the one side it is degraded, on the other it is honored; on the former territory no white laborers can be found, for they would be afraid of assimilating themselves to the negroes; on the latter no one is idle, for the white population extends its activity and its intelligence

to every kind of employment. Thus the men whose task it is to cultivate the rich soil of Kentucky are ignorant and lukewarm; whilst those who are active and enlightened either do nothing or pass over into the State of Ohio, where they may work without dishonor. [98]

The chasm between the two societies was deep and wide and pierced the new country to its core. One society was egalitarian, the other aristocratic. As de Tocqueville noted:

> In the South of the United States the whole race of whites formed an aristocratic body, which was headed by a certain number of privileged individuals, whose wealth was permanent, and whose leisure was hereditary. These leaders of the American nobility kept alive the traditional prejudices of the white race in the body of which they were the representatives, and maintained the honor of inactive life. This aristocracy contained many who were poor, but none who would work; its members preferred want to labor, consequently no competition was set on foot against negro laborers and slaves, and, whatever opinion might be entertained as to the utility of their efforts, it was indispensable to employ them, since there was no one else to work. [99]

The South did not have developed industry or finance and did not want to have them because they believed these activities were the carriers of moral decline and would destroy the rural dream of honest, truthful, landed proprietors—and would inevitably lead to the demise of slavery and the ruin of those proprietors.

This vision was ultimately based on the ideas of Thomas Jefferson, who opposed urbanization, industrialization, commerce, and finance— precisely the harbingers of the new industrial revolution giving shape to the new nation, and precisely the activities that were developing rapidly in the North. Later in life, Jefferson would soften his position and accept that the manufacturer should be placed by the side of the agriculturalist, but he still insisted that an industrial economy in the English fashion, with merchants, bankers, and industrialists, should be considered of far less importance. [100]

In his *Notes on the State of Virginia,* written in 1781–82, Jefferson condemned the industrial revolution, just starting in England:

> Those who labour in the earth are the chosen people of God, if ever he had a chosen people, whose breasts he has made his peculiar deposit for substantial and genuine virtue . . . but, generally speaking, the

proportion which the aggregate of the other classes of citizens bears in any state to that of its husbandmen, is the proportion of its unsound to its healthy parts, and is a good-enough barometer whereby to measure its degree of corruption. . . . The mobs of great cities add just so much to the support of pure government, as sores do to the strength of the human body. It is the manners and spirit of a people which preserve a republic in vigour. A degeneracy in these is a canker which soon eats to the heart of its laws and constitution.[101]

Jefferson also had an ambiguous stance on slavery. In *Notes on the State of Virginia,* he wrote that slavery was possible only because God's justice was sleeping in his time:

For if a slave can have a country in his world, it must be any other in preference to that in which he is born to live and labour for another. . . . This is so true, that of the proprietors of slaves a very small proportion indeed are seen to labour. And can the liberties of a nation be thought secure when we have removed their only firm basis, a conviction in the minds of people that these liberties are the gift of God? That they are not to be violated but with his wrath? Indeed I tremble for my country. When I reflect that God is just: that his justice cannot sleep for ever: that considering numbers, nature and natural means only, a revolution of the wheel of fortune, an exchange of situation, is among possible events; that it may become probable by supernatural interference! The Almighty has no attribute which can take sides with us in such a contest.[102]

Still, he never manumitted his slaves, except for a few he liberated in his will. As governor of Virginia and president of the United States for two terms, he did nothing to liberate slaves or even improve their condition. He adopted the Southern position that, if liberated, African Americans should not be allowed to live in the South. Since sending them back to Africa was not feasible (their population would grow faster than they could be sent), the implicit conclusion was that the only solution was to keep them enslaved.

This appalling contradiction between what many new American leaders said and what they did, especially in the South, was a glaring manifestation of the toxic effect of slavery in the soul of the United States. The country could despise its sin but could not stop committing it.

Thus, in the crucial period from independence to 1860, the United States faced a double opposition to modernity: from those who wished to maintain the institution of slavery and those opposed to industrialization and its financing. Although one form was immoral and corrupt and the other merely economic, they nevertheless coalesced into a single fierce opposition that was most prominent in the South.

This opposition created a growing difference in the level and composition of wealth between the North and the South. Plausible estimates put total wealth per free person in 1860 at $482 in the North and $868 in the South; subtracting the value of the slaves (at market prices), however, the wealth per free person in the North remained at $482 while that of the free person in the South went down to $294.[103]

Free Southerners paid dearly for this wealth differential during the Civil War, when the total wealth invested in other types of capital (railroads, factories, infrastructure) was about three times more in the North than in the South, and the South's lack of infrastructure and industrial resources was one of the main reasons why it lost the war. They paid again at the end of the war, when the liberation of slaves removed two-thirds of their wealth and the South's plantations became unprofitable overnight.[104] White Southerners lost not just the capital they had invested in slavery but also their business model, and it took them a long time to learn a different one. In 1880, fifteen years after the end of the Civil War, the average per capita wealth of the South was $376, much lower than the average in the other states, which stood at $1,086. Individually, all Southern states were at least $300 below the national average. Slavery left a legacy of poverty that lasted almost a hundred years, well into the twentieth century.[105]

Of course, the plight of white Southerners was nothing compared to the suffering of African Americans, who bore the brutality and injustice of slavery and continued to suffer poverty, discrimination, and massive disparities in wealth and freedom during Reconstruction and beyond.

The political scenario of the new country was not auspicious for the development of a modern society. For the first six decades, people who lived, or said they lived, in the Southern tradition dominated American politics. The Democratic-Republican Party, which opposed a national bank and believed strongly in states' rights, held executive power for seven consecutive presidential periods, from 1801 to 1829. Andrew Jackson, who founded the Democratic Party, carried the South and succeeded that Democratic-Republican stretch in 1829. He based his new party on similar principles of agrarianism, opposition to finance, and implicitly slavery. And Jackson's support gave new life to these ideas.

Many Democratic-Republicans and Democrats were opposed to slavery, and the politics of the period was nuanced and complicated; however, the dominant strain in US politics bent toward the South. These politicians respected the rules of the Constitution and the checks and balances that gave form to American democracy. But throughout these years the political representatives of the South, most of them slaveholders themselves, dominated Washington's political circles and worked hard at turning the growing territory of the United States into a predominantly slaveholding country, a country living under the values of the South.

Southern attitudes to slavery had a strong counterbalance. For many years after independence, slavery was legal throughout the United States. Yet by 1819, slavery had been banned in eleven states, all in the North, matching exactly the eleven states of the South where slavery remained legal. In that year, Missouri requested admission to the United States as a slave state, which would upset the equilibrium in Congress between free and slave states. To keep the balance, Congress admitted Maine (which separated from Massachusetts) as a free state and established a boundary between free and slave states that ran across the new territories at the 36°30' parallel. Except for Missouri, all the lands north of this latitude would be free. From that year, the difference between the North and the South became sharper.

The North was becoming a modern commercial, financial, and industrial power—the cradle of what became the United States of our times. The South might dominate the halls of Washington, but the North increasingly dominated the markets. This dichotomy was a hopeful sign of the multidimensionality of the United States: the South could not prevent the North and the growing territories and states in the West from reaffirming their horizontal vocation. If Southern politicians had been able to control the economy of the North, the country could have sunk into tyranny and destructiveness.

The political hegemony of the South seemed to be increasing. When the Supreme Court's chief justice, John Marshall, died, President Jackson appointed Roger Brooke Taney as his successor. Taney, who remained chief justice for thirty years, is remembered primarily for the Court's infamous verdict in the 1857 case of *Dred Scott v. Sanford*. Sanford had taken two slaves, Dred Scott and his wife, to the free states of Illinois and Wisconsin for extended periods. Scott claimed that he and his wife should be granted their freedom because they had lived in these free states for four years. Based on the principle that "once free, always free," which had been applied for twenty-eight years, a judge decided for Scott and his wife. When the case reached the Supreme Court, it ruled that any person descended from Africans, whether slave or free, was not a citizen of the United States and therefore could not possess the legal standing required to bring suit in a federal court. Taney further justified his Court's sentence, arguing that Congress was prohibited by the Fifth Amendment from depriving individuals of their private property without due process. The Scotts were the private property of their owners, who could take them anywhere in the United States without impairing their ownership.

The decision not only defeated the efforts of Scott and his wife but also killed the principle that states could decide to forbid slavery in their territories. It also nullified the Missouri Compromise, federal legislation passed to ensure that slavery would not be adopted by new states in the West. Taney's decision declared this legislation unconstitutional, opening the door for continued expansion of slavery.

This decision was the ultimate turn of the screw for resistance to change. The forces of slavery had been able to command the strongest of the institutional checks and balances and pervert the meaning of the Constitution to perpetuate slavery. The decision signaled a sinister destiny for the nation. Abraham Lincoln saw it clearly: the country would have to go one way or the other, and he trembled at the prospect of the entire country debased by slavery. On June 16, 1858, the delegates to the Illinois Republican Party chose Lincoln as their candidate for the Senate, running against Democrat Stephen Douglas, author of the Kansas-Nebraska Act, which allowed western states south of the Missouri Compromise line to decide whether they wanted to be slave or free. On that occasion, Lincoln delivered a speech that clearly spelled out his concern that slavery would destroy the country. He pointed to the increasing agitation for slavery; warned about the approaching crisis that such agitation would bring; and, with amazing clarity, passed judgment on the slaveholders' invocation of self-government to enslave a minority. In the most famous part of the speech, he predicted what would happen to the United States if this process continued:

> A house divided against itself cannot stand. I believe this government cannot endure half *slave* and half *free*. I do not expect the Union to be *dissolved*. I do not expect the House to *fall*. But I *do* expect it will cease to be divided. It will become *all* one thing, or *all* the other. Either

the *opponents* of slavery will arrest the further spread of it, and place it where the public mind shall rest in the belief that it is in course of ultimate extinction; or its *advocates* will push it forward, till it shall become alike lawful in *all* states, *old* as well as *new*, *North* as well as *South*.[106]

Of course, the Civil War, with all its suffering and carnage, including the death of Lincoln himself, would follow. And though the war delivered emancipation for slaves, after a brief period of transition, the period of Reconstruction, the states of the South passed Jim Crow legislation that formalized institutional discrimination against African Americans, politically, socially, and economically. And the federal government would fail to address this legislation for nearly a hundred years. By the turn of the twentieth century, African Americans were living in what Isabel Wilkerson called "a feudal caste system." African Americans emigrated to the North in massive numbers. In *The Warmth of Other Suns*, Wilkerson described the conditions that pushed the African Americans to migrate:

> From the early years of the twentieth century to well past its middle age, nearly every black family in the American South, which means nearly every black family in America, had a decision to make. There were sharecroppers losing at settlement. Typists wanting to work in an office. Yard boys scared that a single gesture near the planter's wife could leave them hanging from an oak tree. They were all stuck in a caste system as hard and unyielding as the red Georgia clay, and they each had a decision before them. . . . [The migration] would become a turning point in history. . . . It would force the South to search its soul and finally to lay aside a feudal caste system. [107]

By 1970, when the Great Migration ended, six million African Americans had moved from the South to the great cities of the North. By that time, 47 percent of all African Americans were living in the North compared to only 10 percent when the Great Migration started.[108] The Jim Crow regime persisted in the South from the 1880s to the 1960s, when it ended as a result of a confrontation between the black population, national civil rights organizations, and the federal government on one side, and a substantial portion of the population of the South on the other.

Of course, discrimination throughout the United States has remained a crucially destructive force in the otherwise multidimensional US society. Slavery remains a stain on US history, just as imperialism blighted British history. Yet historically, the Civil War ended slavery and opened the West for the development of an enormous horizontal society. The transformation that US society went through in the seventy or eighty years after the end of the war created an entirely new country and strained US society drastically. There were many confrontations between the forces for change and those who resisted it. However, never again would either align with a political party or with a geographic location. The country could not be split, as it had been during the years leading up to the Civil War, into two definite camps—at least up to the present day, when the red–blue divide of American politics is drifting dangerously close to vertical confrontation.

Native Americans

Another vertical dimension to US society in the nineteenth century caused immense destruction: the way the country treated Native Americans, who, for most of history, have been seen as enemies of the country's Manifest Destiny. As enemies, they needed to be dominated and defeated, and over time America's European immigrants and their descendants exiled most of the continent's original inhabitants, offering them a stark choice (when they didn't kill them) of either being assimilated into the European culture or moving to inferior and alien territory in the West. By the end of the nineteenth century, Native Americans had been expelled from almost the entire country, including the barren lands of the West, and banished to remote reservations.

In 1824, President James Monroe said that moving the Indians (as they were called at the time) west of the Mississippi was an absolute necessity. His secretary of war, John C. Calhoun, said that the great difficulty was not the savagery of the Indians but the progress they were making toward civilization.[109] In Georgia, 15,000 Cherokees, who were not nomads but farmers, had established a representative government, judicial courts (including a supreme court), a police force, schools, and private property. They had formed a republic with a senate and a lower house. In 1827, they had enacted their own constitution, based on that of the United States, enfranchising all free male citizens excepting those of African descent. They had begun to industrialize. They had two thousand spinning wheels, seven hundred looms, thirty-one gristmills, and eight cotton gins. Their capital, New Echota, was a clean and nice city. Like the country at large, however, they had 1,500 black slaves.[110]

That year, Georgia demanded that the federal government remove the Cherokee people. President Jackson declared that he did not want to allow the Cherokee to create a different country inside the United States. Other well-ordered communities emerging at the time were treated with respect. The Cherokee republic's racial origin was deemed unacceptable. Utah, which had a religious origin, would show in time that the country could accept new states based on different principles, but racism was so deeply ingrained in the American experiment that the culture could not accept a separate, equal community of Native Americans.

In 1830, Congress passed the Indian Removal Act, which authorized the federal government to move any Indians still living east of the Mississippi across the river, by force if necessary. With the help of some whites, the Cherokees appealed to the Supreme Court. In *Cherokee Nation v. Georgia,* one of the last suits it considered, the Marshall Court ruled that the Cherokee tribe was not a nation in the sense meant by the Constitution and therefore could not bring suit. The federal government herded the Indians across the Mississippi.[111]

In his 1831 peregrination through the United States, de Tocqueville witnessed such a forced migration and wrote about it:

> At the end of the year 1831, whilst I was on the left bank of the Mississippi at a place named by Europeans, Memphis, there arrived a numerous band of Choctaws (or Chactas, as they are called by the French in Louisiana). These savages had left their country, and were endeavoring to gain the right bank of the Mississippi, where they hoped to find an asylum which had been promised them by the American government. It was then the middle of winter, and the cold was unusually severe; the snow had frozen hard upon the ground, and the river was drifting huge masses of ice. The Indians had their families with them; and they brought in their train the wounded and sick, with children newly born, and old men on the verge of death. They possessed neither tents nor wagons, but only their arms and some provisions. I saw them embark to pass the mighty river, and never will that solemn spectacle fade from my remembrance. No cry, no sob was heard amongst the assembled crowd; all were silent. Their calamities were of ancient date, and they knew them to be irremediable. . . . Half convinced, and half compelled, they go to inhabit new deserts, where the importunate whites will not let them remain ten years in tranquility.[112]

The feeling of Native Americans was captured by de Tocqueville in this moving passage:

> The social tie, which distress had long since weakened, is then dissolved; they have lost their country, and their people soon desert them; their very families are obliterated; the names they bore in common are forgotten, their language perishes, and all traces of their origin disappeared. Their nation has ceased to exist, except in the recollection of the antiquaries in America and a few of the learned in Europe.[113]

American Populism

The United States in the nineteenth century was rife with injustice, but the country did establish the foundations of a multidimensional society that provided the ongoing means of addressing that injustice and working toward becoming a free and fair society.

At the end of the Civil War, the railroad and the telegraph created a national market that opened the door to an expanded national industry, with increasing returns to scale, and mass production and huge savings in overall costs. Initially, industry was concentrated in two main corridors, the Atlantic seaboard between Baltimore and Boston, and the Great Lakes, but the railroads extended industrial impact to the whole country. It was a period of huge growth but also huge risk. The post–Civil War boom was followed by a giant bust that would lead to the country's first great populist movement.

Like today, the distribution of income and wealth deteriorated sharply in the 1890s, financial crises became frequent, and the economy slowed down. The deterioration of income and wealth was at both ends of the social spectrum: some people reached unprecedented levels of wealth, while some were impoverished. Among those hardest hit were farmers. And like today, these problems were rooted in a technological revolution.

Before the crash, new technologies and machines had enabled cultivation of the dry lands of the West. The productivity of land and labor skyrocketed, and the United States became the granary of the world. As the productivity of land increased, so did land prices, affording large capital gains to farmers, many of whom became land speculators and often earned large profits.

Technology turned against the farmer, however, at the end of the century. Modern transportation had helped farmers to integrate into the huge emerging US market, but it also created a global market, allowing countries like Argentina and the British dominions to become large exporters of agricultural products that competed with US agricultural products. In the 1890s, worldwide oversupply brought about a global agricultural crisis that proved deadly for many farmers. Many of them discovered that they had borrowed too much, believing that the price of land would always continue to rise. When the price of their products crashed, the price of land collapsed as well. Bankers took advantage to charge extremely high interest rates on their loans. As described by C. Vann Woodward, under the crop-lien system then in fashion,

> the farmer pledged an unplanted crop for a loan of an unstipulated amount at an undesignated but enormous rate of interest averaging about 60 per cent per year. Trapped by the system, a farmer might continue year after oppressive year as a sort of a peon, under debt to the same merchant and under constant oversight.[114]

Because many farmers could not service their debts under these conditions, creditors foreclosed many mortgaged properties, and a wave of bankruptcies desolated rural areas. The stress and discontent of farmers gave birth to a radical political party, the People's Party, also known as the Populist Party, which flourished in rural areas at the turn of the twentieth century. This party's ideas were eerily similar to those of the *Volk* movement in Germany and of other populist ideologies of the twentieth century. They were manifestations of resistance to change.

The populist credo had several points. First, it saw history as a one-dimensional confrontation of two forces, one good and the other bad. The good people toiled under the natural harmonies of the old, agrarian ways of living. The bad lived under the perverse principles of urban industry and finance.

Second, the good people were many while the bad people were few, a small parasitic minority. As a populist manifesto said, "On the one side are the allied hosts of monopolies, the money power, great trusts and railroad corporations. . . . On the other are the farmers, laborers, merchants, and all the people who produce wealth and bear the burdens of taxation. . . . Between these two there is no middle ground."

Third, the dangerous state of the world was the result of a massive international conspiracy of the few aimed at enslaving the many. The 1892, the People's Party platform said: "A vast conspiracy against mankind has been organized on two continents, and it is rapidly taking possession of the world."

Fourth, in a sinister tone, the Populists thought that the conspirators were Jews and people they dominated (mainly, according to them, the British). In 1896, an Associated Press reporter noted that one of the "most striking things" in the national convention of the Populist Party was "the extraordinary hatred of the Jewish race." [115]

These beliefs are almost identical to those that drove the *Volk* movement in Germany. They convey the same nostalgia for an idealized agrarian world, the identification of an evil enemy using industry, trade, and finance as weapons to destroy good people. There is even the mention of an apocalyptic struggle between good and evil. All the elements are there. In Germany these ideas were destructive, while in the United States they proved eventually to be ephemeral.

In the 1896 presidential election, populist William Jennings Bryan, who had successfully won the Democratic nomination, faced Republican William McKinley. Bryan focused on a single demand that he believed would unify the coalition needed to win the presidency: replace the gold standard as the basis of the monetary system with a mix of silver and gold. The populists ended up focusing on a single monetary issue, almost a technical demand. Bryan lost, and the movement disintegrated. Much of what the populists believed in was driven sincerely by hardship and unfairness. But what in Germany would become a bulwark of resistance to change that helped the Nazis to gain power fizzled out in the United States.

The New Threat to Multidimensionality

While populism was a real threat to multidimensionality, a corresponding threat came from the opposite side of the social spectrum: the rich industrialists or robber barons who were driving what became known as the Gilded Age. The increasing returns to scale characteristic of the second stage of the industrial revolution combined with the enormous size of the country to nurture new megaenterprises. These large enterprises included the national railroads, Carnegie Steel, Standard Oil of Ohio, the giant mail order companies like Sears Roebuck and Montgomery Ward, and the large New York financial houses. The colorful characters who managed and owned them, dubbed robber barons for their enormous wealth and acquisitive methods, were a novelty at that time in US society.

The king of the robber barons was John D. Rockefeller, who thought that competition was a waste of resources. For him, building monopolies was the right and moral way to reintroduce order into what had become a chaotic competitive landscape. He watered down the value of stock; fixed prices and tariffs; squeezed smaller competitors by lowering prices below costs; and bribed government officials, judges, and senators. In *The Story of a Great Monopoly*, first published in the *Atlantic* in 1881, Henry Demarest Lloyd wrote, "Standard [Oil] has done everything with the Pennsylvania legislature except refine it."[116] In most cases, Rockefeller offered to buy the companies he had squeezed at bargain prices. He often offered Standard Oil shares, turning victims into partners. He called this a method of cooperation, which he believed should replace competition as the main relationship between entrepreneurs in the same field.

In 1879, Rockefeller organized a gigantic trust, centered around Standard Oil of Ohio, made up of companies that had competed against it. He was not the owner of the conglomerate but the trustee, and the former competitors, now cooperators, were the trustors. He managed these companies as if Standard Oil owned them and distributed the profits in accordance with arrangements he had defined. Other barons created gigantic trusts in industries like copper, iron, sugar, tin, paper, and coal. Thus, the name *trust* came to be associated with large attempts at cornering the market through an association of all or many of the producers supplying that market—very much like what German industry was doing with its industrial associations.

Political opinion turned against the robber barons, and in 1890, Congress passed the Sherman Act, which declared illegal every contract, combination, or conspiracy to restrain trade across state lines, and made it a misdemeanor for any person to monopolize or attempt to monopolize any part of such trade, or trade with other countries. The Sherman Act did not forbid monopolies—only monopolistic practices. Still, the public interpreted the creation of trusts as evidence of a conspiracy to establish monopolies, so trusts acquired a bad name. In spite of the Sherman Act, the trend toward concentration remained strong, and in the late 1890s and early 1900s, mergers and consolidations, many of them engineered by the robber barons, continued to produce giant firms with very large market shares.[117]

On the other end of the income distribution spectrum, labor problems became serious as unemployment increased to unheard of levels, particularly after financial crises. Recessions hit labor hard. It was estimated that in the depression that followed the panic of 1873, about 40 percent of the labor force was unemployed, and an additional 20 percent worked half-time. People living in shantytowns gathered around industrial cities numbered three million nationwide.[118] Poverty and homelessness became highly visible.

With low wages, long working hours, unstable employment, and dire working conditions, workers were prone to protest. While in Germany and other European countries such protest became ideological, in the United States it was pragmatic and mainly focused on specific enterprises and specific issues. Still, many of them were violent and negatively affected the reputation of trade unions.[119] There was no precedent for these conflicts in the United States.

Labor unrest and the growing political and economic power of the robber barons provoked a reaction in the press and the population. In 1902, Ida Tarbell published the first of nineteen articles about Standard Oil in *McClure's* magazine, which inaugurated the era of the so-called muckrakers, who wrote articles and books denouncing the robber barons with feverish diligence.[120] The muckrakers succeeded in drawing public attention to the robber barons' abuse of market power and maltreatment of workers, and in the early years of the twentieth century, the political pressure to control these abuses became very strong.

These denunciations coincided with the rise of progressivism. Progressives worried that the unchecked predominance of the robber barons would threaten the mutual independence of economic and political power. Far from being anticapitalist, they asserted the power of the democratic state to preserve the independence of the two powers and the multidimensional nature of American society. In Theodore Roosevelt they found a president who would reaffirm the power of the state without actually increasing it.

Roosevelt publicly humiliated J. P. Morgan; spoke badly of the robber barons; and disbanded Northern Securities, a holding company formed by Morgan and the investment bank Kuhn, Loeb & Co to monopolize railroad traffic in the West. While these actions did not directly affect the economic structure of the country, they were very important psychologically: the democratically elected government remained independent of the institutions that controlled the economy. Having illustrated the power of the federal government, Roosevelt moved in a different direction by focusing on the press virulence against big business. On April 15, 1906, he gave a speech known as "The Man with the Muck Rake." He cited John Bunyan's *Pilgrim's*

Progress, which describes the man who cannot lift his eyes from the filth he rakes on the floor:

> There is filth on the floor, and it must be scraped up with the muck rake; and there are times and places where this service is the most needed of all the services that can be performed. But the man who never does anything else, who never thinks or speaks or writes, save of his feats with the muck rake, speedily becomes, not a help but one of the most potent forces for evil.[121]

This speech was the source of the term *muckraker,* and Roosevelt's coinage was a death sentence. From that year on, muckraking began to decline, but not just because of Roosevelt's words. The muckrakers themselves were already changing their view. They became more moderate and complemented criticism with an assessment of the positive things that modern companies were bringing about in the US economy. Even Ida Tarbell found good things to say of the new industries.[122]

The trustbusters in the federal government kept working through the administrations of Roosevelt and William Howard Taft. They filed only a few lawsuits under the Sherman Act, but those had a huge impact on Standard Oil and American Tobacco.[123] The dismemberment of these monopolies was the high-water mark of the antitrust movement. The relationship between government and big business and finance then took a 180-degree turn. In 1909, just when the antitrust suits were being fought, the United States demanded an equal share in a $25 million syndicated loan that European banks had negotiated with the Chinese government to finance the Hukuang Railroad. The State Department appointed a group of American bankers led by J. P. Morgan. The big banks had arrived. The federal government, which hitherto had seen them as an economic liability, now saw them as national assets.[124]

In the midst of their malfeasance, the robber barons and smaller industrialists left a large and productive legacy. They consolidated new markets and created highly efficient companies that contributed to national and global progress and formed the backbone of the US economy well into the twentieth century. At the same time, Teddy Roosevelt, a free press, and the population at large reaffirmed the multidimensional nature of US society by reasserting the power and independence of the US government.

THE GERMAN QUESTION

Divisiveness in Germany

Germany at this time, although it shared many characteristics with the United States, followed a very different path. How could Germany, a democratic country and one of the most industrially advanced and cultured countries in the world, adopt an ideology of naked power and destructiveness in the twentieth century? Why did Germans accept Hitler and his destruction of their social order? Why did intelligent, refined people, in touch with the world at large, accept subservience to an absolutist rule? The answer is that pre-Nazi Germany was a deeply fragmented and divisive society that had come to the conclusion that it needed verticality to keep the unity it had achieved with such difficulty only a few decades earlier.

Germany entered the nineteenth century as a collection of thirty-nine small states that were members of a useless unifying institution, the so-called German Confederation, created at the end of the Napoleonic Wars. During the first seven decades of the nineteenth century, the most cherished objective of the German population was unifying the country under a democratic regime. Twice they failed to do so—in 1815, after the defeat of Napoleon, and in 1848, during the wave of revolutions that temporarily toppled several European governments. On both occasions, the endangered princes promised to grant constitutions and work for the unification of the country if they were kept in power. They recanted as soon as the waters calmed. To make things worse, Austria blocked all efforts to unify Germany.

Then, an 1862 speech by the prime minister of Prussia, Otto von Bismarck, captured the hearts and minds of all Germans:

> The position of Prussia in Germany will not be determined by its liberalism but by its power. Prussia must concentrate its strength and hold it for the favorable moment, which has already come and gone several times. Since the Congress of Vienna in 1815, our frontiers have been ill-designed for a healthy body politic. Not through speeches and majority decisions will the great questions of the day be decided—that was the great mistake of 1848 and 1849—but by iron and blood.[125]

With those words, Bismarck discarded democracy and individual rights as the road to unification in favor of a strategy of war. He waited for an opportunity, which France unwittingly provided in 1870 when it declared war against Prussia over an issue regarding the royal succession in Spain. Prussia called for an alliance of all German states against France.

This external objective unified the German will. Germany invaded France in record time, advancing as far as Versailles. In the enthusiasm of victory, the rulers of the German states accepted Bismarck's proposal to unify the country under the king of Prussia. On January 18, 1871, while their cannons bombarded Paris, Germans founded the Second Reich of Germany in the Hall of Mirrors in the palace of Versailles. It was a lesson in what worked to unify: the kaiser, the army, blood, and iron.

The Second Reich was nominally a constitutional monarchy, but it was not democratic. The constitution mixed an absolutist structure with a powerless federal legislature. The king of Prussia was enthroned as the absolutist kaiser of the German empire. The legislative branch had two cameras: the Bundesrat, which represented the unelected rulers of the states (archaic kings and nobles), and the Reichstag, which was elected by the people. The unelected Bundesrat was far more powerful. The Reichstag could not even propose laws. It could only consider and approve or reject laws proposed by the chancellor and the Bundesrat. As a manifestation of its superiority, the Bundesrat, with the kaiser's agreement, could dissolve the Reichstag.

Together, these bodies had the power to approve new taxes, allocate their proceeds, and question ministers. As had been the case in Prussia, however, executive power was in the hands of two men unelected by the people: the kaiser and a chancellor appointed by him. Neither was accountable to the representative institutions. The kaiser's power was supported by the army, which swore loyalty not to the constitution but to the kaiser personally. So the kaiser and his chancellor decided the country's destiny, and the constitution therefore imposed an absolutist regime on the newly unified Germany.

Under this new regime, Germany industrialized at breakneck speed, but in the context of dramatic division—Protestant northerners against Catholic Bavarians, farmers against urban dwellers, democrats against supporters of autocracy, and workers against capitalists.

Resistance to Change

The confrontation between workers and capitalists was particularly vicious in a country that had opted for a vertical regime to control its divisiveness. The verticality that framed Germany's politics was transferred to its economic organization as well, creating conditions for one-dimensional conflict that eventually led the country into a world war, a Bolshevik revolution, and a Nazi regime.

As in other areas in Europe, before the industrial revolution, the economy of the German states had been organized around the old medieval guilds. These had disappeared in the middle decades of the nineteenth century under the sway of the first stages of industrialization. Soon after, however, German entrepreneurs re-created the guilds as so-called industrial associations, which were cartels that replicated the strict control of the economy the guilds had exercised in the feudal economy.

These associations killed competition among the new industrial enterprises. Entrepreneurs coordinated their policies through the associations, including pricing, use of raw materials, wages offered to workers, and other key policies. The associations formed associations of associations, until they organized the *Centralverband Deutscher Industrieller* (CVDI), which unified all of them. They used these associations to influence the government, which rapidly became their ally—or their servant. Economic and political power were amalgamated. The newly unified Germany became a one-dimensional society, as its component member states had been.

One of the main objectives of the new associations was to present a unified front for the negotiation of wages and other working conditions. This provoked a reaction from the workers. Recognizing that they confronted an almost invincible hybrid of political and economic power, in 1863 workers created a nationally unified trade union and in 1869 a political party, the Social Democratic Party (SDP). Established before the unification of the country, these organizations became stronger in the newly unified Germany.

The alignment of two opposing forces fighting for both the political and economic dimensions of power within an absolutist regime gave a dangerous one-dimensional, polarized quality to Germany. Employers and workers entered an all-or-nothing struggle for absolute power that lasted for decades and made compromise almost impossible. The struggle became violent. In 1878, when radical social democrats twice tried to assassinate Kaiser Wilhelm I, people blamed the social democrats. Within weeks, Bismarck passed through the Reichstag the Law against the Public Danger of Social Democratic Endeavors. The law banned trade unions and any other group aimed at spreading social democratic principles. Social democrats could run for public office but could not generate propaganda. This law polarized the struggle even more. Without legally established trade unions and without the political party they had created to counter the domination of entrepreneurs, workers felt that government and business were trampling on their rights. Workers went underground in their proselytism and the government repressed them harshly, generating a poisoned environment that was splitting the country.

Bismarck tried to steal the socialists' thunder by offering workers social benefits while still keeping in place the ban on trade unions and the SDP. In 1881 he created a social security system, the first in the world, which was to be paid for by the industrialists. In exchange, he protected the industrialists from foreign competition, which would allow them to increase prices without competitive concerns. This arrangement was facilitated by the "iron and rye" pact of 1879, under which industrialists and farmers supported the imposition of import tariffs on both agricultural and industrial products.

Both measures—social security and protectionism—aimed at producing stability in the midst of an unstable transformation. Industrialists and workers accepted the system. They also accepted the central role of the state in achieving stability and in managing economic and social relations. It was a one-dimensional solution to a problem that had been generated by the one-dimensional verticality of German politics. And it was very much like what many people are proposing today: a one-dimensional regime to keep a divided society in order.

One-Dimensional Germany

The 1879 protective tariffs combined with the increasing returns to scale characteristic of the second stage of the industrial revolution to spur the emergence of huge monopolies that swallowed or destroyed smaller competitors. Within a single generation, Germany gave birth to many large companies with impressive market power, domestically and abroad, companies we are familiar with today, such as Siemens, Krupp, BASF, Bayer, Hoechst AG, Agfa, Daimler Benz, Thyssen, and AEG.

Leading these enormous enterprises and their banks were men comparable in their wealth and economic power with the robber barons. But the robber barons could not compare with them in terms of political power. Industrialists such as Gustav Krupp von Bohlen und Halbach, Walter Rathenau, August Thyssen, and Hugo Stinnes, and the bankers financing them, were not just influential. They intermeshed with the government in a regime that took it for granted that the government had to protect their enterprises against smaller competitors and their own workers.

The vertical shape of the economy brought about unprecedented stability to the industrialization of Germany. The coordination of cartels and government gave the Germans an edge in its competition with Great Britain in the capital-intensive activities of the second stage of the industrial revolution (steel, chemicals, heavy machinery). However, this coordination had terrible social and political costs that would become evident only in the future. The CVDI, the most powerful of German industry's political arms, still

> maintained a consistent hostility to all proposals for the conciliation of organized labor. This meant not only opposition to trade union recognition, welfare legislation and reform of the Prussian suffrage. It also meant the active pursuit of new legal restrictions on both the unions and the Social Democratic Party. . . . [By comparison with Britain] it was precisely the most "modern" and "progressive" aspects of Imperial Germany's capitalist development—namely, the higher levels of concentration, the rapid investment in new plant and technology, the experimentation with more sophisticated divisions of labor—that first permitted the repressive labor relations.[126]

In this way, the fusion of economic and political power also brought a fatal rigidity to the country's economic and political behavior. Gradually, Germany developed a maze of governmental and quasi-governmental structures to manage its economy that set the stage for Hitler's new absolutism, which would come a half century later. Aggressive in restraining what they called the "destructive effects of all-out competition," these cartels numbered more than fifteen hundred by the beginning of the twentieth century. They colluded in all sectors to set prices and regulate the levels of production of individual firms. Different from Britain and the United States, where cartels became illegal, cartel contracts were legally binding in Germany. In this way, competition, the most important force of capitalism, was harshly restricted. In the end, the economic fate of German citizens was in the hands of huge organizations that worked politically to enhance their own influence on government policy.

Even more baffling was the mix of absolutism with the independent judicial system, which provided the rule of law but not the protection of individual rights. The law defended the state, and Germany became an "industrial, but not a capitalist society."[127] It was not democratic either. While extremely successful in its economic undertakings, the country lacked the two dimensions of freedom—political and economic—that are essential for a harmonious adjustment to rapid social change.

The wealthy and the middle classes in Germany accepted this rigidity because they believed that preventing the collapse of Germany required the strong will of an emperor, and, if he failed, the strength of an institution—which was the army—that would not allow the destruction of the country. So the army came to be seen not only as an institution to defend the country against foreign enemies but also as a bulwark against domestic sedition. Militarist absolutism became acceptable, even desirable.

This preference for vertical order permeated the entire institutional setting of the country. It was difficult for any German to escape from its influence. In the midst of creating a modern industry, Germany became politically archaic with no opening to modernize itself.[128] The German historian Fritz Fischer described clearly how this resistance to change took and kept the most strategic positions in the country:

> The Germans were the only people who did not create the state from below by invoking the forces of democracy against the old ruling groups, but "accepted it gratefully" at the hands of those groups in a defensive struggle against democracy. The Prussian state, the power and prestige of the Prussian crown, the constitution which made the Prussian king German Emperor and the Prussian Prime Minister Chancellor of the Reich, the composition of the Prussian Diet (a Lower House elected on a restricted franchise and an overwhelmingly feudal Upper House), the bureaucracy, the schools, the universities, the established Protestant churches and not least the armed forces, directly subordinated as they were to the kings of Prussia, Bavaria, Saxony, etc.—all these were factors which guaranteed the predominance of the conservative elements against the pressure of the rising forces of democratic liberalism and later of democratic socialism.

For the kaiser and the army, the main enemies were the democratic and socialist ideas coming from abroad, which were getting support from some sectors of the population. They worked hard to eliminate those enemies by aligning institutions against them. They were helped by nostalgia for the old preindustrial order that was taking hold of Germany. Soon, the Jews would join the list of these enemies.[129]

German Populism

Nostalgia for an idealized rural past was part of what Germans called the *Volk* culture—a concept that idealized past customs as a way of shaping the future. Volk culture was opposed to "civilization," the customs and mores coming from the West along with industrialization that were said to be disrupting the idyllic reality of rural Germany. In reality, Volk culture was a desire for feudalism. Its advocates maintained that peasants, artisans organized in local guilds, and aristocratic landlords were the soul of the country. In their view, the newly emerging industrialists, the industrial proletariat, and the bankers were foreign creations, alien to the German soul.[130]

The Volk culture was immersed in the realm of magic. It was in fact apocalyptic, portraying a struggle in which supernatural forces of good fought against those of evil for the future of the world. Its adherents associated all that was moral, healthy, and strong with the rural Volk culture, and everything that was debasing, disruptive, and unclean with urban civilization imported from the West. It was eerily similar to the populist movement in the United States. But where the reign of populism was brief and limited in scope, Volk culture set down deep roots and became one of the pillars of national socialism.

As the Volk culture took shape, it developed racial and proto-Nazi connotations. The honest peasant was a blond Aryan, a strong man emerging from the primeval forest, full of natural virtues, Friedrich Nietzsche's "Blond Beast," now being forced by foreigners to live in an urban environment and work under oppressive conditions.[131]

According to many supporters of the Volk culture, the main architects of "civilization" were the Jews, a people that, being uprooted, wanted to uproot Germans and reduce them to slavery. Wilhelm Heinrich Riehl, a Bavarian professor, wrote in the 1860s that this was the secret purpose of creating cities: they were places where people became as rootless as the Jews. Uprooted Germans had become subject to the domination of a worldwide web of cities controlled by the evil Jews.[132]

Throughout the nineteenth century, but particularly in the second half, a flood of novels, essays, and other writings inundated Germany with these ideas. *The Foundations of the Nineteenth Century*—a rabidly anti-Semitic book published in 1899 by Houston Stewart Chamberlain, a naturalized German—was a best seller that went through twenty-four editions between its first publication and 1938, selling about half a million copies. Both Kaiser Wilhelm II and Hitler became great fans of Chamberlain.[133]

Militarism

As the elites came together in a wide alliance to form a vertical society, the idea that Germany's problems could be solved by military conquest became part of the intellectual mainstream. Great Britain, France, Holland, Russia, and even Belgium had large empires that provided them with raw materials, markets for industrial goods, and space and work opportunities for their growing populations. Germany envisioned an empire that would be like Canada, Australia, and New Zealand for Great Britain, or the western states for the United States: a place where German peasants could settle and feed the home country and from which German industries could extract raw materials. Because there were no more available lands in the developing world, the German idea to provide this space, or *lebensraum* (living space) as Germans would later call it, was to the east—primarily Russia. With time, Germany would add industrialized Belgium and other neighbors to provide iron, steel, and other industrial goods. As a manifestation of the one-dimensionality of the Second Reich, these ideas came from various groups of the elites, including the big entrepreneurs and the academy, which were part of the large alliance that supported the vertical shape of the German state.

These ideas were part of a larger strategy aimed at turning Germany into a bulwark of the old order in Europe, based on the elimination of democracy and socialism in Germany proper and the conquest of European territory to feed the growing German population. These two objectives and the word lebensraum have been identified with the Nazi regime of twenty or thirty years later. However, they were central to German policy since the exit of Bismarck from government in the 1890s. Germany's population was growing quickly. It went from 48 million in 1871 to 68 million in the second decade of the twentieth century. The idea that the progress of the country would be constrained by the lack of territory became very common among the population and the elites. It became one of the few bonds linking most members of German society.[134]

Stopping Change

The strategy of the commanding elite of the Second Reich thus had three interlinked goals: the preservation of a vertical structure of government, the elimination of democratic and socialistic trends, and the creation of an all-powerful Germany through the annexation of neighboring lands.[135] The first goal was also the ultimate objective of all three—to stop change and keep the old elite in power. Annexation was needed to give the population what they missed, the return of an agrarian way of life. And the elimination of democratic and socialist trends eliminated the feared collapse of the existing elites. Everything had become focused on stopping change.

In this way, by the early twentieth century, while the industrial revolution continued to create new social classes and change the relations between them, Germany resisted change and remained fixedly absolutist, bureaucratic, and militarized—as rigid a combination as Russia. The consequences of these attitudes became painfully obvious in the early decades of the twentieth century and included World War I.

THE LESSONS

The difference between Germany and the United States of the Gilded Age was not economic. Both countries industrialized quite rapidly and both attained what today are called economic miracles. The difference was in how each country managed the divisiveness brought on by transformation; in the political freedom of the population; and in the capacity to create a free, modern, liberal democracy. The price for Germany's failure to create this new social order was huge.

In Germany, the development of the economy of high returns to scale served to worsen the country's one-dimensionality, to worsen divisiveness, and to spur the forces that would eventually lead to the worst tragedy of the twentieth century. By contrast, in the United States, the interaction between the industrial elite, the federal government, industrial workers, the press, and public opinion, entities that did not exist fifty years earlier, created a competitive environment for these new activities. Even if there are periodic accusations that the robber barons manipulated the government and that the government stifled the creativity of new industries with its intervention in monopoly cases, the independence of the political and the economic spheres was maintained in the long run, and the multidimensional society survived the challenges of this most difficult adjustment.

In both countries there was substantial controversy over the growing power of hugely rich industrial entrepreneurs. In the United States, the objective of such controversy was to find a new balance of interests and principles. The controversy took place in the open, via newspaper articles and other opinion pieces, within the country's institutional setting. In Germany, however, the objective of the controversy was to impose a way of life on the opposing side, and, on the side of the government and its supporters, to silence the workers and negate their right to participate in politics. This was the response of a one-dimensional society to the challenges posed by the emergence of new groups associated with the industrial revolution. For decades, the two sides confronted each other in one dimension of conflict. In the United States, the conflict played out in the society as a whole, everyone participated, and the population at large contributed to define the outcome.

Up to the turn of the last century, the differences between Germany and the United States were known but not dwelt upon. People saw the two countries as the avatars of modernity. In fact, many people thought that the most modern country was Germany. What showed how different they had become was World War I, the most terrible war up to that moment and, in many ways, the worst war ever fought.

WORLD WAR I

World War I was the pivotal event of the industrial revolution. It marked the end of the old elites, who, having resisted change for such a long time, collapsed while their societies slipped into chaos. As the old institutions fell, the power vacuum created a storm that led to the most destructive period in modern history.

The war was fought by two great blocs: the Triple Entente, which included Great Britain, France, and Russia, against the Central Powers, including Germany, the Austro-Hungarian Empire, and the Ottoman Empire. Italy entered on the side of the Entente in 1915. In 1917, the United States joined the Triple Entente and helped decide the war in its favor. Many smaller countries joined these alliances.

The rate of killing was sobering. The Entente powers had about six million soldiers killed and about four million civilians dead from military action, malnutrition, and disease, for a total of ten million. The

Central Powers had a total of eight million deaths, of which about half were soldiers.[136] How this tragedy came to pass has remained a matter of controversy for more than a century.

For years European governments risked triggering this terrible war, responding to obscure political reasons we still fail to understand fully. The decision to prepare for war and then engage in it must have been taken in an environment in which all the participants thought that war—which they knew would be costly in material and human losses— was the lesser of the potential evils they thought they confronted.

The cold manner in which the politicians weighed such costs against obscure reasons was evident in the words pronounced in 1913, a year before the start of the war, by Theobald von Bethmann-Holl- weg, German chancellor from 1909 to 1917. He said, "No human being could possibly imagine the dimensions as well as the misery and destruction of a world conflagration . . . no responsible statesman would think of lighting the fuse that ignited the powder keg without careful consideration."[137]

What were the reasons that would make it worthwhile to ignite this powder keg, even if only after careful consideration? The reasons were related to the incongruities lurking beneath the apparent security of the nineteenth century, first manifested in the rise of imperialism as a solution to the problems of unemployment, lack of raw materials, and the political turmoil that these problems triggered, all of them related to the industrial revolution.

The war was foreshadowed by the competition for empires that prevailed among the industrializing countries in the second half of the nineteenth century. This race created an explosive environment as new potential imperialists joined the competition while lands available for conquest outside Europe were becoming scarcer. By the turn of the century, Germany was complaining that its empire was too small relative to its new industrial power. The developing world had been completely colonized, so the idea that Germany should compensate for this disadvantage by grabbing lands in Eastern Europe became popular in Germany.

These problems were worsened by another incongruity. The newly massive urban populations were demanding political participation. Yet some empires remained autocratic, and even the most democratic coun- tries were still ruled by agrarian, traditional elites that attached great impor- tance to one's birth, heritage, and religion as the forces that kept the world in place. The modernization of the nineteenth century had removed many of these men from the commanding heights of the economy. Politically and militarily, however, they still dominated the scene. And they saw the war as a lesser evil than their own demise. As it turned out, this was a false conclusion. The war assured the fall of the old elites.[138]

As we have seen, the German elites saw war was an attractive possibility to resolve their domestic crises.[139] Other rigid societies thought like the Germans. The historian Pieter Judson has described the situation at the time for the Hapsburg Empire in this way:

> The elite mood of existential pessimism in 1914 was one factor that encouraged some members of the General Staff and Diplomatic Corps to risk taking Austria-Hungary to war. Believing that a cataclysm like a war offered them their last opportunity to silence political conflict at home and forestall further damage to the empire's great power status abroad, they embraced it. As the single individual most responsible for war, Chief of the General Staff Conrad von Hotzendorf (1852–1925) himself wrote to Joseph Redlich of his caste's fears, "It is very difficult to improve the internal situation of the monarchy peacefully."[140]

Regarding Russia, historian Richard Pipes has summarized the motives of this country for entering the war: "Long before 1914 Russia had a good notion of the designs Germany had on her. These called for the dismemberment of the Empire and her borderlands."[141] Yet the government also "counted on a quick triumph and surge of patriotism to silence the opposition to bury their differences in face of a foreign enemy."[142]

The climax came with the Great War of 1914. Arno Mayer describes well how, through the war, the elites of Europe were presenting a last stand against the political changes brought about by the industrial revolution:

> Eventually, in July–August 1914, the governors of the major powers, all but a few of them thoroughly nobilitarian, marched over the precipice of war with their eyes wide open, with calculating heads, and exempt from mass pressures. Along the way, not a single major actor panicked or was motivated by narrow personal, bureaucratic and partisan concerns. Among the switchmen of war there were no petty improvisers, no romantic dilettantes, no reckless adventurers. Whatever the profile of their populist helpers or harassers, they were men of high social standing, education, and wealth, determined to maintain or recapture an idealized world of yesterday.[143]

The destructiveness unleashed by the war and its sequels can be traced to the maladaptation to the transformations triggered by the industrial revolution, domestically and internationally. Rather than looking at free trade among equals, countries aimed at subjecting other countries to both political and commercial domination, which opened the door to the destructive regimes of the twentieth century.

When the crown of the tsars rolled in the streets of Moscow at the end of the war, it was picked up not by democrats but by communists, who then led Russia to almost a century of suffering. Mired in chaos, Italy's government asked Mussolini to form a government in 1922. After its autocratic kaiser fell, Germany had a Bolshevik revolution in 1918 and 1919, stabilized for a while, and then fell into a Nazi dictatorship in 1933. Destructive regimes took over country after country in the 1920s and 1930s.

During the industrial revolution, resistance to change led to rigidity, which led to the collapse of obsolete institutions that refused to change, which led to chaos, then led to the emergence of destructive leaders from obscure corners, then led finally to totalitarian regimes. The collapse itself, at the end of the war, was the result of imperialism, a symptom of maladaptation—the search for solutions to internal problems through the domination of other countries.

9

DARKNESS AT NOON

Death is a master from Germany.
Paul Celan

Extraordinary conditions do not create or enlarge constitutional power.
Supreme Court of the United States

THE INTERWAR PERIOD

World War I did not resolve any of the economic, social, and political problems that affected the industrial countries in the prewar years. However, it mortally wounded the old order that had regulated the destinies of Europe and the world throughout the nineteenth century. The power of the land—with all its structures based on blood and tradition—finally gave way to the still unstructured power of industry. The spirit of national unity that had prevailed in the early months of the conflict vanished without a trace. Economic instability remained in place and actually worsened. The old social divisions returned with unusual strength. Demobilized soldiers went back to their civilian life only to find that they were unemployed. And Lenin dashed from Switzerland to Russia to set in motion the first of the bloody revolutions of the twentieth century.

This postwar turbulence would extend for two and a half decades: a deep recession in 1920, a long boom in the next ten years, the Great Depression in the 1930s, and finally World War II and the Holocaust in the early 1940s. World War I had opened a Pandora's box.

This period witnessed an acceleration of the radical transformation that had started during the Gilded Age in the industrializing economies. This was quite similar to, but deeper than, that which accompanied the Great Recession, when the structure of employment shifted from low to high skills (which we discussed in Chapter 3). The products demanded after the war were radically different from those demanded when the twentieth century dawned. The same can be said of the methods used to produce them. To accommodate these changes, some old activities had to die (along with the physical and human capital used to produce them) and new investments had to create new activities that were replacing them in the aggregate demand. This created three problems. First, the structure of supply would have to change to accommodate the structure of demand, leaving many people jobless and many investors bankrupt, while others had to emerge. Second, the population had to be somehow protected against unemployment and the accompanying suffering. Third, this should be done within the ideals of liberal democracy that had been growing during the previous two centuries.

Although there are many parallels between today and the Gilded Age, the period that most resembles ours is this interwar epoch. The interwar problems are the same problems that we are confronting today. This is scary because the 1920s and 1930s are the years that led to the worst tragedies of the twentieth century. And as we shall see, societies reacted very differently to the interwar crises, with dramatically different historical outcomes.

How countries responded to this turbulence was significant. Some tried to shield citizens by protecting the existing economic structure, trying to force the survival of old companies and activities that were becoming obsolete—so that nothing would change, investors would suffer no losses, and people would not be left unemployed. These policies backfired because it was impossible, except with the coercion of one-dimensional tyranny, to oppose the tide of change. The other principal approach was to protect the public from the effects of change through social security. Countries that adopted the first method did not stop change and often fell prey to totalitarianism. Those that chose the second course did better economically in the long term and preserved freedom and liberal democracy. We are faced with a similar choice today.

THE WEIMAR REPUBLIC

The vertical mindset often produces self-fulfilling prophecies, and the one-dimensional confrontation of late-nineteenth-century Germany would shape the country's future in the first half of the twentieth. Within fifty years of Germany's creation, the fragmenting forces of its society— which had given shape to the verticality of its institutions—succeeded in throwing the country into total chaos. The rigid institutions that had resisted the onslaught of political change for decades suddenly collapsed, leaving the country in absolute disarray.

In late 1918, the German army was showing the same signs of demoralization that the Russian Army had shown before its collapse the previous year. Yet the government's propaganda had convinced the German people that they were winning the war, and some events seemed to support their claim. On March 3, 1918, Russia had signed the Treaty of Brest-Litovsk, and with it ceded to Germany 750,000 square kilometers, 26 percent of its population, 37 percent of its harvests, and 75 percent of its coal and iron deposits.[144] This was the lebensraum the Germans had been expecting from the war.

The German general Erich Ludendorff secretly asked the Allies for an armistice. President Woodrow Wilson stated quite clearly that he would not negotiate unless Germany became a democracy. To meet Wilson's conditions, Ludendorff offered the majority parties in the Reichstag a constitution that would turn Germany into a democratic state, on two conditions. One was that the parliament would assume the control of the government immediately, announcing that there had been a revolution and that Germany would be, from then on, a full-fledged constitutional democracy. The other condition was that, once in power, they should immediately ask for an armistice with the Allied powers, seeking the signature of a peace treaty soon afterward. This would put the blame for the defeat squarely on the politicians, particularly on the Social Democrats.[145]

The Social Democrats naïvely accepted. Ludendorff then informed the kaiser of his decision, and the kaiser had no alternative but to accept it. A member of the royal family, Prince Max von Baden, was appointed chancellor. And then, on October 5, 1918, the new government announced to the startled public that there had been a socialist revolution, Germany had been defeated and now it was a parliamentary democracy, and Germany was asking the United States for an armistice.

As a result of Ludendorff's machinations, when democracy finally arrived in Germany, it came associated in the minds of the Germans with the international humiliation that followed and with the economic disarray of the years following the war. In the popular imagination, the people who were managing the new democracy had betrayed their country. As a result, the nascent democracy, called the Weimar Republic, never commanded the moral authority it needed to solve the difficult postwar problems.

Chaos ensued. Germany went through a Bolshevik revolution that took the government nine months to eradicate. The rebels included sailors, soldiers, and workers. On November 7, 100,000 workers with red flags marched in Munich against the Royal Palace. Ludwig III, king of Bavaria, fled, abandoning the throne that the Wittelsbach family had occupied for one thousand years. The Bavarian Independent Socialists took over the capital and appointed Kurt Eisner, a music critic, as chief of state.

The fall of the House of Wittelsbach had a snowballing effect throughout the country. The twenty-two heads of the German states—lesser kings, princes, grand dukes, and dukes—fell within twenty-four hours. Soviet republics were created in Cologne, Munich, Leipzig, Stuttgart, and Frankfurt-am-Main. The only crowned head remaining was the kaiser himself, who abdicated within a few days.

For several months, frenzied Bolshevik regimes ruled in many of the German states. The mobs that commanded these regimes resembled those that ruled Paris during the Commune of 1871. They ransacked the capital cities, took hostages, and dethroned leaders they had just put in power. Some of the rebels were groups of deserters, but others controlled army units—including those stationed close to Berlin. Mobs of supporters of the soviets wandered about the capital city. The rebels even took possession of the barracks of the imperial palace and cut the telephone lines of the chancellery.

A confrontation between the communists and voluntary groups of veterans led by imperial officers acting unofficially (called the *freikorps*) was enacted throughout Germany. The superior discipline and organization of the *freikorps* prevailed. They liberated city after city until the entire territory was recovered, and by the end of 1919 the German Bolshevik Revolution was finished.

As in Russia, the rigid structure of the Second Reich channeled social conflicts created by the industrial revolution into a vicious one-dimensional confrontation, which led to chaos. One vertical institution, the army, saved Germany from this chaos, seeming to justify the choice the Germans had made for verticality in the nineteenth century. Yet in reality the army had saved Germany from the chaos that verticality itself had spawned.

The end of this revolution did not bring about stability. The victors of World War I imposed enormous reparations payments on Germany. Unable to finance a growing fiscal deficit, partly due to the reparations payments, the government resorted to printing money, generating one of the worst cases of hyperinflation ever recorded. Prices at the end of November 1923 were 10,200,000,000 times the prices in August 1922.[146] The central bank stopped the hyperinflation by creating a new currency and refusing to print it to finance the government. After this episode, the economy recovered but remained dependent on loans from abroad, mainly from the United States, to keep going.

None of the problems of the Weimar Republic was worse than the internal confusion caused by the adoption of a political system—democracy—that nobody wanted. Germans accepted it with discipline. Their loyalty to it was thin, however, as they proved when unemployment exceeded 25 percent during the Great Depression. The country's divisiveness exploded, chaos ensued (again), and we all know what followed.

A Deadlocked Country

While the Weimar Republic resembled the Second Reich in many ways, it did not inherit its discipline and order. The changes that the war brought about accentuated the vertical shape of the economy. The largest trusts (as they were called in Germany, using the American word) were created in those years. The *I. G. Farbenindustrie* (the German Dye Trust) was created in 1925 by merging the six largest corporations in the field, which, in turn, had been created by the amalgamation of other large companies. It employed 100,000 people. There were very large mergers in coal and steel and other sectors as well.

Ominously, the motivation behind those big mergers was not to exploit economies of scale, as it had been during the Second Reich, but to avoid the closure of failed enterprises. Even in the booming 1920s, Germany's industrial capacity was grossly excessive in many fields as a result of the distortions created by the war, when production was biased toward military goods and when Germany had to produce many things it did not have comparative advantage to produce. These enterprises could not compete in a peace economy. The least efficient companies, which would have failed in a free market, were protected from bankruptcy by the high prices maintained by the trusts—a policy that, as we will discuss in the second part of this chapter, closely resembled that of the National Recovery Administration (NRA) during the First New Deal in the United States.[147]

Weimar created an economy that kept loss-making firms alive. People did not want to confront changes to become more productive—and they did not become so. In the process, they delayed necessary adjustments to the productive capacity (Schumpeter's creative destruction) that then took place, all at the same time, during the Great Depression, leading to huge unemployment rates.

Governments tended to be weak coalitions of diverse interests. Frequently, the Reichstag deadlocked in crucial decisions, unable to form a majority one way or the other. The constitution provided a solution for this problem: in case of deadlock, the president was empowered to rule by decree without consulting the Reichstag. Consequently, Germany was increasingly ruled by executive decree—as it had been during the Second Reich. The problem became worse with time, until it became critical at the end of the 1920s. It took a year to form a government after the 1928 elections. It was even worse in 1932, when the Reichstag was dissolved three times.

Through the 1920s, the communists used brute force to intimidate their adversaries and people in general. The right responded in kind. Hitler's German Workers' Party—the forerunner of the National Socialist Party—created the Storm Troopers, known as the SA, a group of bullies that dealt with enemies of the Nazis violently. In 1925, Hitler created the Protection Squad, known as the SS, a more disciplined body that attained a perverse notoriety in the 1940s as executioners of Jews. From 1925 to 1929, the calmest period of the Weimar Republic, the sight of armed SA and communist squads beating people in the streets was familiar in Germany. The country was retreating to a savage past.

These problems became a huge crisis with the onset of the Great Depression in 1929. Very quickly, Germany's unemployment rate rose to close to 25 percent, and the democratic social order began to dissolve.

The Thriving Extremists

The Nazis thrived in this environment, offering a vision of a new Germany unified under a single will. Figure 8 shows how, from May 1928 to November 1932, as the Great Depression started and worsened, the two parties offering tyranny instead of democracy (communists and Nazis) increased their votes from 4.0 to 17.7 million, going from 13 to 50 percent of the total votes. In this way, in scarcely four years, Germany turned from a country where the extremes represented just about

Figure 8
German Elections: The Flight to the Extremes

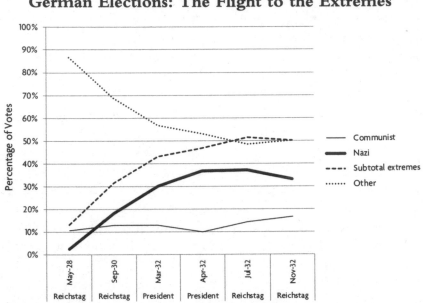

Source: Samuel W. Mitcham, *Why Hitler?: The Genesis of the Nazi Reich,* Westport, Conn.: Praeger, 1996.

10 percent of the votes into one where 50 percent of the voters wanted to destroy democracy through either Nazism or communism.[148]

Voters in the nonextremist 50 percent were increasingly demoralized about the system. The only thing the Germans seemed to agree on was that democracy and freedom were not the solution to their problems. The democratic Weimar Republic was being killed by the fragmentation that had characterized German politics since the unification of the country and by a set of values that deprecated democracy. Finally, after a local election in the small state of Lippe confirmed the rising popularity of the Nazis, the German president, Marshal von Hindenburg, decided to call Hitler to form a government in January 1933. That was the beginning of the end.

Germany justified its decision with the argument that liberal democracy had failed. But what had failed was the liberal will of the German people. The speed of the process is a warning. It shows how long-standing divisiveness, mixed with severe economic, social, and political disruption, broke the apparent normality of a government celebrated for its democracy and cultural prowess and delivered a terrible tyranny, supported by the people who happened to be tired of the divisions they themselves had created.

Dismantling Democracy in Seven Months

On January 30, 1933, President von Hindenburg, suppressing his distaste for Hitler, appointed him chancellor in a cabinet in which the Nazis would have three of the eight positions. Hitler moved at lightning speed to grab total power. The fact that he had only three positions in the cabinet was no obstacle. He called for new elections in March 5, 1933, and increased the share of the Nazi party in the government from 33 to 44 percent. Even if he did not get a majority, Hitler immediately started behaving as if he were the dictator of Germany.

He was helped by a random event, the burning of the Reichstag building on February 27, 1933, by a mad individual who happened to be a socialist. Hitler used this as an excuse to obtain from the Reichstag the power to govern by decree. He immediately used this power to abolish freedom of speech and justify the persecution of political enemies. Then, without much trouble, he eliminated the autonomy of the German states and concentrated all power in himself. He appointed Nazi Reich commissars to substitute for local authorities and gave them ample powers.

Then the Reichstag changed the Weimar constitution by enacting the Enabling Law of March 24, 1933, with the necessary two-thirds majority. Less than three months after Hitler became chancellor, this law transferred legislative authority from the Reichstag to Hitler, consolidating all power in Hitler's hands.

Next Hitler disbanded the state parliaments and took over the courts of justice. In May 1933, he announced that trade unions were illegal. In their place, the government created a new organization called the Labor Front, which would represent not only the workers but also employers and professionals. The institutional setting resembled what Mussolini had imposed on Italy. Strikes and collective bargaining were forbidden. Government representatives in each enterprise—ironically called labor trustees—would set wages. In a weird process that took place in June and July 1933, all political parties, including the Nationalists, the Nazis' partners in government, dissolved themselves. Finally, on July 14, Hitler abolished all political parties and movements except National Socialism and established prison terms for transgressors.

Within six months, the Nazis dismantled the rule of law and an entire set of democratic institutions without any considerable opposition, illustrating the shallowness of the roots of the rule of rights and democracy in Germany. William Shirer, author of *The Rise and Fall of the Third Reich,* wrote about his surprise at the ease with which liberal democracy ended in Germany:

> In the background, to be sure, there lurked the terror of the Gestapo and the fear of the concentration camp for those who got out of line or who had been Communists or Socialists or too liberal or too pacifist, or who were Jews. The Blood Purge of June 30, 1934, was a warning of how ruthless the new leaders could be. Yet the Nazi terror in the early years affected the lives of relatively few Germans and a newly arrived observer was somewhat surprised to see that the people of this country did not seem to feel that they were being cowed and held down by an unscrupulous and brutal dictatorship. On the contrary, they supported it with genuine enthusiasm.[149]

Shirer's words should remind us of Mark Mazower's observation from Chapter 2 that the crucial step in the installation of a tyranny is the destruction of the prestige of liberal democracy.

The Squanderers

The end of the Third Reich was a Wagnerian grand finale in the Nietzschean spirit. Hitler's bunker beneath the chancellery was his Valhalla. Germany was consumed in the flames of its own hatred for the sake of the Reich of a Thousand Years that a squanderer had offered them. This was the man the Germans thought was the most German of all Germans, an Austrian corporal they called their führer.

Certainly, there were Germans who opposed the criminal policies of the Nazis. However, they were few—as is shown irrefutably by the small number of Aryan victims of Hitler's terror. There was never a popular uprising against Hitler, even in the early days of his reign when he had not yet developed his machinery of terror. There was never anything like Hungary in 1956 or Czechoslovakia in 1968, when the unarmed population confronted Soviet tanks in the streets. There was nothing like the peasants' resistance to collectivization in the Soviet Union. Hitler destroyed the trade unions, the judiciary, the autonomy of the states, freedom of speech, and a parliamentary system within six months of his accession to power, and he did it without major trouble. Nazi terror was never directed against the ethnic Germans—it was not necessary.

With their return to the past, the Nazi and communist regimes became more rigid than the regimes they replaced. They were the last bulwarks of absolutism and feudalism against the forces of modernization that the industrial revolution had unleashed. They created worlds where, as the title of Arthur Koestler's novel says, there was *Darkness at Noon*.

THE UNITED STATES: THE FIRST NEW DEAL

Toward a One-Dimensional Society

In June 1933, in the midst of the Great Depression and three months after his first inauguration, President Franklin Delano Roosevelt passed through Congress the National Industrial Recovery Act, which did four things. First, it created the Public Works Administration (PWA), which would manage an extraordinary program of public investment aimed at extricating the economy from the Great Depression by increasing domestic demand. Second, it created new labor rights such as fewer working hours and a minimum wage. Third, it forbade price cutting, implicitly imposing minimum prices for all industrial goods. Fourth, it created the National Recovery Administration (NRA), perhaps the oddest institution ever created in the United States. It is taking away nothing from Roosevelt's New Deal achievement to say that, in the search for solutions to the daunting challenges Roosevelt was facing, he initially took some actions that were dangerously one-dimensional. The mark of his greatness was that he abandoned these once their negative effects became evident. He embodied democracy's ability to correct.

The NRA was in charge of ensuring that companies followed better labor and trade practices. In addition to shorter hours and higher wages, banning child labor, establishing collective bargaining, and strengthening trade unions, "better labor practices" also meant the total subordination of the commercial operations to the instructions of the managers of the NRA and the elimination of price competition. Under the new law, enterprises would fix prices with their competitors. Once the NRA had approved these prices, they would become mandatory. Different from what is normally done, the NRA established minimum, not maximum prices. The idea was that prices should be kept high to allow companies to pay high wages, which the government thought was essential to keep demand strong. To allow price fixing, the law suspended antitrust laws.

Without saying it explicitly, the new system would lead, one way or the other, to central planning of the economy. As many advocates of the New Deal understood, the prices fixed for each sector would have to be consistent with those of other sectors, and this implied the need for a central authority that would coordinate the fixed prices. Because these prices would have to clear demand, in the sense that they would not lead to excess supply or scarcity, the central price authority would first have to determine what would be consumed by the population, in what quantities, and with what technologies and inputs. One thing led to the next. The First New Dealers never said it in so many words, but they thought centralization was necessary. The NRA would be the planning institution for the industrial sector.

The design of the NRA was driven by Rex Tugwell, a member of Roosevelt's brain trust. In early 1933, he had proposed the control of enterprises through existing private trade associations and trade unions, as in fascist Italy. The idea was adopted. Each of these associations would have a planning office, and a national board would merge their plans into a coherent national plan.

The participation of the private sector in the management of the new system was conditional on behavior, however. Donald Richberg, general counsel and later executive director of the NRA, put it this way:

> There is no choice presented to the American business between intelligently planned and controlled industrial operations and a return to the gold-plated anarchy that masqueraded as "rugged individualism."
> . . . Unless industry is sufficiently socialized by its private owners and managers so that great essential industries are operated under public obligation appropriate to the public interest in them, the advance of political control over private industry is inevitable.[150]

That is, if the private sector did not cooperate with the new system, politicians should take control of private industry. The New Dealers never said if this would be done through fascism (taking control but leaving the ownership of the companies to private individuals) or through communism (taking control by expropriating the enterprises).

Colluding with Resistance to Change

These ideas were embodied in the NRA and the Agricultural Adjustment Act (AAA), a twin institution that the government created for the agricultural sector; they gave shape to what eventually was called the First New Deal. While controlling the private sector through trade associations was a continuation of the past in Italy and Germany, it represented a radical change in the United States, where guilds had not existed and competition had been considered part of the American life-style since the foundation of the colonies. Arthur M. Schlesinger, one of Roosevelt's best-known biographers, has described the rationale for this radical change succinctly:

> The tenets of the First New Deal were that the technological revolution had rendered bigness inevitable; that competition could no longer be relied on to protect social interests; that large units were an opportunity to be seized rather than a danger to be fought; and that the formula for stability in the new society must be combination and cooperation under enlarged federal authority. This meant the creation of new institutions, public and private, to do what competition had once done (or was supposed to have done) in the way of balancing the economy—institutions which might well alter the existing pattern of individual economic decision, especially on investment, production and price.[151]

This approach was totally different from the liberal, hands-free economic regime that had prevailed in the United States since the inception of the thirteen colonies three hundred years earlier. It was also radically different from the aims of the progressives such as Teddy Roosevelt and Woodrow Wilson, who had introduced state intervention in the economy to protect competition. Now, rather than trying to prevent anticompetitive practices, legislation was being used to foster collusion and use the resulting monopolistic powers for the benefit of the people. The NRA would be the core of this new approach.

The logic of the market was not totally excluded from the operations of the NRA. Its managers knew that the way to increase prices was to cut supply. In the midst of the Great Depression, when production had fallen drastically, the NRA decided that, to cure underproduction, production should be curtailed even more. In this way, prices would go up, which would, in turn, increase demand and thus end the downturn. It was for this reason that the NRA established *minimum prices* and *maximum production quotas* on most industries. The law also empowered the NRA to issue (and of course deny) licenses needed to operate a business. It had the power to close any company that refused to comply with its mandates by refusing to license its operation. This plan, of course, did not work as expected. With ceilings on output, the Depression worsened.

The AAA replicated this strange philosophy in the agricultural sector. In a country where people were going to bed hungry, the AAA began to pay farmers to produce less. Farmers began to plant less grain and killed what the new agency thought were excess animals. The AAA got its power from the licensing system, which was similar to that of the NRA: it required farmers to get a license to operate a farm, and the failure to get one would result in a fine of $1,000 a day.[152]

On June 20, 1933, just four days after the president had signed the National Industrial Recovery Act, the institution's appointed chair, Hugh S. Johnson, announced that the NRA would go to work right away. Fearing that the licensing powers the law had given the NRA could be unconstitutional, Johnson decided not to use them. Instead, he proposed to establish voluntary codes for each branch of economic activity, which would prescribe the way the signatories would behave in terms of wages, prices, production volumes, and labor practices. The NRA negotiated 550 codes with corporate lawyers working for business associations. The sectors with codes included everything that the economy produced.

The supporters of the New Deal portrayed themselves as agents of necessary change and accused the defenders of market competition as reactionaries who were trying to defend an archaic way of life. In fact, the New Dealers defended the status quo. Of course, the kind of social order based on production quotas and price fixing that they were proposing was new in the United States. But their effect was to leave things as they were. With production that could not be increased, and prices that could not be reduced, they guaranteed the survival of the economic power of the establishment, eliminating the threat that more efficient newcomers could pose to their positions in the market. Regardless of its original intentions, the NRA became an instrument to defend the inefficient but politically powerful against change.

For this reason, the ideas of the National Industrial Recovery Act found much support among some of the largest entrepreneurs in the country, who saw this kind of "cooperation" as the only solution to the problems that the furious competition of the second stage of the industrial revolution posed for them. Bernard Baruch, a millionaire broker and a close presidential adviser; Henry Harriman of the Chamber of Commerce; and Gerard Swope of General Electric supported the idea of using trade associations to restrict competition and impose a uniform behavior on industrial companies.[153]

They had their own theory about the origins of the Great Depression. They believed that competition, which they called "cutthroat competition," was killing industry. They believed that reducing prices or improving quality at the same price introduced disequilibrium in the economy. Thus, overcoming the Great Depression required the elimination of competition—which was the same as eliminating their competitors. Organized labor concurred. Sidney Hillman of the Amalgamated Clothing Workers said: "Cutthroat competition makes the unscrupulous employer the leader in each industry and the rest willingly or otherwise follow."[154]

These were the same arguments that the robber barons had used to justify the creation of their trusts thirty years earlier. Nobody explained the rationale for the NRA of the 1930s better than John D. Rockefeller two or three generations before, when he argued for the creation of private trusts. At the time, the progressives had attacked those arguments furiously. Now they supported them, although this time the leaders of the trusts would not be J. P. Morgan and his equals but state bureaucrats.

At a time of rapid innovation, and therefore rapid reaccommodation of market share, the production quotas included in the codes relieved the big enterprises of the concern that smaller and more aggressive competitors posed. The lawyers that negotiated and drafted the codes usually worked for the trade associations, which were controlled by the large enterprises. This was cooperation, but of the wrong kind, the kind that the famous eighteenth-century economist Adam Smith was referring to when he said:

> People of the same trade seldom meet together, even for merriment and diversion, but the conversation ends in a conspiracy against the public, or in some contrivance to raise prices.[155]

The code system killed innovation. For example, the textile enterprises established in the South were more modern and efficient than those in the North. They were in a position to expand and gain market share. However, the textile codes made such expansion impossible. The country had to pay higher prices for textiles just to keep the northern producers profitable.[156] This part of the New Deal was a manifestation of resistance to change, similar to what had happened in Germany, where the government also protected existing large, inefficient, and politically influential companies through the business associations and their trusts. The historian Michael Bernstein put it this way:

> The available evidence indicates that it was precisely in the industries where economic conditions were worst that the industry codes were

> most welcome. And it tended to be the older, larger firms that were most eager to secure government regulation. . . . Steel firms with high overhead and excess capacity welcomed the codes, whereas smaller fabricating companies accepted them only reluctantly.[157]

No doubt many of the people who worked at the NRA were well intentioned, but it would be naïve to believe that some of the bureaucrats who controlled the process were not attracted to the possibility of wielding awesome economic power by means of a political appointment. It was a search for economic power through political means. In this respect, multidimensional US society was becoming one-dimensional and vertical.

The Blue Eagle

Because he had discarded the use of licenses, Johnson had to find a way to entice enterprises, even those unwilling to establish limits on themselves, to join the system of codes. In a few days he came up with the idea of a sign of compliance, which any enterprise joining the system could stamp on its products and propaganda, so consumers could tell who was helping the country by complying with the codes of conduct and who was not. The sign would be a blue eagle with a legend saying: "We do our part."

Johnson launched the Blue Eagle with great fanfare. Consumers formed an organization of their own and signed a pledge to patronize the products bearing the Blue Eagle. In early September, the NRA paraded in New York, cheered by a million and a half supporters. The parade was the nice side of this campaign. Johnson also used a threatening tone that was rarely, if ever, heard from an American public servant:

> Those who are not with us are against us, and the way to show that you are a part of this great army of the New Deal is to insist on this symbol of solidarity exactly as Peter of the Keys drew a fish on the sand as a countersign and Peter the Hermit exacted the cross on the baldric of every good man and true. This campaign is a frank dependence on the power and the willingness of the American people to act together as one person in an hour of great danger.[158]

More than two million employers signed up for their respective codes. Henry Ford refused to sign, however, and the NRA did not dare do anything to him. But the institution did a lot to smaller enterprises who failed or were accused of failing to comply with the codes. The fourteen hundred inspectors could recommend fines of up to $500 and up to six months of jail for each violation. After a crackdown on dry cleaners in December 1933, the NRA brought 150 of them to Washington to respond to supposed code violations.

By the end of 1933, the NRA had formally acquired total control of the industrial sector of the United States. Most of the big enterprises had agreed to their codes and the rest had no choice but to comply. Besides, the law had empowered the presidency to turn any of these codes into law. Everything was working, except that the depression was becoming worse.

Within a year, Roosevelt, with very strong popular support, had been able to carry out a series of changes that could have transformed the United States into a completely different country from that which the Founding Fathers had envisioned—and quite different from the country we know today. These reforms had been carried out as a result of the anguish produced by the worst economic crisis in history. Such anguish had molded attitudes that did not correspond to those prevailing in the United States either before or after the depression. They were influenced by fear.

If these reforms had taken root, the United States could have been turned into a fascist country. The NRA and AAA were the kind of instruments that governments in other countries had used to concentrate both economic and political power in the government as a prelude to tyranny. They met the objectives of the institutions that Mussolini created in Italy.

Four sets of checks and balances stopped this from happening, reversing this one-dimensional process: a negative turn in public opinion, litigation that entrepreneurs brought against the NRA, growing opposition in Congress, and a Supreme Court ruling that the act establishing the NRA was unconstitutional.

The Negative Turn of Public Opinion

The ineffectiveness of the National Industrial Recovery Act in bringing about recovery was one of the reasons why people stopped supporting it. The idea that administrative controls would be better than the market to regulate industry proved to be unrealistic. In the absence of competition, firms maximize their profits by increasing prices, even if their sales volume goes down. There is a point where further price increases do not compensate for the reduced sales volumes. But the prices at that point are higher and the volume of production lower than those existing in a competitive environment. That is why monopolistic practices are bad. That is why governments intervene to eliminate them.

But with the government on the side of increasing or keeping prices high, the temptation to increase them was too strong. Its only countervailing force was a weak consumer advisory board. It was easy to fool them with figures to get the prices increased. As prices increased, demand weakened further.

People also became conscious of the negative effects of the lack of price competition. Senator Gerald Nye of South Dakota made a speech accusing the NRA of breeding monopolies, citing several sectors—electronics, cement, and pulp and paper—in which the NRA was allowing big conglomerates to take advantage of the suspension of antitrust laws to crush competitors. As a result of his intervention, the National Recovery Review Board was created to investigate the influence of the codes in increasing monopolistic behavior. The board was headed by a veteran criminal lawyer with a reputation of being a civil libertarian, Clarence Darrow. One of the board's principal findings was the following:

> [In] virtually all the codes we have examined, one condition has been persistent, undeniable and apparent to any impartial observation. It is this, that the code has offered an opportunity for the most powerful interests to seize control of an industry or to augment and extend a control already obtained.[159]

At the same time, the AAA, worried that increasing industrial prices would annul the effect of its own efforts to increase the prices of agricultural goods over and above industrial prices. The AAA had wanted to change the terms of trade between agricultural and industrial products, so that, say, tractors would become cheaper in terms of agricultural goods. But the NRA increased the prices of industrial goods as quickly as those of agricultural products. One side of the new bureaucracy turned against the other. Also, the PWA was concerned that the increase in industrial prices was raising the cost of construction. Assistance to the poor became more expensive because of the high prices of essential goods.

Although they never recognized it, the creators and managers of the NRA began to understand the complexity of the price system and the hornet's nest awaiting those who have the fatal conceit of believing that they can control them.[160] They finally seemed to have understood that higher prices worsened the Great Depression and reversed their position. General Johnson, speaking before the National Retail Dry Goods Association, showed his desperation at seeing that his success in creating a monopolistic system was destroying the economy:

I only have nine words with which to address you, I would rise here and say: "Keep prices down—for God's sake, keep prices down."[161]

The NRA was losing credibility and the power to enforce the codes and the benefits the code system could bring to the population. The Civilian Conservation Corps (CCC) opened a bid process for five hundred trucks. Ford made the lowest bid, $169,000 less than the next best offer, which came from Chrysler, which, unlike Ford, had signed the code and therefore displayed the Blue Eagle. Embarrassingly for the NRA, Ford paid higher wages than Chrysler and was able to sell at a lower price.[162]

Roosevelt entered the fray. He announced in his next fireside chat that going forward the government would buy only Blue Eagle goods. From then on, Ford was left out of government purchasing. Still, Ford sales went up during the year, as consumers kept buying Ford products even if they didn't have the Blue Eagle. Given the great visibility of its products, the high performance of Ford became a source of embarrassment for the NRA and its eagle.

The idea that prices were better set by the market than by administrative decisions gained support from an unexpected corner: the young professionals working in the NRA itself. These professionals began to express their strong opinion that the NRA should forget about price fixing and concentrate on enforcing the prohibition of child labor, reducing the number of working hours, and maintaining higher wages. What happened next was very revealing. While the NRA professionals wanted to go back to market freedoms, big business became a passionate defender of price fixing.[163]

Many people started to see the similarities between the NRA and fascist institutions. General Johnson reinforced this impression by invoking the "shining name" of Mussolini in his farewell speech when he resigned as executive director, and by giving Frances Perkins, the secretary of labor, a copy of a fascist book.[164] James Whitman, a professor at Yale Law School, has written:

> Nor was General Johnson alone in the early New Deal years. A startling number of New Dealers had kind words for Mussolini. Rexford Tugwell spoke of the virtues of the Italian Fascist order. So did internal NRA studies. And the President himself expressed interest in bringing the programs of "that admirable Italian gentleman" to

> America. . . . To supporters and critics alike, General Johnson's NRA,
> a vast scheme for delegating governmental authority to private cartels,
> seemed akin to the "corporativism" of Italian Fascism. [165]

Of course, fascist delegation of power to private entities was a sham.
The Italian government retained those powers by directly managing anything that went out of line. The NRA took the same approach. If the
codes of any industry were not satisfactory to the NRA, the president
had the authority to impose whatever codes he wished. When Mussolini
learned of this aspect of NRA legislation, he said, "*Ecco un ditatore!*"
("Behold a dictator!").[166] Of course, Roosevelt never reached the standards of arbitrariness that Mussolini established, but the power to do so
was there before being subjected to the test of checks and balances.

Checks and Balances

It was time for the Supreme Court to act. The opportunity came when
the NRA brought a lawsuit against a small chicken company that
included sixty counts of violating the National Industrial Recovery
Act. One of the accusations was that the company did not engage in
"straight killing," which meant that they allowed their customers to
choose the chickens they wanted to buy and kill. According to the
code, the sellers should not allow the buyers to choose. The chicken
sellers were handed a prison sentence and a stiff fine. They appealed
up to the Supreme Court.

After a sensational trial, the Court unanimously declared the poultry
code unconstitutional because it was based on a law, the National
Industrial Recovery Act, which was unconstitutional in two ways. First,
Congress had violated the constitutional separation of powers by del-
egating its power to regulate trade to the executive branch. Second,
Congress did not have the power to regulate trade in this case, which
did not involve interstate trade. The Court added that the NRA had
abused the chicken company and other enterprises through unconstitutional coercive exercise of lawmaking power. Justice Louis Brandeis,
known as a man of the left, told Roosevelt's aides at the end of the trial:
"This is the end of this business of centralization, and I want you to go
back and tell the president that we're not going to let this government
centralize everything. It's come to an end."[167]

The NRA dropped about five hundred lawsuits against supposed
violators of the codes. In the months that followed, the Supreme

Court declared unconstitutional several other laws that were crucial for the New Deal.

Roosevelt was furious. He decided to try to pack the Supreme Court—that is, to appoint additional justices sympathetic to his ideology. However, by the time of the Supreme Court's decision, he had already noticed how many people worried that the country was veering toward a form of society very different from what it had been in the previous century and a half. So he changed tack.

The Second New Deal

Assessing popular opposition to his early radical moves, Roosevelt designed a different program of reform, called the Second New Deal. Announced in January 1935, the new program included the creation of a social security system to help older Americans, combat unemployment and illness, clear slums, and establish a national welfare program. The NRA would have lapsed in July 1935. In February 1935 Roosevelt asked for a two-year extension of the act. Senate offered ten months. Roosevelt declined, and the NRA ceased to exist.

The Second New Deal changed the country forever, giving the economy a new flexibility that helped it to avoid the political chaos that the enormous rates of unemployment could have eventually caused. By 1935, when the Second New Deal was launched, the rate of unemployment had declined from its 1933 peak of 25 percent to 20 percent—still too high and falling too slowly. With the shift from the First to the Second New Deal, Roosevelt changed strategy. Instead of trying to reduce the rate of unemployment by manipulating the economy against the market, he shifted to a strategy of reducing the social impact of unemployment, retirement, and incapacity by means of social security. This strategy not only reduced the risk of a social explosion but also helped revolutionize modern capitalism by reducing the pain of inevitable economic cycles. In 1911, the United Kingdom had established an unemployment insurance scheme under the Liberal government of H. H. Asquith, with the enthusiastic support of Winston Churchill. Significantly, communists criticized the British scheme, thinking that it "would prevent workers from starting a revolution."[168]

In 1936, based on this new platform, Roosevelt was reelected in a landslide. His Democratic Party controlled 64 percent of the Senate and 73 percent of the House. This gave him tremendous power. He attempted to use it in his fight with the Supreme Court. In mid-1937, he proposed a law that would have increased the number of justices by one for every incumbent over seventy years old, up to fifteen total justices. If approved, his law would allow him to appoint the six members he wished right away. His own Democrats joined the Republicans to defeat the law, however.

Yet Roosevelt's 1936 landslide reelection nevertheless had an unexpected effect on the Court. Two justices, Charles Evan Hughes and Owen Roberts (who held the balance of power in the Court between liberal and conservative), abandoned the principle of enumerated powers, which said that the federal government had only those powers spelled out in the Constitution. The Court began to uphold laws that were based on attributions of the federal government that were not mentioned in the Constitution.[169] This shift resulted in sentences that favored the federal government. Furthermore, in the next few years, Roosevelt appointed four new justices in accordance with the existing law. The new Court then upheld many laws that would have never been accepted in previous years.[170]

The move from the First to the Second New Deal was dramatic and significant. Roosevelt shifted from a one-dimensional approach to another that was consistent with the multidimensional nature of the United States. Over time, the First New Deal was forgotten as the government focused on providing better social services and investing in human capital. Slowly, the radicals in favor of central planning were weeded out of the government.

At the same time, however, Roosevelt maintained what appeared to be a campaign of abuse against the private sector, which surely played an important role in deterring investment and growth. Roosevelt portrayed entrepreneurs as his enemies, depressing the mood in the private sector. Although almost impossible to quantify, such a shift must have had a negative impact on investment. Joseph Schumpeter has written:

> [Investors] realize that they are on trial before judges who have the verdict in their pocket before hand, that an increasing part of public opinion is impervious to their point of view, and that any particular indictment will, if successfully met, at once be replaced by another. Again, we may differ in our estimates of the importance of both this factor and the functions it tends to paralyze, but it should not be overlooked.[171]

Also, Roosevelt tripled taxes during the Great Depression, including the 1936 tax on undistributed profits. Such profits were the main source of investment funds, especially for small firms. By the late 1930s, Roosevelt began to pay a price for his aggressiveness against investors. On June 16, 1939, Congress approved by 357 to 1 a bill that, among other probusiness measures, abolished the undistributed profits tax by not extending it.

THE LEGACY

There are three great puzzles associated with the Roosevelt administration: the first is how people have forgotten how the First New Deal flirted with corporatism and the slippery slope that leads to fascism. In the words of James Whitman:

> For a generation thereafter, historians preferred to ignore the italo-philia of the early New Deal years. Perhaps understandably, the history of American interest in Italian "corporativism," an ill-defined industrial policy involving official state sponsorship of industry cartels and labor unions, remained something of a taboo topic. . . . But about fifteen years ago [he was writing in 1991], both the scholarly climate and the political climate began to change. In 1973, two prominent historians published articles suggesting that early New Deal government had resembled government in fascist central Europe.[172]

This void, understandable as it is, is crucial to understand the period—and the search for the solution to the terrible disruptions that the industrial revolution inflicted on industrial countries. Filling the void with the facts is essential to see how US citizens went to the brink in the midst of this transformation, looked over the edge, found what they saw alien to their nature, and pulled away from it. This is a period crucial to understanding the anguished search for solutions in whatever place they seem to be while facing the disruptions of a technological transformation. Today's crisis presents the country with a similar brink and the same danger of a search for false solutions.

The second puzzle is that most people believe Roosevelt's economic policies saved the country from the Great Depression. In fact, the United States did not escape the Depression until World War II, when demand increased exponentially as a result of war operations. One of the most controversial questions regarding the Great Depression is why it lasted so long. Britain and Germany exited their depressions much earlier than the United States.

Of course, there were two different periods in terms of economic policy. As we previously discussed, the First New Deal is frequently ignored in the discussions of this subject. But looking at the First New Deal as it was is indispensable to drawing the lessons needed to deal with the challenges we are facing in the twenty-first century. As Michael A. Bernstein has shown, the NRA and its associated policies delayed this painful adjustment and therefore the resolution of the Great Depression:

> In the slower-growing industries, those experiencing transformations in the strengths of their markets because of long-term changes in the structure of American consumption, the response to the crisis was essentially one of output restriction and price maintenance. Such policies, of course, interfered with the efforts of firms in newer industries, or of newer firms in the older industries, to compete effectively and penetrate the market. On this basis it can be argued that the [First] New Deal apparatus, as exemplified by the N.R.A., obstructed the recovery of the American economy in the crisis of the thirties. But insofar as the code authorities themselves were dominated by the older firms within the older industries, the failure of the [First] New Deal in this respect cannot be ascribed simply to ignorance of economics, or to willful and misguided obstruction of the workings of enterprise. Indeed, such an indictment of the New Deal can be made only if one ignores the peculiar and powerful constellation of material interests thrown up during the crisis of the thirties that made effective government intervention problematic.[173]

In fact, even after the first, failed state of their program, New Dealers made it more expensive for employers to hire people; they discouraged economic growth and employment creation with a constant harassment of investors; and, while the economy was weaker than at any other time, they increased taxes from $1.6 billion in 1933 to $5.3 billion in 1940, thus reducing the private economy's ability to create capital and jobs. Together, these measures delayed economic recovery. Yet the notion of investing in the population through social policies, central to the Second New Deal, transformed capitalism for the better, enabling it to adjust more easily to cyclical fluctuations and radical transformations, like those we are experiencing today. It also lent capitalism legitimacy, allowing it to help in the solution of the pressing problems that the population was facing.[174]

Roosevelt always insisted that he had saved capitalism by providing a space for people to vent their frustrations and anguish during the Great Depression. He might have played that role, but not through his economic policies. His historic interventions were in the social and political spheres.

The answer Henry Morgenthau gave his son when asked what the New Deal had achieved, quoted earlier, was true: "The United States had come through this terrific turmoil and . . . the individual in this country still had the right to think, talk, and worship as he wished."[175] This truth was a great achievement for Roosevelt and for the country he led.

Much of his leadership was personal. At times his language could be divisive, but his impressive charisma was a unifying factor for the nation as a whole. People idolized him. His fireside chats, listened to every Sunday evening throughout the country, kept alive a sense of togetherness and made people feel that, even in the midst of the Depression, they were the citizens of a great country. He held their hands through one of the most painful and uncertain periods in its history. With all his sins and defects, he was one of the great leaders of the twentieth century. When we look at how he is remembered, his legacy was unifying.

The third puzzle is something that did not happen. For several years, Roosevelt controlled the three branches of government. When he became president in 1933, Democrats had majorities in both the Senate and the House. These majorities increased in subsequent years and peaked at 80 percent in both chambers in 1937 and 1938. Democratic majorities remained in place until Roosevelt's death in 1945.[176] He also controlled the Supreme Court from 1937 onward through the normal appointment of magistrates. He was in an ideal position to turn the United States into a one-dimensional tyranny. But it didn't happen.

Even had Roosevelt wanted to impose a tyranny, it wouldn't have happened. Even if Roosevelt controlled the three branches of government, he did not control two additional levels of checks and balances, neither of which is mentioned in the Constitution. One was the separation of the economic and political power, which always remained wide enough to ensure the multidimensionality of US society. The second was the liberal democratic conviction of the American people, which guided and supported the liberal conviction of the judicial and legislative branches.

These obstacles were insurmountable. Even Democrats made it clear to him that there were limits to the lengths they would go with him. Montana senator Burton K. Wheeler, a Democrat, told Roosevelt when he tried to pack the court in 1937:

> Create now a political Court to echo the ideas of the executive and you have created a weapon; a weapon which in the hands of another president could . . . cut down those guarantees of liberty written by the blood of our forefathers.[177]

The senators who rejected his proposal to pack the court showed that they would not allow a president to violate the spirit of the independence of the United States. If Roosevelt had tried to go beyond these limits and attempted to establish a true dictatorship, which was unlikely, his own aides would have thought that he had lost his mind.

This is what never happened in Germany, Italy, or Russia, where government was the seat of power rather than the people themselves. The difference between the pre-Nazi and American approaches to the emergency posed by the Great Depression can be summarized in two quotations. Carl Schmitt, the top Nazi judicial expert, said that "sovereign is whoever decides what constitutes an exception." These words, which imply that there were exceptions to the sovereignty of the people, justified government by decree, and ultimately Hitler's dictatorship. At about the same time, the Supreme Court of the United States asserted, very clearly, that "extraordinary conditions do not create or enlarge constitutional power."[178] That reaffirmed the rule of the Constitution.

These lessons are important for our time. Intervening in the economy to keep things as they are backfires. On the contrary, investment in human capital, as it was done with the GI Bill for veterans after World War II (the Servicemen's Readjustment Act of 1944), is the right way to facilitate adjustment. The most important lesson, however, is that all this can be done, and better, within liberal democracy.

The United States survived the crisis of the Great Depression because it was multidimensional and wanted to remain so. The institutional checks and balances worked because people wanted them to. There was nothing automatic in the institutional setting of the United States. There is nothing automatic in liberal democracy, or in any other system, that ensures people will behave in a particular way. The ultimate check against absolutism came from the American people, who exercised their power through their votes. That is the mark of a great country. The big question for today is: Will the United States still have the will to stick to the liberal principles that bestowed on it this greatness?

10

THE WELFARE STATE AND COMMUNISM

If it is true that absolute power corrupts absolutely, it is also true that absolute powerlessness corrupts absolutely. Without the ability to make decisions there can be no choice to act morally. Powerlessness corrupts by eroding the sense of personal, not public, responsibility. That is central to ethical conduct.

Nina Witoszek

THE COLD WAR

The three or four decades that followed the end of World War II were extraordinary. After more than a century of turbulence, the world reached a new equilibrium. It was as if the challenges of the industrial revolution had at last been settled. Industry and services supplanted agriculture as the mainstay of the economy, while agriculture adopted industrial technologies. The large migrations to the cities and to developing countries, which gave an outlet to the people who were left unemployed by the industrialization of agriculture, had already taken place. The grossest manifestations of class war, so intense up to the 1930s, disappeared in most developed countries along with financial crises. The distribution of income and wealth, which had been such a source of concern at the turn of the century, became substantially more equitable.

Life became more predictable as the end of the war marked the end of the industrial revolution. It was not that innovation stopped. The rate of technological growth may have actually increased. But new inventions did not disrupt the industrial social order. On the contrary, they reinforced it by confirming the apparently perpetual progress in the multiplication of the power of muscle. New technologies buttressed the old ones without changing the direction of progress. Jetliners and rockets do the same thing as propeller planes and even the same thing as the early railroads invented at the beginning of the industrial revolution. The new inventions were more of the same things that had been characteristic of the industrial revolution.

The dynamic world of empires in which Britain, Germany, France, the United States, Japan, and Russia had competed for global domination gave way to a more static world of two superpowers locked in something called "the Cold War," which actually provided long-lasting stability. With some exceptions at the fringes (Korea, Cuba, Vietnam, Cambodia), the areas controlled by the communist bloc and those that were liberal democracies remained stable for decades. Then, suddenly, at the end of the 1980s, the Soviet Union began to betray symptoms of a deep economic and political sickness, and within a few years, it collapsed.

We are now in the midst of the connectivity revolution. Inequality and instability have returned to the entire world, including liberal democracies, and people are focusing again on the role of social order. In the new competition of systems now emerging, attention has turned to bring back socialism, which many people believe is the model used in Sweden, where it was well implemented, as opposed to that which existed in the Soviet Union. In this vein, many people think that Swedish or Nordic socialism should be introduced in the United States. Let's compare the social orders of Sweden and the Soviet Union to see if the difference is one of degree or of essence.

Sweden

Early Development

The crucial fact in the history of Sweden is that its welfare state emerged from an individualistic argument: the need to liberate individuals from the most basic tasks in life so that they could develop their higher capabilities. This happened in three stages: a moderate period of change in the 1930s and 1940s; the radical 1970s; and the period from the 1990s to today, which has represented a retrenchment from the extremes reached in the late 1980s.[179]

Sweden's social and economic progress is closely associated with its early investment in human capital. Its development depended in part on the work of outstanding inventors and businesspeople, who became immensely rich as a result of important innovations that could only have been the product of an educated culture. As a result of this human capital, Sweden, a small country, has many world-class enterprises that successfully compete internationally with companies that operate in very large domestic markets.

By 1920, Sweden had established the basic infrastructure of a developed economy and began development of its welfare state in two dimensions: social care and labor relations. In the 1930s, the Swedish parliament approved reforms to provide unemployment support, insurance, childcare centers, a government employment service, housing for families with children, and one week's statutory leave. These measures did not immediately result in a substantial increase in the size of the national government. The cost of social services was covered by the municipal and county authorities, which funded them with local taxes, and were not very large in any case. The social policies were still in the hands of the citizens, in a very local way—as they had been when the parish managed them in the nineteenth century.

Employers and their workers structured their relations in a centralized way that closely resembled that which created so much rigidity in Germany. But this centralization did not lead to the conflicts it created in Germany. In the 1920s, Sweden had more labor unrest than any other country in Europe, but with time, the challenges were solved via quiet, rational dialogue without government interference.[180]

In 1938, the Swedish Employers Association and the Swedish Trade Union Confederation signed the Saltsjöbaden Agreement, which recognized employees' right to an "equitable" share in the results of production, while the workers recognized the employers' right to "direct and allocate work."[181] The workers recognized that better wages could be obtained only through improved productivity. The creation of more jobs at higher wages was possible only if industries were profitable and free of labor unrest. So they decided not to seek conflict and to support industrial modernization. The employers supported the unions, fired strikebreakers, and accepted the construction of the welfare state. Both sides did what they did on their own because they didn't want the government to intervene in their affairs.[182]

As a result of the government's detachment from labor issues, to this day there is no officially set minimum wage in Sweden. Salaries and working conditions are still negotiated by the associations of employers and employees without government participation. The right to strike was not abolished, but the two sides agreed to suspend it for the life of each of the periodic agreements. If unions want to strike, they first have to reject the standing agreement, an action that requires advance notice of at least two weeks to deflate emotions. There have been strikes after the agreement, especially in recent decades and especially in the public sector, but the spirit that led to their suspension is still there, and most labor conflicts are resolved without recourse to strikes.

In the same spirit that they displayed in the provision of social services in the early twentieth century, Swedes found the solution to their labor problems in the private sphere. All sides showed restraint. This was one of the ways in which Sweden saved itself from the terrible social and political divisiveness that overtook Germany in 1933.

Sweden shifted gears in the 1970s as it increased the size of the welfare state. Pushed by the radical left, new reforms posed a threat to Sweden's liberal democratic tradition as the government seemed to be positioning itself to control the economy. From 1970 to 1990, Sweden seemed to be moving toward socialism.

This second, more radical welfare state of the 1970s was based on an even more individualistic notion. Jonas Love Almqvist published a novel in 1838 that criticized the web of relationships that tie families together. The argument of the novel was that many of these ties were false. People portrayed them as manifestations of love, but in reality they were the result of unhealthy economic dependencies, which had to be eliminated. Human links should be driven only by true love.[183]

More than a century after the publication of Almqvist's novel, the intellectual Alva Myrdal convinced the government that all dependencies should be abolished so that, if a family stayed together, it was because there was love, not just economic or psychological dependencies. To abolish these dependencies, the government had to take under its wing the mutual responsibilities of family members. That is, the state should replace the father and the mother as providers of each other and as providers of their children. This would eliminate the influence that they could have on each other, on their children, and on their parents. People had to be independent of human relations to focus on their own happiness without paying attention to that of others. To do so, of course, they had to become dependent on the state. But the state was happy to take that responsibility. In the early 1970s, the Social Democrats issued a manifesto arguing that "all adults shall be financially independent of their next of kin."[184] The drive to create this dream coincided with a drastic radicalization of the left, subsequent to the 1968 leftist revolts that convulsed Europe.

In 1971, the government abolished joint taxation of couples, eliminating the fiscal incentive to marry or remain married. In 1973, it abolished legal alimony payments to ensure that women would be independent from their former husbands and that men would not feel responsible for the maintenance of children or their former wives. Women would not need the alimony because the state would provide child support and subsidize their primary needs. The children, in turn, did not need either father or mother, and older citizens did not need to have any relationship with their offspring to survive. The state took care of them all.[185] In a famous documentary, Erik Gandini called this kind of reasoning the Swedish Theory of Love. It seemed like socialism, but ultimate control of the process remained tightly under the control of citizens, which they eventually exercised in the direction of freedom and the rule of rights.

This is not to say that the reforms of the 1970s were costless in economic, social, and political terms. The country took a sharp turn to the left. Contradicting the spirit of the Saltsjöbaden Agreement, the Social Democratic government intervened in the labor market, passing laws to satisfy radical workers' demands. The payroll tax increased from 12.5 to 36.7 percent of salaries to cover more social services. Other regulations further increased the cost of labor. As a result, salary costs increased by 45 percent during the mid-1970s. High taxation (which reached 80 percent at the margin), combined with tax deductions of interest expenditures to create powerful incentives for debt financing while profits were falling. Worse still, as these measures broke the back of many enterprises, the government began to subsidize unprofitable industries to protect uncompetitive labor. With that, they moved toward the rigidity that had so badly served Germany during the Weimar Republic.

The most alarming of the 1970s Social Democrat initiatives was embedded in the so-called employee funds. These funds would buy shares of Swedish companies listed in the stock exchange, funded with new taxes on a portion of the companies' profits. Over time, workers would own the publicly traded companies and the trade unions' representatives would control them.[186] It would have been like Gorbachev's idea of socialism, whose failure we discuss later in this chapter.

As the future of liberal democracy darkened under the prospect of such unification of economic and political power, the Swedes confirmed their liberal vocation in two very powerful ways. In October 1983, opposition mobilized the largest demonstration ever to take place in Sweden. Between 80,000 and 100,000 people protested in Stockholm against the employee funds.[187] The funds were quickly discarded. As concern that government power was becoming too strong deepened, the Swedish parliament passed a new constitution that reaffirmed the country's liberal values, emphasizing the protection of the rights of the Swedish citizens against government encroachment.[188] Even when expanding the welfare state to its historical zenith, Sweden reinforced the rule of rights.

The Crisis and the Decline of the Social Democrats

By the 1990s, the welfare state had become incredibly expensive. General government expenditures represented 68 percent of gross domestic product (GDP). Fiscal deficits increased, and profits went down all over the economy. More ominously, job creation came to a halt and even became negative in many years. Innovative enterprise creation, key to Sweden's riches, came to a halt. The excessive taxes that financed social expenditures were taking their toll.[189] Worse still, excessive monetary creation unleashed a bubble in housing.[190]

A new social and political divisiveness became visible as well. In 1986, the nation was shocked by the assassination of Prime Minister Olaf Palme, the first political assassination in almost two hundred years. The housing bubble burst. The central bank could not prevent a catastrophic fall in international reserves, and a full-fledged financial crisis exploded. The central bank bailed out several banks at very high cost. All this worsened the impression that Sweden was falling apart.

The crisis induced a reappraisal of the direction that the country was taking. It resulted in many deep reforms, all in the direction of liberalizing the economy.[191] The ratio of the government expenditures to GDP fell by about twenty points, from 68 percent in 1993 to a stable 48 percent in 2008.[192] The Social Democrats, which had once had a majority of seats in parliament, now commanded less than a third of them, and they remained in power only through agreements with parties to its right, which imposed liberal reforms as a payment for their support. While the issue that seemed to decide the 2018 election was migration, the new minority government was forced to recognize that it had to continue liberalizing the economy and further reduce the social engineering embedded in the welfare state.

The Capitalist Nordic Countries

Sweden's history shows how fundamentally individualistic and liberal the country is. Unlike truly socialist countries, Sweden created a welfare state not to increase the power of the government but to increase the freedom of the citizens by liberating them from poverty and economic dependencies. Without these burdens, its citizens were freer to pursue their happiness in all dimensions of life. And throughout their history, they have kept political and economic power separate. As a result, Sweden is one of the freest economies in the world, and this is true of all the Nordic countries. Denmark's Prime Minister Lars Lokke Rasmussen clarified this point to a Harvard audience in 2015:

> I know that some people in the US associate the Nordic model with some sort of socialism. Therefore I would like to make one thing clear. Denmark is far from a socialist planned economy. Denmark is a market economy. The Nordic model is an expanded welfare state which provides a high level of security for its citizens, but it is also a successful market economy with much freedom to pursue your dreams and live your life as you wish.[193]

Notice the prime minister's emphasis on the key words: *freedom to pursue your dreams and live your life as you wish*. That is the essential motivation of the Nordic welfare state rather than an exotic doctrine or the will for power. He knew what he was talking about, not just about Denmark but also about the other Nordic countries.

Table 1 shows the global ranks of these countries in terms of their overall economic freedom and of their protection of property rights, compared with those of the United Kingdom and the United States. Sweden is third in the world in terms of protection of property rights (after Singapore and New Zealand) and number 15 (out of 186 countries) in terms of overall economic freedom, three positions ahead of the United States. All the Nordic countries are ahead of the United States

TABLE 1
Rankings in Terms of Economic Freedom and Protection of Property Rights

	Rank Economic Freedom	Rank Property Rights
Sweden	15	3
United Kingdom	8	5
Finland	26	6
Iceland	11	10
Norway	23	11
Denmark	12	13
United States	18	24

Source: Heritage Foundation Economic Freedom Index, 2018, https://www.heritage.org/index/.

in terms of protection of property rights, and three of them are ahead in terms of overall economic freedom. Marx would turn in his grave if he heard these countries called socialist. If socialists want to imitate Sweden, they imitate a version of capitalism.

Another common misconception about Sweden is that it has a dismal record of growth, relative to the less welfare-oriented capitalist countries. Data belies this misconception. By 2016, the German economy was 404 percent of its size in 1960; the Swedish economy, 390 percent; the United Kingdom, 323 percent; and the United States, 294 percent.[194]

Sweden's wealth distribution is such that a few extremely rich families own an overwhelming majority of the country's wealth, while many others own nothing. The richest 10 percent own 58 percent of the country's wealth; in the United States, the richest 10 percent own a comparable 64 percent.[195]

The Paradox

The history of Sweden shows how a very individualistic country may end up with a social order that many people think is a socialist one. Surprisingly, the country adopted this social order for individualistic and social interest reasons—they wanted to create a system where everyone could pursue their destiny while being free from poverty. Sweden as a nation shows how flexible and diverse liberalism can be. Superficially,

Sweden is completely different from the cradles of liberalism, Britain and the United States. Yet all three countries, as well as other liberal democracies around the world, share an identical set of core beliefs: the separation of economic and political power, a belief in democracy and freedom, and the rule of rights. These are the essential features of liberal democracy. The rest are details, adjustments of the basic model to the preferences of the population.

This is completely different from classic socialism, as it was applied in the Soviet Union, which we discuss next.

THE SOVIET UNION

The Two Kinds of Markets

In the late 1980s, while the rush to socialism in Sweden was faltering, the Soviet Union was collapsing as well, posing some fundamental questions: Why did it collapse? And why did it fall so quickly, so catastrophically? More broadly, what went wrong with socialist economies in general? Did the system contain some fatal, internal flaw that led irremediably to its own failure? Or was the collapse the result of a particular way in which the system was managed?

It is difficult to imagine a wider difference than that between the idyllic visions of socialist theoreticians and the hard reality of these countries. Rather than becoming a worker's paradise, these countries developed regimes held together by terror alone, a contrast that provides weight to the argument that socialism was a perversion of the original intentions of the creators of the system. If this is true, then it could be argued that the system did not fail; the way it was put into practice was the source of the failure.

A closer look at those original visions, and particularly at the problems of their implementation, reveals a clear relationship between theory and reality. Trying to apply socialist principles had to lead to the results observed. This does not mean that there was a historic force at work that condemned the countries of Central and Eastern Europe to their sad experience. Contrary to what Marx believed, the flow of history is not inevitable. However, there are causes and effects. In following the socialist road, these countries had to go through the checkpoints that the logic of socialism signaled. As it happened, chaos, terror, or both dominated these stages. They were the result of an essential conflict that a socialist economy creates for its participants.

The conflict is ingrained in the socialist vision of what makes people work and carry out economic activities. Capitalism works on the premise that self-interest is one of people's natural motivations. Individuals meet the needs of others—serving social ends—because the only way in which people can survive and increase their economic well-being is by producing and selling something that is useful to others. As a result, people strive to identify needs they can fulfill for others and then work to fulfill them. In capitalist societies, egoistic motivations are thus harnessed to produce benefits to society as a whole. Socialism, in contrast, is based on a rejection of self-interest as a legitimate motivation for economic activity. That is, socialist theoreticians believed that social interest, which must be a complement to self-interest in a multidimensional society, would become the only motivation in a socialist economy—an assumption devoid of common sense.

Having rejected self-interest, socialist theory had to be based on the assumption that people will behave in ways defined as socially responsible, putting their egoism aside in the pursuance of the collective good. The main contention of socialism is that such change in motivation can be accomplished through the prohibition of private ownership of the means of production. Without the possibility of owning capital, people should stop working to accumulate wealth. Rather, they should work for the benefit of society.

Under this system, people, one way or another, have to surrender the fruits of their economic activity to an abstract entity—society. Society, in turn, would take care of maximizing the income and wealth of the collective and would distribute their benefits in a socially fair way. The expectations of such unselfish behavior are obvious in the vision of communist utopia, where the state withers away and people work under the motto "From each according to his ability, to each according to his needs." Social benefits are supposed to be related to the work performed, although each individual has to depend on society for the direct or indirect provision of capital and for job opportunities, which in turn leads to the social determination of all sources of income in the country. While society supposedly allocates its resources in a spontaneous fashion, in fact everything is controlled by the state. Rather than withering away, the state becomes all-controlling.

Expectations of this kind of behavior—giving to the pool to receive from it—were superimposed on the natural economic motivations of people, which remained predominantly individualistic. The conflicts created by this social arrangement were obvious in many ways. On the productive side, socialist enterprises suffered from what in economics is called the *principal-agent problem*, the conflict of interest that exists whenever an individual (the agent) manages the property of someone else (the principal). Agents tend to manage the assets for their own, not the owner's, benefit. In extreme cases, in which the principal is absent or busy doing other things, the agent may even steal the assets. If, as in a socialist economy, the assets cannot be stolen because there is no private ownership, the managers can still appropriate the rents produced by those assets. They can't steal the cow, but they can steal the milk.

The possibility of appropriating rents, however, is not limited to the people managing physical assets. It can also be done by the bureaucrats managing any part of the complicated apparatus needed to administer the separation of the fruits of one's work from one's consumption.[196] According to socialist doctrine, these problems would not exist in a socialist economy because people would behave as socialists; they would be unselfish.

Rather than promoting the emergence of a new, unselfish human being, unrestricted social pooling encouraged unbounded consumption without providing the incentives to produce the goods and services needed to fill such consumption. The combined effect crushed the economy. In a nutshell, the demise of socialism was caused by its basic irrationality. The collapse of the Soviet and other communist economies should have been no surprise to anyone.

One thing is surprising, however. The irrationality of the system is so marked that it should have not lasted as long as it did. The chaotic tendencies that brought down the socialist regimes in the former Soviet Union and Central Europe are natural results that could have been expected from the system from the very beginning. But the system lasted for seventy-five years.

The fact that the Soviet Union could survive for so long with such an irrational economic system prompts two questions. First, what was the glue that kept socialism together and thus prevented its downfall until very recently? Second, why did this glue disappear in the late 1980s, leaving the system vulnerable to its own irrationality?

The glue was terror. The construction of socialism was built on the basis of coercion and violence. Because people's behavior contradicts socialist economic objectives, the coercion needed to make them behave as true socialists had to be so encompassing and pervasive that its appropriate name was terror. Lenin, Stalin, and Lenin's fellow Bolsheviks used it to destroy what they called the enemy classes, to force peasants to surrender their crops, to eliminate trade, to break any remnants of economic initiative and to create scapegoats for their economic mistakes. Then they used it to force peasants to join collective farms and to force compliance with production targets.

For reasons we will see, however, communist leaders had to reduce terror, and the effectiveness of that which remained declined. This is what killed the Soviet Union.

The Nemesis of Communism

The fundamental problem of communism was the principal-agent problem, which became manifest in the corruption of the workers shortly after the 1917 revolution. As soon as Lenin nationalized enterprises, the workers and their controllers started to use them for their own, not the nation's, benefit. They increased their salaries and pilfered goods, machinery, and equipment to sell on the black market. Without capitalists, the natural advocates for capital, the workers drained all the capital from the enterprises. The economy declined sharply in the following months.

The Bolshevik leaders felt betrayed. The masses did not understand what was better for them and kept on engaging in trade and other sinful economic activities. More important in Marxist terms, the dictatorship of the proletariat was running out of proletarians. Industrial employment was falling. People fled from urban areas, looking for food and trying to escape the control of revolutionary cells and the hatred that prevailed in the cities. The government tried to stop these migrations by force, introducing roadblocks and armed detachments in the factories, all in vain. As workers abandoned their workplaces to migrate en masse to the countryside, industrial employment fell from 2.6 million in 1917 to 1.2 million in 1920.[197] Industrial production in 1920 was just 20 percent of its 1913 level, and that of transportation was 22 percent.[198] Lenin was alarmed.[199]

The most intellectually restless among the Bolsheviks, Leon Trotsky and Nikolai Bukharin, came out with parallel diagnoses of the problem and a single solution. They reckoned that people would never voluntarily comply with the socialist work ethic—working for nothing. Therefore, what was needed was to force people to work—not for a while but forever. Trotsky, then the commissar of war, advocated for the militarization of labor, which he thought people would actually enjoy.[200]

Bukharin made a more sophisticated argument. In *The Economics of Transition,* published in 1920, Bukharin argued that established economic systems have an internal consistency that gives them stability. He maintained that, in capitalism, such equilibrium was provided not just by market relations but, fundamentally, by capitalist ownership, which disciplined the enterprises. Market forces in turn disciplined the capitalists. Hiring and firing and compensation policies are how capitalists disciplined the labor force.[201]

As a result of the introduction of socialism, capitalists and market forces had disappeared in Russia. Without them, and in an environment of generalized labor corruption, state coercion was the only way to make people work and to allocate labor to the activities where it was needed. Bukharin thought that this coercion would be needed forever because the tendency toward equilibrium would never return in the absence of market incentives. In this way, Bukharin stated the principal-agent problem with utmost clarity. He advanced a solution that would be adopted by all communist regimes: terror. Before he was killed during the Great Terror of the 1930s, Bukharin wrote in the 1920s:

> Proletarian coercion in all its forms, beginning with shooting and ending with labor conscription is . . . a method of creating Communist mankind out of the human materials of the capitalist epoch.[202]

Grigory Zinoviev, another of the original revolutionaries killed in 1936, said:

> We must carry along with us 90 million out of the 100 million Soviet Russian population. As for the rest, we have nothing to say to them. They must be annihilated.[203]

The Commission on Labor Obligation was created under Trotsky in late December 1919, and the militarization of labor was approved by the Ninth Party Congress in March 1920.[204]

By choosing this path, socialist regimes turned the conflict from one between expected and actual behavior into one of citizens against state and words against deeds. This conflict generated the hypocrisy characteristic of socialist regimes. Under Soviet communism, socialist ideas became an instrument of power for small minorities to impose a harsh rule on the population, not a system to improve the lives of the people, as happened in Sweden.

The most spectacular example of the confrontation of revolutionaries with their own constituency came with the uprising of the Kronstadt Island naval base in February and March 1921. Kronstadt Island is near St. Petersburg, which had been renamed Petrograd after the revolution. This uprising was not only a serious challenge to the government but also carried with it a strong symbolic message. This base had been part of the revolution that put the Bolsheviks in power. Now, the sailors at the naval base rebelled in protest against the dire living conditions of the Petrograd population, which they did not share because they had better rations. In early 1921, reacting to news coming from the mainland, they sent a delegation to investigate what was happening in the city. Afterward, they claimed that the revolution had been betrayed.

The uprising convinced Lenin to change his strategy. As the Red Army moved on the frozen sea to storm Kronstadt, Lenin made a speech to the Tenth Congress of the Communist Party. He said that the policies of the past few years had been forced on him by the state of war that Russia had suffered continuously since the revolution; that these policies, which he called "War Communism," had been mistaken; and that he intended to launch a new strategy that would redress these mistakes. The new strategy would be called the New Economic Policy (NEP). Under it, free trade would be allowed in agricultural products and in some consumer goods, some private property would be permitted, and foreign investment would be invited. The attempt to plan the economy centrally was abandoned for the time being.

The government adopted these ideas, and the NEP became not only official policy but also the new orthodoxy. Lenin's sycophantic companions competed with each other to show how liberal they were. The most famous of these new liberals was Bukharin, who had argued that communism must be built with violence and labor conscription. He told the peasants, *Get Rich!*[205] It was the deepest economic liberalization that the Soviet regime was to effect in its history—in many ways deeper than that carried out by Gorbachev under perestroika.

The NEP ended, however, when Stalin, who succeeded Lenin after killing the competition, launched his Second Socialist Offensive, which established the regime that would last until Gorbachev. He forced peasants onto collective farms; strengthened central planning, which had survived under the NEP, and turned it into the ultimate economic authority; and imposed terror on managers and the population at large as the means to control society, implementing in this way the original ideas of Trotsky and Bukharin. During the so-called offensive, the communists killed more than twenty million people. After communism was thoroughly reimposed, Stalin arranged for the killing of the Old Bolsheviks, the original communists who had fought alongside Lenin during the revolution and who had carried out those twenty million murders. Stalin's purge was called the Great Terror, and although the death toll was under a million (compared with twenty million) it was nevertheless socially devastating because it was carried out against communists themselves.

This regime of terror lasted as long as the country existed. It was there during the peasant rebellions of the late 1910s and early 1920s, when Lenin confiscated grain from agricultural workers, and it was there for all the gulags, which existed right up to the 1980s. The peak of the terror was in the 1930s, as the Soviet Union was becoming an industrial power, and after the defeat of the Nazis in World War II, Stalin seemed to have succeeded in creating a superpower permanently founded on terror.

Stalin's victory, however, was not permanent. The system he bequeathed to his country carried with it the seeds of its own destruction. As much as the escalation of terror can be explained by the logical necessities of the socialist system, the ultimate collapse of the system can also be explained by the dynamics that total terror sets in motion in society. A system whose economy can work only on the basis of terror is obviously very weak. If, for any reason, the level of terror has to be reduced, the chaotic trends created by the lack of economic incentives for production take over and productive capacity falls. Soviet leaders confronted this situation after the death of Stalin. For reasons that we will shortly explore, the rulers became unable to maintain the levels of terror that had made socialism possible. As terror declined, the cracks in the socialist construction became fractures, leading to the demise of the system in a long process that spanned almost four decades.

When Stalin died in 1953, the process that had taken place after Lenin's death nearly thirty years earlier was reenacted as the top leaders attempted to determine who would succeed him. Knowing his comrades, Lenin had been concerned about what would happen to the party after his death. His main concern was that a fight for individual leadership would lead to a split, which would be disastrous for the regime. For this reason, he wanted them to establish a collective government. In his testament—written just before he died—he named six men as the most outstanding members of the party, highlighting their qualities but also their defects. Analyzing their characters, he came to the conclusion that none of them would be a good leader if acting alone. In this way, he tried to convince them that they needed each other and that a collective government would be the best.

Lenin's concerns proved unfounded. There was a single heir to his power, and there was no split of the party. As if following a plot invented by Agatha Christie, one of the men on his list killed the other five— along with thousands of prominent communists, hundreds of thousands of grassroots communists, and millions of others.[206] The assassin was Stalin, the person the Old Bolsheviks had entrusted to manage their machinery of terror against the population. The Old Bolsheviks were killed by the assassin they had created to impose their terror. In this way, Stalin showed communist leaders that they were not omnipotent and that terror can have negative consequences for those who practice it.

When Stalin died, the deadly game that had been played out after Lenin's death was played again. But this time, most of the heirs were determined never again to allow the power of any individual to grow to levels that would endanger their own lives. This meant that the power of the machinery of terror had to be curbed. The new leaders started the implementation of their decision by killing the head of the NKVD (the secret police organization that would become the KGB), Lavrenty Beria, who had the best shot at becoming a second Stalin and was working toward that end. After that, Nikita Khrushchev denounced the terrorist methods of Stalin and gained the individual leadership of the country. The party, however, never allowed him, or any of his successors, to attain absolute power.

The Decline of the Effectiveness of Terror

Stalin's successors did not abandon the use of violence to impose their will. Khrushchev used brute force to crush the Polish and Hungarian rebellions in 1956, as Brezhnev did against Czechoslovakia in 1968 and—with much less strength and effectiveness—Mikhail Gorbachev did against the Baltic countries in the late 1980s and early 1990s. Soviet leadership continued sending dissidents to Siberia and to mental hospitals, and the KGB continued hunting defectors worldwide. This violence was enough to discourage any effective challenge to the socialist regime and its ruling elite. However, the regime had been weakened by its leadership's decision not to allow any individual to accumulate as much power as Stalin had, and this weakness curbed the extent to which the leadership was willing to go to terrorize the population. As people realized that their leaders would refrain from the massive killing and deportation of the Stalin years, the level of subjective terror was gradually eroded.

Coercion and terror did not remove the communist system's tendency to chaos but only submerged it temporarily. State terror certainly forces people to do what the government wishes them to do, but only for those behaviors where the leaders can measure compliance. But most individual behavior is not so easily monitored, and people can keep on bending the rules in ways that frequently render state control meaningless. Although severely restricted in many respects, citizens of regimes based on terror can enjoy secret freedoms that they exploit to their advantage.

For example, terror cannot be used to prompt creativity. Terror is a negative instrument, which can prevent people from doing what they want to do but without the ability to encourage the positive but complicated activities needed to run a modern economy efficiently. Terror can force effectiveness but not efficiency. This problem becomes more difficult when military might depends on creativity. It was much easier to force an individual to put a screw in place than to force him to invent a new integrated circuit.

These two sets of factors—those reducing the level of terrorist actions the government was willing to undertake and those reducing the population's response to terror in a more complex society—interacted with each other to accelerate the process of decay. As people exercised their small freedoms, they pushed to see how far they could go without being stopped. New generations, which had not suffered directly the impact of naked violence, were willing to push harder than their parents. Without repressive force being applied periodically, coercion gradually lost its effectiveness.

CORRUPTION

Exploiting the State

As terror and its effectiveness declined, party officials and workers in general bypassed the absurd restrictions of socialism by engaging in pervasive corruption—using state-owned assets for private gain. Workers stole products from their shops in such volume that pilfering became a national problem as early as the 1970s. Party officials and bureaucrats used their positions as if they were their capital, demanding personal payment for procedures they had to authorize. Managers hid substantial parts of their production from the central planners and sold them on the black market. They extracted payments from the workers they hired. They even invented imaginary transactions to get payments from the central planners, which they then used to increase their salaries. In this way, huge chains of imaginary products were created—imaginary cotton used to produce imaginary textiles, which then were transformed into imaginary clothes. The enthusiastic participants in these chains confirmed the figures provided by other participants, and received payments from the central planners, who were not able to ascertain the falsity of the pretended productions—or who, when discovering such falsity, traded their silence for a take in the booty.[207]

Thereafter, the nature of socialism was shaped by pervasive corruption. A communist regime progressed into a system in which a single abstract principle was exploited by all those who acted as agents for it. In fact, because the state could get only as much resource as it could from its citizens, these citizens were in fact exploiting each other and reducing their collective income because of their goal of working as little as possible. Driven by these incentives and constrained by socialist institutions, an extremely distorted market economy emerged with unprecedented strength in the Soviet Union during the 1970s. It erupted in the black markets, inside enterprises, and in the relationship between enterprises and planning agencies, as well as other enterprises. These problems were the consequence of the absence of an advocate for capital in each enterprise. Everybody was interested in how to extract rents from the enterprise capital; no one was interested in how to protect and increase it.

Gradually, the symbiosis of socialism and terror was substituted by the symbiosis of socialism and corruption. Without corruption, the economy would come to a screeching halt. But allowing corruption to exist would eventually bring an end to the system. Thus, corruption became to the socialist economy what the drug is to an addict: an indispensable companion and a path to death. This was the terrifying truth that Yuri Andropov and Mikhail Gorbachev realized in the 1980s. The problem was not that self-interest was not at work but that it was channeled in ways detrimental to the functioning of society as a whole. Socialism succeeded in creating a system where self-interest was consistently opposed to social rationality.

The Crippling of the Soviet Union

By the late 1970s and early 1980s, there was a sense within powerful groups inside the Communist Party that corruption and inefficiency were destroying the country. The Soviet Union was trailing Western countries not only in the social and economic welfare of the population—which they had known for decades—but (more important for them) in military power. The main symptom of this process was not active opposition to the regime but the encroachment of apathy and corruption. Simultaneously, the economy's ability to grow was checked, and the initial signs of what would become the anarchy of the Gorbachev years started to emerge. One thing led to another.

Around this time, technological advance shifted toward the immensely complicated field of gathering, processing, and transmitting information in real time—computerized communications. In a world where several powers were able to destroy the entire planet, speed of response became crucial. The West advanced at breakneck speed in this area, but the Soviet Union suffered from not only its traditional lack of incentives for innovation but also from the challenge of developing communications technology in a country where authorities feared that people would use communications to topple the government.

These problems were crippling. The Soviets watched with horror as the technology of microcomputing and communications leaped forward in the West, to the point where some toys and computer games were included in the US government's list of products that could not be exported to the Soviet Union or its satellites. The controlling mechanisms of some radio-controlled toys were better than those installed in Soviet tanks. The connectivity that developed with the new technologies prompted the current explosion of scientific and technological progress in all areas of human knowledge. But the communist countries were out of it.

The Fight against Corruption

These problems prompted an agonizing reappraisal of the course that socialism was taking. Unsurprisingly, this reappraisal started in the Soviet institution with the most complete worldview: the KGB. Its director, Yuri Andropov, decided that the time had come for a drastic change. The situation was so desperate that he decided that reversing the decline of the country was worth a pact with the capitalist devil: he was willing to grant some limited openness of communications and individual incentives for production.

Andropov forged an alliance of KGB forces to advance his idea and put together a team of leaders not tainted by corruption to put it in place. Knowing that he had only a few years to live, he chose a bright man to lead the team, Mikhail Gorbachev. He then used his brief tenure as secretary general to effect changes in party staffing that would ensure Gorbachev would be elected secretary general after the brief reign of Andropov's successor, Konstantin Chernenko, the last representative of the old, corrupt leadership.

Liberation through Chaos

The new leaders identified central planning as the culprit of the country's economic woes. They conceived a system that would still forbid the private ownership of the means of production and would still keep the government in control of the main trends in the economy, but would decentralize many day-to-day decisions in the enterprise. It was to be like a market, except that there would be no owners and enterprises would have to deliver most of their production to the state. This was proof of how vertical minds fail to understand how the market works. They never realized that it was the same system Peter the Great installed in the early eighteenth century. They launched these reforms with great enthusiasm, but they were a complete failure.

The Gorbachev reforms effectively dismantled the centralized mechanism that Stalin had put in place fifty years before. The effect of such dismantling, however, was not the one that the reformers had been expecting. To his chagrin, Gorbachev discovered what should have been obvious from the start: that the only economic structure under which socialism can possibly work is central planning because that is the structure consistent with the application of terror, the only incentive that socialism can provide to its citizens. Decentralization can increase efficiency only when the economy has built-in incentives to promote efficiency at the individual level, which can be provided *only* by private property. Rather than increasing efficiency, decentralization of decisions without private ownership of the means of production actually worsens the principal-agent problems—the conflicts of interest between the owners of the enterprise and the people managing it.

Rather than improving the economy, the Gorbachev system of reforms destroyed it. For the managers and workers, perestroika ("restructuring") was a legitimization of an illegal system they had been operating for many years. Managers and workers went to the predictable extreme, ignoring central planners altogether. They raised their own salaries, stopped their deliveries of state orders, and sold all their production on the black market. The entire Soviet economy was turned upside down. The official distribution system for both production inputs and consumer goods collapsed. Official stores ran out of products. Everything became scarce—falsely so, in fact, because the products were there, but they were on the black market. Frequently, the same official stores that were saying they did not have official goods at their front door sold them out the back door.

Even so, finding food and other essential products became extremely difficult for the average Soviet citizen because the availability of black-market goods was unpredictable. Sometimes a specific product would be available in one place, sometimes in another. Simply gathering information about the place one should go to get a particular product took hours a day. And people needed more than one product. Workers abandoned their jobs in the frantic search for food and other essential products. With wages increasing fast while production was at best stagnant, inflation on the black market was rampant while lines at official stores were lengthening. Black market vendors refused to take rubles after a time: they asked for other goods.

Wholesale bartering then developed, intermediated by the enterprises on behalf of their workers. Enterprises started to get basic goods for their workers through complex barter transactions. For example, a company making shoes would barter its production for, say, vegetables. It would distribute some of these vegetables among its workers and barter the rest for clothing. Part of this clothing would then be bartered for milk and eggs, part of which would serve in turn to get cooking oil and sugar, and so on. Many enterprises institutionalized their barter, reaching strategic alliances with companies producing consumer goods. Thus, a car factory would deliver so many cars per month to a farm in exchange for a monthly supply of eggs and chicken. Enterprises sent bartering delegates over the expanse of the Soviet Union to find supplies for their workers. Sometimes they had to get their goods in some faraway corner of the country, while equivalent goods were produced in their own neighborhood but bartered with a distant partner.

In this game, the companies producing consumer goods had a competitive advantage because they produced something in high demand. At the other extreme, companies producing high-tech military and scientific products were at a disadvantage. Nobody wanted to exchange consumer goods for abstract mathematical papers or spacecraft components. Many of these companies shifted to produce goods in demand, at terrible cost. For example, in the neighborhood of Nizhny Novgorod, I visited a factory making space vehicles that had reached an agreement with a local dairy farm. It produced a pasteurizing plant for the farm in exchange for milk delivered over five years. The pasteurizing plant must have been the most expensive ever. It was built with materials that withstood high-speed reentry into Earth's atmosphere. Workers and scientists who were not able to produce anything immediately useful were left out in the cold, literally. They, the unemployed, and the retired were populating the long lines outside the official stores, on freezing winter days, hoping to get a share of one piece of cheese or a fraction of a liter of milk.

Managers and workers started to carry out what was called spontaneous privatization. This was another name for stealing the company's capital goods or even the entire company. If the government was not able to supply them with inputs and consumer goods, why should they need the government? At the time, private ownership of capital goods was still prohibited, so spontaneous privatization really meant ransacking the enterprises.

In this chaotic environment, organized crime grew exponentially. Wide networks of corruption that had developed in the previous decades streamlined their respective organizations and expanded their operations to include not just distribution of goods on the black market but also protection—Mafia style—to stores, restaurants, factories, and common citizens. If people did not pay, they were harassed, their stores were destroyed, or sometimes they were killed. In the final years of Gorbachev's leadership, organized crime substituted for the government as providers of citizen security. The chieftains of these mafias were local party leaders, the same people who every day declared that buying and selling on the black market were illegal and punished some of their own customers from time to time to keep up appearances.

This chaos destroyed the legitimacy of Gorbachev's regime. It was not that people reneged on communism. It was not that they wanted to become capitalists or democratic. It was just that the government, which they expected to provide for all their needs, was failing to deliver even the most essential ones.

This is the crucial fact about the fall of the Soviet Union. Gorbachev, communist up to his last day in power, did not understand how to manage a communist society. As should have been predicted, the workers used the new autonomy that Gorbachev gave to them not to improve the conditions of their enterprises but to increase their salaries, and steal machinery and goods, and sell on the black market. As they diverted production toward the black market, the official chains of supply in the economy collapsed. Food disappeared from the official stores. Within five years, the economy went back to its original chaos, destroying the complicated machinery that the communists had used to control the population at the individual level. The irony of it all was that, by giving the power to the workers in the enterprises, Gorbachev led the Soviet Union to its destruction.

THE IRONY

On December 9, 1991, Boris Yeltsin paid a visit to Gorbachev and informed him that the Soviet Union had ceased to exist. This meant not only that Gorbachev's position as unelected president of the defunct state had become extinct but also that he would have to vacate his quarters in the Kremlin. Yeltsin was courteous and did not press the point at that moment, and he even told Gorbachev that there could be a job for him in the new Commonwealth of Independent States that he, Yeltsin, had created among Russia, the Ukraine, and Belarus. Gorbachev was not pleased and did not accept the dismantling of the Soviet Union. How could he recognize that the tremendous power he had acquired just six years before had vanished together with the country he was supposed to run?

I was in Moscow on the evening of Yeltsin's December 9 visit. I saw the news on CNN and went out of my hotel into the bitterly cold evening to see how Muscovites would receive news of the demise of the Soviet Union. After a metro ride, I walked into Red Square. It was a beautiful night. A wintry light diffused by the snow illuminated the Kremlin and St. Basil's Cathedral from below.

I wondered what Gorbachev could be thinking about inside the Kremlin walls. He must have been thinking of the irony of it all. Nobody had been more prominent in the dismantling of communism than Gorbachev, and now that the work was done, he was being sidelined. But then I thought of the ambiguity of his situation: if Gorbachev had intended to fool Andropov and always wanted to destroy communism, the irony would be that his ultimate victory as a statesman had brought about his own personal defeat. However, if he had been true to his original alliance and had been sincere when he wrote in his book *Perestroika* that he wanted to save communism, the irony was much more bitter: in his blind fight for renewing and strengthening the power of the Communist Party, he had destroyed the very source of such power. Both positions were tragic. One was like Churchill being voted out of power after World War II. The other was like Ivan the Terrible crying over the corpse of the son he had killed in a senseless rage.

The events of the Gorbachev years will be the subject of speculation and analysis for many years to come. The fall of communism was an event of staggering magnitude, the implications of which we are barely starting to understand, and scholars of the future will be fascinated by the same questions that led me to write this book, including the reasons for the fall of the Soviet Union. I believe that Gorbachev's perestroika will continue to provide a hint about why Gorbachev's decentralization led to the demise of communism.

Certainly, Gorbachev's reform contained no economic reasoning, no economic analyses, no economics at all. At most, his reforms were statements of economically naïve desires. However, in a country where the study of economics consisted of learning Marx by heart, naïveté was the basis for the new economic program on which the success of the whole process of reform would depend. Andropov, Gorbachev, and their fellow reformers built the foundations of their construction on quicksand. This was the source of the providential blindness that fooled them into destroying the system they wanted to perpetuate.

But Gorbachev's ignorance of the most elementary principles of economics and the lack of common sense that permeated his reforms were shared by all the economic plans that were ever drawn in the Soviet Union and other communist countries—including both the centralized and decentralized models. What was the difference between Gorbachev and the previous leaders of the Soviet Union? Why did Gorbachev destroy the Soviet Union while the others did not?

Returning by metro to my Moscow hotel on the evening of that memorable day when Yeltsin paid a visit to Gorbachev, I asked myself that question. While insisting that workers enthusiastically controlled not only enterprises but everything else, the old leaders never tried to put these ideas into practice. The proponents of perestroika, by contrast, believed that the rhetoric was for real, that they could make communism work by decentralizing it while keeping the power firmly in their hands. This was the ultimate irony of Gorbachev's tenure as the last communist leader. He and other late-day reformers fooled themselves with the same simplistic notions and harebrained ideas that their predecessors had used to fool others.

～

Why have I spent so much time analyzing the experiences of the Soviet Union and Nazi Germany? It is unfortunate, but these experiences are not that far from our own. It's hard to imagine either of those one-dimensional regimes returning, especially in a country like the United States with its liberal democratic tradition. But before those regimes came to power, it was equally difficult to imagine them. If anything, Soviet Russia and Nazi Germany were less imaginable before their rise than they are today because nothing comparable had occurred in history. We have the advantage, however, of knowing twentieth-century history. We've seen the tragedies and how they were primed by environments very similar to ours. We have also seen how nonlinear history is; small happenings, like the assassination of an Austrian grand duke in Sarajevo, can escalate within a few weeks into a terrible war and then within a few years into chaotic revolutions and terribly destructive regimes doing things that nobody could have anticipated a few years before.

Stanley Baldwin, three times prime minister of Britain in the 1920s and 1930s, wrote:

> Civilization is but the ice formed in process of ages on the turbulent stream of unbridled human passions, and while this ice seemed to our fathers secure and permanent, it has now rotted and cracked.[208]

The German film director Werner Herzog has said something similar but more sharply: "Civilization is a thin layer of ice upon an ocean of chaos and darkness."

Seventeen years after the end of World War I, four before the beginning of World War II, the British journalist George Dangerfield wrote a book about the old Britain that perished in 1914, *The Strange Death of Liberal England*. The book ended with a paragraph full of nostalgia for the world that disappeared in those years:

> All the violence of the pre-war world has vanished, and in its place there glow, year into backward year, the diminishing vistas of that

other England, the England where the Grantchester church clock stood at ten to three, where there was Beauty and Certainty and Quiet, and where nothing was real. Today we know it for what it was; but there are moments, very human moments, when we could almost find it in our hearts to envy those who saw it, and who never lived to see the new world.[209]

Those few sentences give the feeling of the brutal change that the disruptions of the previous technological revolution brought to the world between the nineteenth and the twentieth centuries. The current revolution has the power to cause a difference as great in the early twenty-first century if we do nothing to keep alive the spirit of liberal democracy that saved the world after it fell through the thin layer of ice into the ocean of chaos and darkness.

PART III

No theoretical forms, no form of government can render us secure. To suppose that any form of government will secure liberty or happiness without any virtue in the people is a chimerical idea.
James Madison

11

TOWARD COMPLEXITY

Thus we are led to conclude that the same nonlinearities may produce an order out of the chaos of elementary processes and still, under different circumstances, be responsible for the destruction of this same order, eventually producing a new coherence beyond another bifurcation.

Ilya Prigogine and Isabelle Stengers

THE CONNECTIVITY REVOLUTION

The Origins

Computers have been around since the 1930s, but it was a Massachusetts Institute of Technology (MIT) mathematician, Norbert Wiener, who first conceived, in the late 1940s, how computers could interact to create a new world in which technology would multiply the power of the mind so that machines might communicate with humans and facilitate communication between humans and between machines. Decades before it became reality, Wiener saw that the road of progress had shifted from the tangible to the intangible:

> [The] thought of every age is reflected in its technique. . . . If the seventeenth and early eighteenth centuries are the age of clocks, and the later eighteenth and nineteenth centuries constitute the age of steam engines, the present time is the age of communication and control.[210]

In 1949, in an unpublished article, Wiener described with humbling lucidity how the new machines would use what today we call artificial intelligence to learn on their own and how they would be able to "control entire industrial processes and [would] even make possible the factory substantially without employees." Then he warned about the problems of adjustment to this new world:

> These new machines have a great capacity for upsetting the present basis of industry, and of reducing the economic value of the routine factory employee to a point at which he is not worth hiring at any price. If we combine our machine-potentials of a factory with the valuation of human beings on which our present factory system is based, we are in for an industrial revolution of unmitigated cruelty.[211]

Wiener's vision was received with skepticism in many quarters. Although dismissed as vague, his theories and concepts—information, message, feedback, and control—provided a basis for understanding the connections between sciences that had been considered separate, like biology and economics, computing and thermodynamics. He foresaw that something invisible—interactions—would lead a technological revolution. As he predicted, the resulting new technologies are rocking the world's social order and posing the same questions he pondered.

In the following decades, the development of computers, electronics, and communications started to converge to create modern connectivity. Computers began to be connected in networks to maximize their power. The internet, invented in the early 1980s, created a network of networks, and the World Wide Web, introduced in 1990, allowed the linkage of documents. Over the next two decades, connectivity made the world unrecognizable, unsettling the equilibrium it had reached in the industrial era. This new revolution was set in motion by the power to manage complex tasks from afar in real time, an ability that the combination of computers, telecommunications, and fast transportation has made possible. This revolution is the core of the new economy, formed by international supply chains and based on knowledge and information. Slowly at first and then at amazing speed, the march of progress shifted from multiplying the power of the muscle to multiplying the power of the mind.

The challenge presented by this transformation has been unprecedented. Unlike the industrial revolution, the connectivity revolution is principally concerned with the adjustment, as Wiener identified, not to machines but to other human beings, and to their relationships and communications. While the technologies of the revolution are embedded in physical equipment, the revolution itself is in the changes of behavior that these technologies are triggering. And these changes are in the most intimate space: the acquisition and management of knowledge, the shape of the structures framing relationships with other human beings, values, and self-control.

The Network of Knowledge

This change has moved us toward an economy where human capital is by far the most crucial source of wealth. Human capital includes not just knowledge but also the ability to coordinate complex tasks at a distance and to cooperate in creative groups. This is true of every level of employment. We are moving toward a network economy, in which coalesced groups are linking with others to form sophisticated chains of supply.

Knowledge has always been a basic factor of production. The industrial revolution was based on knowledge—on scientific knowledge, inventions, and manufacturing skills. That knowledge was embedded in machines, which multiplied the power of muscle. With the connectivity revolution, however, knowledge has become so prominent in economic activity that it has been decoupled from the material and gained an independent life, to the extent that the economy is becoming a space where knowledge is produced and from where it flows in infinite ways. Information embedded in tangible and intangible goods and services is the only thing our economies now produce.

The information and skills necessary to give life to such an economy (data, scientific knowledge, technological prowess, the links between experts, and managerial capacity, among others) are embedded in the enterprises and the institutions. Development is a function of the amount of information embedded in these repositories of knowledge. As happened in Germany and Japan at the end of World War II, a society remains rich and developed as long as it keeps those repositories alive, even if all their physical facilities are destroyed. They carry the wealth of the country. Once you have that knowledge, you can secure everything else you need to produce anything.

In fact, some of today's most successful companies have built their business model around the essential elements in the creation of wealth—knowledge, coordination capacity, and connectivity. Uber, for example, has no cars, drivers, or parking places at its disposal, and it has only a few buildings for the employees who control the cars, drivers, and locations of the people they coordinate. The same is true of Airbnb and many other companies that sell coordination and ideas. It is also true of the core of many other companies that produce software, companies that outsource the components of their products under a proprietary design, or those that buy the knowledge they do not have. In the process, the international economy has been taking the shape of a giant network of knowledge. Such knowledge, not machinery or money, is the substance that moves the global network of production that sustains the world's economy.

Networks, Pyramids, and Social Investment

This society of networks, the successor of the pyramidal economies of the twentieth century, has some other important features. The pyramid was a vertical organization that increased the knowledge you had to contribute as you climbed it. In this organization, it wasn't important if some at the base of the pyramid were outside the productive economy or were too poorly educated to be employable in high-value-added positions, which were relatively few. Captains of industry could create highly successful businesses with very low levels of education if they invested massively in machinery. In a network of knowledge, the situation is different because the organization is more horizontal, and success depends on having educated employees at many nodes of communication. A network with voids instead of links is a weak network. If a company lacks educated people to take responsibility for those links, there is no way to create a high-value-added, profitable business. You cannot have a profitable company if you don't have a well-educated, healthy workforce. This need has changed the social role of investment in human capital. From being a desirable activity from the social and human point of view, it has moved to become an essential part of economic strategy.

In the industrial revolution, added value depended on machines; social expenditures were seen as a complementary activity, undertaken not to improve production but to take care of fellow human beings. Here is another way to put it: let's produce first and distribute later. In the knowledge economy, you cannot produce without high levels of human capital. Only a healthy and educated labor force will produce high added value. So the ordering of activities is the reverse. First, investment in human capital is necessary, which is then used to produce wealth. We can express this in a different way: health and education have become public goods whose provision benefits all in society. The idea, for example, that education must be the concern of only those who have children is obsolete. Education and health of all, like national defense and policing, must be the concern of all.

The true wealth of the United States is its highly educated population. As a society, however, its networks of educated people have enormous problems. One is the presence of voids. Every person outside an economy is a void instead of a link. In those voids, the United States is wasting opportunities. The country must find a way to invest in its own citizens to ensure the maintenance of a strong economy. Moreover, divisiveness becomes more dangerous in a society that is moving toward the network model. The voids become more dangerous because a network is easier to rip apart than a pyramid. Today, for a variety of reasons (which are not the subject of this book), many people of all classes and races and on both sides of the ideological divide feel left out, which contributes to the divisiveness that is so perilous to liberal democracy.

These are the circumstances that have resulted in the return of the "ghosts" I reviewed in Chapter 2, including social restlessness and widespread disenchantment with capitalism and liberal democracy. Inside this disenchantment is a much deeper anguish summoned by the uncertainty about the direction history will take in the future, which suddenly has become so uncertain. The challenge of this transformation is different from that posed by the industrial revolution. It is more intimately human.

From Outward to Inward

In the midst of the angst that pervaded the 1930s, the scientist Alfred Ewing posed an intriguing question that is equally relevant today:

> Whither does this tremendous procession tend? What, after all, is its goal? What is its probable influence upon the future of the human race?[212]

The British historian Arnold Toynbee, who dedicated his life to the study of social change, hypothesized that civilizations are born and grow in response to the challenges they face. When they succeed in producing a positive response, they are ready for the next challenge. The nature of these challenges shifts, however, as society meets them. They move from problems posed by nature or external enemies to problems presented by the increasing complexity posed by the relationships between members of society. Using this as a context, Toynbee proposed a response to Alfred Ewing's questions:

> We conclude that a given series of responses to successive challenges is to be interpreted as a manifestation of growth if, as the series proceeds, the action tends to shift from the field of an external environment physical or human to the *for intérieur* of the growing personality of civilization. In so far as this grows and continues to grow, it has to reckon less and less with challenges delivered by external forces and demanding responses on an outer battlefield, and more and more with challenges that are presented from itself to itself in an inner arena.[213]

The industrial revolution gradually brought us together in spite of geography. The connectivity revolution brings us psychologically close. Now, we are left with the internal challenges—how to deal with each other in this new world.

The problems now besieging society have besieged us before, and we have solved them, but embers from earlier fires remain and are flaring again as the world experiences its latest deep transformation. Racism, for example, enabled slavery, but outlawing slavery did not get rid of racism. It still exists, deep inside individuals, and the evidence is in the continuing culture of discrimination. The horrifying racism that led to the Holocaust was resolved on the surface, but anti-Semitism in particular and racism in general is again on the rise.

The repetition of these problems reminds us of Toynbee's thesis that our challenges are moving from external to internal, from simple to complex, from inner secrets to open realities. The connectivity revolution enables the inner convictions of individuals to surface and to disturb the equilibrium of society in countless ways. And in this dimension, we seem to be losing, not gaining territory. In Toynbee's conception, if the challenges posed by reality are not addressed, they will return again and again, in ever more difficult and complex ways, until they are overcome. If they are not overcome, they can destroy society. This is not as far away as it sounds. The most daunting problem of this transformation is that it is forcing us to confront ourselves, our prejudices, and our values or lack of them, to make our society viable among people we have seen as "others" for generations—racially, sexually, socially, politically. It is a problem of divisiveness. It comes from within.

In his essay "The Crack-Up," F. Scott Fitzgerald warned against the sly threats that come from within:

Of course all life is a process of breaking down, but the blows that do the dramatic side of the work—the big sudden blows that come, or seem to come from the outside—the ones you remember and blame things on and, in moments of weakness, tell your friends about, don't show their effect all at once. There is another sort of blow that comes from within—that you don't feel until it's too late to do anything about it, until you realize with finality that in some regard you will never be as good a man again. The first sort of breakage seems to happen quick—the second kind happens almost without your knowing but is realized suddenly indeed. [214]

We seem to be on a slippery slope leading to a serious crack-up.

THE SLIPPERY SLOPE

The divisiveness that is plaguing developed countries has two compo-nents: that which naturally emerges from the disruptions of change and that which is introduced by so-called populist leaders to turn the majority against a minority. The second kind appears only when the first kind is already grave. This second kind generates hatred, was at the core of the destructiveness of the twentieth century, and is reappearing today.

The 2016 presidential campaign reframed the immigration issue in a different and very dangerous way. Immigrants were, and continue to be, blamed for the economic decline of the Rust Belt, the country's drug problems, and criminal activity. Donald Trump and other pop-ulists attack immigrants in ways reminiscent of attacks against Jews in Nazi societies and the bourgeoisie in communist countries—that they defile women and are despicably weak but at the same time so powerful that they can destroy society.

Of course, there are legitimate issues regarding immigration. It is unreasonable to expect that any country should allow unlimited immi-gration. In Europe, immigration is causing severe national security con-cerns. Portraying anyone who is not ready to support unlimited immi-gration as a Nazi-fascist is counterproductive and can push moderates to support extremist leaders who are sowing hatred. Many who vote for these populists are extremists, but many others are people who have not found moderate leaders who would pay attention to their concerns about migration.[215]

Hatred triggers hatred, and even supporters of populists can become the object of discrimination and abuse. Social media has exacerbated the acrimonious tone of extremists from all ideological positions. Unhinged hatred is a symptom of a country at risk of drifting into chaos, with potential for the terrible consequences we have seen in our review of the horrid events of the twentieth century.

This sowing of hatred is the main enemy of a smooth adjustment to the current transformation. Unfortunately, it is growing fast. The experience of the interwar years showed how hatred leads to the legitimization of destructiveness. Of course, as I have insisted in other parts of the book, nothing in our current crisis can be remotely compared to the destructiveness displayed by the communists and the Nazi-fascists in their heyday. Saying that we are already on the road to destructiveness would be a distortion of current events. Unlike pre-Nazi, Nazi, precommunist, and communist societies, the United States and other liberal democracies have political and judicial institutions that still have the ability to prevent human rights violations. But the hatred being sown threatens even those long-standing institutions.

A multidimensional system can work in the midst of a society that is showing one-dimensional tendencies as long as the quality of the existing institutions remains in place. There is a moment, however, when, for lack of broad participation, the quality of institutions begins to fade and social order deteriorates—either in the sense of increasing disorder or in the sense of the emergence of a substitute order that is not humane, free, or democratic. If this happens, the legitimacy of liberal regimes can deteriorate.

COULD IT HAPPEN AGAIN?

Could the destructiveness of the twentieth century happen again? The possibility that something as dark and bloody as the events that defined the last stage of the industrial revolution could happen again is so terrifying that most of us automatically claim it could never happen today. But history shows that many Germans said the same thing in the 1930s. Hendrik Willen Van Loon, a Dutch-American historian, wrote the following words in 1939: "[Such] things could not possibly happen [in the US]! Can't they? That is exactly what decent Germans said six short years ago."[216]

But liberal democracy is under attack—it is on a slippery slope. Hatred is on the rise, as are attacks on minorities. Jews in many developed countries feel insecure as a result of public and private threats.

The treatment of immigrant families and children in the United States has become increasingly degrading. The entire world, in fact, seems to be turning insecure—as it was in the 1930s. The threats and insults are not just manifestations of hatred. They aim at dehumanizing the victim, another dangerous threshold now being trespassed. When dehumanization is complete, when people believe that the victims—Jews, immigrants, the bourgeoisie— are no longer human, insult, torture, and murder become easier.

Populist, authoritarian leaders tend to be the first to cross these thresholds. They have an unnerving instinct to find weak spots in the liberal democratic institutional setting that, when pushed, bring down large portions of it. Their words and actions, however malignant, move the goalposts of what is acceptable or legal in society. Long-respected traditions fall under their attacks. They legitimize chaos and authoritarianism as the way to restore order.

The worrying trend is that the hate-inspiring caudillos are finding supporters in large numbers. Worse still, they are not losing their support even when they attack and destroy the liberal institutions that gave birth to the most humane and creative societies in the history of the world. Such attacks were the preamble to the destructiveness of the twentieth century. And, of course, liberal democracies, societies created on the basis of social cohesion, are losing such cohesion precisely at the moment when it is needed more than ever. The environment is becoming explosive.

THE CROSSROADS

The ghosts of the past show that we are as far from equilibrium as our ancestors were a century ago. A new world is emerging, and a new social order is needed to frame it. In this crucial moment, we are threatened by three related trends: the weakening of social cohesion, the return of radical divisiveness, and the growing preference for one-dimensional policies. With declining social interest and increasing divisiveness, the preference for one-dimensional, authoritarian schemes is to be expected. If we do nothing, the dynamics of divisiveness will take us to chaos, and from there, the only possible solution will be authoritarianism. This is the most urgent problem today: how to avoid the collapse of social order—something that sounded unreal a decade ago but today sounds like a clear possibility.

Restoring the vitality of liberal democracy is the only road that we have ahead. Liberal democracy has served its societies well, but its institutions are a blend of principles and the reality of how citizens interact. Relationships among citizens are changing dramatically as a result of the technological revolution. Even the definition of who is a citizen is changing. We must expect changes in the democratic institutions as a result of these transformations.

Having come to this point, we have to define what kind of *liberalism* we should adopt. Of course, we should avoid giving liberalism the meaning that prompted F. A. Hayek, a great liberal thinker, to express "the just irritation with those who used liberal phraseology in defense of antisocial privileges."[217] There are many other meanings of the word—an open attitude to life, a commitment to the rule of rights, or a rigid comprehensive doctrine with an answer for every practical question.

Hayek had very clear words regarding the mistake of taking liberalism as a rigid structure. In his classic *The Road to Serfdom,* he wrote:

> There is nothing in the basic principles of liberalism to make it a stationary creed; there are no hard-and-fast rules fixed once and for all. The fundamental principle that in the ordering of our affairs we should make as much use as possible of the spontaneous forces of society, and resort as little as possible to coercion, is capable of an infinite variety of applications. . . . Probably nothing has done so much harm to the liberal cause as the wooden insistence of some liberals on certain rough rules of thumb, above all the principle of laissez faire. . . . And since a strong presumption in favor of industrial liberty had undoubtedly been established, the temptation to present it as a rule which knew no exceptions was too strong always to be resisted.[218]

And he wrote this about the relationship between classical liberalism and government, which many people who call themselves liberals think of as a natural opposition:

> No sensible person should have doubted that the crude rules in which the principles of economic policy of the nineteenth century were expressed were only a beginning—that we had yet much to learn and that there were still immense possibilities of advancement on the lines on which we had moved. But this advance could come only as we gained increasing intellectual mastery of the forces of which we had to make use. There were many obvious tasks, such as our handling of the monetary system and the prevention or control of monopoly, and an

even greater number of less obvious but hardly less important tasks to be taken in other fields, where there could be no doubt that the government possessed enormous powers for good or evil; and there was every reason to expect that, with a better understanding of the problems, we should some day be able to use these powers successfully.[219]

We must keep Hayek in mind as we design those liberal institutions that will frame our actions in the new connected world. We have to confront the real nature of the relationship between the individual and society. Many people think that it is a confrontational relationship: some believe that the community (of which the government is a part) is a nuisance that impinges on the rights of the individual; many others believe that the interests of the individual are an obstacle for the high goals of the state. Both beliefs lead to one-dimensional societies. But in a multi-dimensional society, we cannot conceive of the individual without the state, and vice versa. A multidimensional society needs multidimensional individuals who understand that we, each of us, can make good use of the state, and vice versa.

12

THE INDIVIDUAL AND SOCIETY

And yet that does not mean that political formulas are mere quackeries aptly invented to trick the masses into obedience. Anyone who viewed them in that light would fall into grave error. The truth is that they answer a real need in man's social nature; and this need, so universally felt, of governing and knowing that one is governed not on the basis of mere material or intellectual force, but on the basis of a moral principle, has beyond any doubt a practical and real importance.

Gaetano Mosca

DRIVES AND THE INDIVIDUAL

The connection between divisiveness and destructiveness is clear because a divided population is more apt to support the imposition of tyranny as the mechanism to make social life possible. Chaotic diversity is replaced by a single, vertical will.

Tyranny is justified with one-dimensional theories of human behavior, based on the assumption that human beings are motivated by a single drive. But this assumption supports the appeal of violence. If you believe there is only one thing that matters in life, you must try to maximize it, and when you find an obstacle you must try to destroy it. Such was the case for Nietzsche's will to power and Marx's drive for economic welfare. Nietzsche thought that people cared only about having power and that they would do whatever was needed to gain it. He also thought that nature demanded that the strong defeat the weak in this confrontation. He lamented that in nineteenth-century Europe, a twisted morality forced the strong to concede defeat and humiliate themselves in front of the weak. A new world should emerge where the strong would prevail and not feel guilty about it. These ideas, built over a one-dimensional conception of life's objectives, prefigured the Nazi morality of power.

Marx also believed that human beings had a single motivation: their own economic benefit. That is why he believed people trample on others to exploit them and impose slavery and tyranny for the sake of their own economic gain. Based on this idea, Marx justified the elimination of private property, thinking that without property, people would forget about greed.

There is another body of thought assuming, like Marx, that the only motivation of human beings is economic gain: market theory. According to this theory, one of the fundamental bases of capitalism, individuals always try to maximize their economic well-being as measured by a quantity called utility. According to Jeremy Bentham, who popularized this school of thought at the turn of the nineteenth century, the fundamental moral principle underlying social order is pursuit of the greatest happiness for the greatest number, with the understanding that happiness is the predominance of pleasure over pain on a one-dimensional scale. He even thought that pleasure and pain could be ranked and then combined into a single index of utility. Consistently with his one-dimensional vision of life, Bentham was not interested in liberty, which was superseded by security in his one-dimensional world. Like all other one-dimensional minds, he was contemptuous of the rights of man. He thought that they were "nonsense on stilts."[220] Bentham's ideas gave one-dimensionality to market economic theory.

Liberal democracy does use the market as the economic component of social order, but it is not one-dimensional. It broadens Bentham's ideas into a multidimensional philosophy. Market theory constrains itself to the analysis of economic behavior *within a given institutional setting*. Liberal democracy defines the setting in a multidimensional way by specifying, for example, that slavery is not allowed or that there are courts for enforcing contracts. Market theory works positively if institutions constraining social behavior under a certain moral framework already exist and have been created outside the market. With these assumptions, market theory can do two things. It can predict the behavior of people subject to different stimuli within the same institutional setting (saying, for example, that people will prefer to earn more money than less for the same job in the same economy). It can also compare what people would do under two different institutional settings when subject to the same stimulus, as we have done when comparing economic behavior in socialist and capitalist economies.

Marx was not interested in these subjects. He was much more ambitious. His concern was the way institutions are created. That is, he did not assume anything as given except for his premise that people are motivated exclusively by economic drive. From this premise, he observed that markets breed competition and that there are strong and weak competitors. Inevitably, as in Nietzsche's intellectual framework, the strong would gain at least a temporary advantage over the weak, would use such advantage to gain political power, and would use that power to create institutions that would perpetuate their domination. Marx went on to build his theory of the state upon this reasoning, asserting that the exclusive purpose of the state is to enforce the domination of one class over the rest. Because it was inevitable that people motivated by self-interest would tend to create institutions for these purposes, he concluded that eliminating exploitation required breeding a new human being devoid of self-interest.

Certainly, Marx's ideas—that human beings could be reengineered to eliminate their self-interest, and the complementary one that this could be achieved in a dictatorship of the proletariat—were absurd, nonsensical. His pretense that capitalist institutions had the exclusive purpose of supporting the exploitation of human beings was a negation of the immediate reality that surrounded him when he, a political refugee, was writing *Capital* in the British Museum. It was not in the interest of British capitalists to admit him as an immigrant to Britain, much less to allow him to use the immense resources of the British Museum to write the most effective attack on capitalism yet. Still, the British government allowed him entry when he was hunted all over continental Europe and gave him freedom of speech to write and publish his main opus.

If one goes with him into an imaginary world where his assumptions are real, however, it is difficult to spot a crack in his prediction that institutions in a world dominated by self-interest alone would have the exclusive purpose of exploiting the weak. Actually, we don't even have to go into an imaginary world to verify his prediction. This perversion of economic self-interest into tyrannical domination is exactly what happened in tsarist Russia many centuries ago. As we saw in Chapter 5, the first tsars acquired absolute power by becoming Russia's owners.

In the pursuance of their self-interest, they found that political power could be obtained through economic power, and vice versa. They and their heirs provided living proof of what Marx eventually said. Other examples of groups using political power to grant economic privileges to themselves are common all over the world and throughout history—including in communist countries founded on Marxist principles.

Marx was wrong not because of a logical fault in his reasoning, not even because his basic assumption about the predominance of self-interest was *generally* mistaken. His problem was that his assumptions, and the reasoning that followed from them, were true in some environments but not in others. Economic welfare, the will to power, or self-interest in general are not our only motivations. They are in some social organizations and not in others. For this reason, institutions associated with markets are instruments to exploit the weak in some countries, while in others they breed progress. Marx missed this crucial fact and, with it, the opportunity to get to the core of the problem of social transformations.

Marx posed the right problem, however. When analyzing the problems of adjustment to a new kind of society, we have to reconsider his fundamental question: how are institutions created?

DO LIBERAL INSTITUTIONS COME FROM SELF-INTEREST EXCLUSIVELY?

As we discussed in Chapter 4, institutions can be seen as capital goods and their creation as a form of investment. The economic analogy is fair. Yet market theory cannot help us in this quest, because it assumes that institutions already exist but cannot tell us how they were created.

Several recent economic theories explain the creation of liberal institutions solely on the basis of self-interest. Their foundation is the observation that liberal principles maximize individual well-being and are therefore rational not only from the point of view of the collective but also in terms of economic self-interest. They begin by saying that individuals are better off when they are organized under liberal principles. From this observation, they jump to the conclusion that liberal institutions were created to maximize self-interest exclusively. Following this approach, they provide explanations based on the narrowest definition of self-interest for the creation of all kinds of institutions, such as marriage, parental care, moral rules, and legal and political systems. Market theoreticians have found in these new theories confirmation of their belief that self-interest is the only force needed to create liberal institutions.

These theories miss the point. If they were true, all societies would have institutions as good as those existing in developed liberal democracies because in all of them self-interest exists and, according to the theories, is the only thing needed to have good liberal institutions. In fact, liberal institutions should be much stronger in developing societies than in the developed ones because their weak social interest leaves the field empty for self-interest to flourish. We know the opposite is true.

Certainly, liberal institutions create a dynamic social equilibrium that maximizes individual welfare for the average human being. Yet this is true only in the end and in general terms. It is not true that liberal institutions maximize utility for *all* individuals at *all times*. Many people maximize their well-being in dictatorial regimes. This is precisely the reason why these regimes exist and survive. People with inclinations to be the next Stalin or to be KGB agents, for example, would be better off in a communist state. Also, inefficient entrepreneurs are better off in a society that restricts the economic freedom of potential competitors. In the pursuit of their self-interest, most people will try to impose dictatorships. When living under the dictatorship of others, most people will always try to remain on good terms with it. Cooperation with a dictator is the most common behavior for people thinking exclusively in terms of their self-interest in a regime of terror.

The maximization of narrowly conceived, short-run, individual utilities may require the corruption of liberal institutions. Imagine a police officer stopping a speeding car late at night in a faraway place and threatening a fine of $100. The economic self-interest of both the police officer and the speeder would be satisfied if the officer accepted a bribe of $50. The damage inflicted to society by any particular bribe is too small to have a negative effect on the services that a particular briber obtains from society. Thus, if self-interest were our only motivation, the only criterion that the driver would use to decide to offer the bribe would be a comparison of the cost of the bribe against the cost of the fine. According to this theory, the decision would be simple. In fact, bribes are natural mechanisms to increase individual utilities at the expense of the rest of society.

The tendency toward corruption and restricting the freedom of others is evident in all societies. Taming them requires constant effort. In fact, as we discussed in Chapter 9, these two problems tell the story of the Soviet Union. The unrestricted pursuit of self-interest led first to a reign of ruthless terror and then to pervasive corruption. If acting alone, unrestricted self-interest will *always* lead to tyranny and corruption, which is close to what Marx said.

Multidimensional institutions are not rooted in economic self-interest even if, on average, they maximize an individual's utility. Instead, they are rooted in the organization of social interest, an acquired characteristic, which is transmitted through values. The differences between the behavior of Britain, the United States, France, Germany, Italy, and so many other countries during the industrial revolution can be traced to the values of their individual citizens that had been handed down through centuries. The liberal order, its checks and balances, its flexibility, and its resistance to tyranny are all based on the values of individuals.[221]

MULTIDIMENSIONAL AND ONE-DIMENSIONAL THINKING

Marxist theory explains how tyrannical institutions are created, using a single variable, self-interest. To explain how liberal institutions are created, we need at least another variable, a social glue that keeps society united in spite of the centrifugal forces of self-interest. This glue is what the Austrian psychologist Alfred Adler called social interest—the desire in individuals to do right in a way that fulfills their own self-interest but also has a positive impact on the lives of the people they love and society in general.

This force—the source of love, friendship, morality, and cooperation—is terribly important in human behavior. Yet it does not exist in the worlds of Marx or market theoreticians—with the crucial but often forgotten exception of Adam Smith.[222] The founders of the sustainable democracies of our times, on the contrary, used social cohesion to convince people to become a social unit.

So what can we do? How can social interest be developed?

The Source of Social Interest

What is the source of social interest? Why do some societies develop it while others lack it? To answer these questions, it is necessary to erase two common ideas. One is that behavior is conditioned by drives or instincts. They exist, of course, but they are not determinant. As Adler put it:

> In real life we always find a confirmation of the melody of the total self, of the personality, with its thousandfold ramifications. If we believe that the foundation, the ultimate basis of everything has been found in character traits, drives or reflexes, the self is likely to be overlooked. Authors who emphasize a part of the whole are likely to attribute to this part all the aptitudes and observations pertaining to the self, the individual. They show "something" which is endowed with prudence, determination, volition, and creative power without knowing that they are actually describing the self, rather than drives, character traits, or reflexes.[223]

The second idea that should be erased is the artificial barrier most social scientists erect between *positive* social science—which is concerned only with *what is*—and *normative* social science—which is concerned with what *should be*. In fact, these two aspects of social science could not be observed in isolation from each other. We cannot understand how societies work unless we understand how values are created and materialized in institutions to give a direction to social progress. The fundamental unity of a society is provided by the nature of the values held by its population. At society's level, it is how values and institutional settings are linked. The tension between what *is* and what *should be* is a crucial variable in the process of building institutions. In all places and epochs, human beings are called good when they relate to other humans in a generally useful way; they are called bad when they act contrary to human interest.

Even most tyrants do not want to think that they are violating a natural code of values regulating social behavior. Nietzsche and Marx when spreading hatred, and Lenin, Stalin, and Hitler when reaping the perverse fruits of such hatred, said and often truly believed that they were helping humankind. Hitler saw himself as a great liberator. Many of the executioners of Jews during the Nazi era said that, in killing them, they were making a sacrifice for the sake of humankind. These protestations of human kindness are private and perverse, of course, but they illustrate the importance of the ethical dimension to social science.

This ethical issue, the definition of good and evil, establishes the dividing line between healthy and destructive institutional development. People who behave ethically, in ways that contribute to the common welfare, develop a healthy institutional setting.[224] Destructive institutions develop in people motivated by self-interest exclusively, the mark of unethical behavior. [225]

Social and Private Meaning

Why do some people develop a positive social meaning for their actions while others develop only private meaning? These differing attitudes emerge from an individual's degree of adaptation to the realities of life. We all have an urge to integrate with the pack, but some of us succeed while others fail. Successful integration takes place only when individuals develop social interest, the capacity "to see with the eyes of another, to hear with the ears of another, to feel with the heart of another."[226] Empathy, another name for this capacity, is what oils the natural contraposition of individual self-interest, creating the possibility of mutually satisfying human relations. *By opening a space for willful sacrifice for the sake of the interests of others, social interest converts social life from a destructive, one-dimensional confrontation of self-interests into a multidimensional space where harmonious pursuit of self-interests can be carried out.*

When people feel that they can relate to other people empathically in the essential dimensions of life—work, communal life, and love— they direct their energies toward the use of cooperation in meeting their self-interest. By doing so, they naturally help in the satisfaction of the self-interest of others. The urge to integrate becomes a sense of belonging, of being useful to others, which eventually acquires an intertemporal dimension. People become interested in the long-term fate of their society, which then translates into an urge to create long-lasting institutions based on the same self-reliance that has given them their success in life. In this way, the urge to belong becomes an urge to grow, to develop the entire society.

In contrast, when people feel that they cannot adapt to human society, they reject any attempt to cooperate with others, something they consider impossible because they cannot believe that anyone could be interested in the fate of others. They think that there is no such thing as a free lunch and behave accordingly. Their world becomes one-dimensional. They come to see social life as a Nietzschean game where the gain of one is always another's loss. In this world, one is either on top or on the bottom, a master or a slave. Their urge to grow is then perverted from being recognized as a useful member of society into achieving the status of a master. They turn to a goal of personal superiority and adopt methods consistent with such a goal for meeting their self-interest. Such methods can vary widely, but all of them share one feature with each other: they are based on some form of dependency. According to Adler:

> In the investigation of the neurotic style of life we must always suspect an opponent, and not he who suffers most because of the patient's condition. . . . The life plan of the neurotic demands categorically that if he fails, it should be through someone else's fault, and that he should be freed from personal responsibility; or that, if his triumph is prevented, it should be by a fatal detail only. . . . In certain forms of psychosis, and also in neurotic patients, the attack and accusations are not aimed at one single person, but at a number of people, the opposite sex, occasionally at the whole of humanity, or to the entire world order. [227]

Adler's language is sometimes old-fashioned, but his meaning here is clear and can help us understand how, for example, German attitudes after World War I resulted in seeing treason and the actions of Jews and foreigners as the reason for everything bad that happened in Germany. This attitude prepared German society for Hitler's leadership philosophy: create an opponent and blame everything on him.

Negative master-slave thinking can emerge in many when one-dimensional circumstances put them in positions of command, the other end of dependency relations. They often use their authority to impose their unrestricted will on those beneath them. The exercise of this power, however, does not raise self-esteem. In their one-dimensional world, the price for being the master of others is that of being the slave of others. No better example of this exists than the combination of servile subservience to Hitler and cold cruelty to the Jews that prevailed in Nazi Germany.

In extreme cases, people who fail to recognize the importance of social interest and act solely out of self-interest, without the context provided by liberal democratic institutions, don't stop at crime. When confronted with the proof of their misdeeds, they explain their actions in a logical, even if amoral, way. They justify stealing based on their need for things they could not afford, murder on the obstacles that the homicide victim posed for them, rape on the temptation to violate the victim. In all cases, their justification is that they had no other option but committing the crime in order to meet what they consider to be their legitimate self-interest. They blame it on drives. Frequently, they blame or deprecate their victims, asserting that they were inferior and deserved their death or the disgrace they inflicted on them. They do not show any consideration to the interests of their victims. The only thing that matters is their own interest. Can we think of a better way of describing the Nazis or the communists in the Soviet Union?

Like thieves who justify stealing by arguing they could not buy what they wanted, pre-Nazi Germans accepted the idea that Germany had to enslave its neighbors because it needed "living space." Like assassins who justify their crimes by arguing that the victim was inferior, Nazis and Soviets accepted and supported genocide on the basis that non-Germans and "class enemies" were inferior.

Self-Victimization and Self-Discipline

The Soviet Union, with all its tragedies and misery, was also a society in which most citizens refused to cooperate with each other, believing that the state should meet all their needs. They refused to see their own failures and always found a culprit for them. Like Germans during the Nazi regime, they blamed the victims for their own problems of adjustment. This is why it was so easy for Stalin to create his regime of terror and for Hitler to murder so many of the Jews of Europe. Germans and Russians created an imaginary world of their own and justified crime for the sake of their private fiction. Those among them who did not participate in the massacres tolerated them as long as they themselves were not among their victims. They accepted the morality of amorality, expressed so powerfully by Lenin in the following words:

> To us, all is permitted, for we are the first in the world to raise the sword not in the name of enslaving and oppressing anyone, but in the name of freeing all from bondage. . . . Blood? Let there be blood, if it alone can turn the grey-white-and-black banner of the old tyrannical world to a scarlet hue, for only the complete and final death of that world will save us from the return of the old jackals.[228]

The first few words of this statement contain the essential asymmetry of a tyrant's view of the world: *to us, all is permitted.* . . . Of course, the tyrant does not permit anything to *others*—not even their right to live. The ethics of the tyrant are the ethics of naked self-interest, essentially divisive, which lead societies to their own destruction. It is not a coincidence: divisiveness begets destructiveness.

Lenin's quotation also exposes quite clearly the reasons why societies based on self-interest exclusively cannot develop the capacity to install a social order based on cooperation. They lack the natural restraint that individuals moved by both self-interest and social interest provide to their own societies. Reliance on social values, the willingness to cooperate and establish horizontal relationships, the maintenance of political and economic freedom, and the discipline to respect the rights of your neighbors are manifestations of the same entity: a healthy, mature, creative society.

THE FUSION OF SELF-INTEREST AND SOCIAL INTEREST

One-dimensional economic thinking is common. Even economists interested in institutions can see them one-dimensionally—believing that Alexander Hamilton, Thomas Jefferson, Benjamin Franklin, John Marshall, and others who created democratic institutions and the rule of rights in the United States did so only with their own economic interests in mind. Many economists also believe in the superficial notion that *there is no such thing as a free lunch,* which ignores the multidimensionality of liberal societies and fails to recognize the true value of social interest.

Economics was not always so superficial. Adam Smith, who is normally considered the intellectual father of modern capitalism, did not believe that there is no such thing as a free lunch. He wrote a book on social interest and thought it his best work. *The Theory of Moral Sentiments* begins with these words, which introduce Smith's multidimensional vision of society:

> How selfish soever man may be supposed, there are evidently some principles in his nature, which interest him in the fortune of others, and render their happiness necessary to him, though he derives nothing from it except the pleasure of seeing it.[229]

That is social interest. Furthermore, Adam Smith did not believe in attributing behavior, moral or immoral, to any single drive. He attributed it to the interrelations of various factors, some of them linked to the *nature* of morality (propriety, prudence, benevolence, and licentiousness) and the rest to the *motive* of morality (self-love, reason, and sentiment). Like Adler, he believed that a free will controlled the decisions of human beings.

In their book *Humanomics: Moral Sentiments and the Wealth of Nations for the Twenty-First Century,* Nobel Prize winner Vernon L. Smith and Bart J. Wilson discuss the role of trust, caring, generosity, and empathy in the normal conduct of the economy and society in general.[230] They note that economic self-interest cannot be the source of the "rules to be followed," the institutions that frame a liberal society. Instead, they wrote:

> Fundamentally, it is the human capacity for sentiment, fellow feeling, and a sense of propriety that is the stuff of which human relationships, and the general rules-to-be-followed, are made.[231]

They follow with a scathing criticism of how modern economics has deviated from the classical thinking of Adam Smith, which included ideas and people in economic analysis:

> The new equilibrium concepts were defined too narrowly over out-comes, a substitution that seemed superior in the context of institutions-free general equilibrium market analysis and the partial-equilibrium analysis of game theory. At some point even the human being was dropped as the subject of our general inquiry as a social science. . . . We have lost sight of the fellow feeling by which human beings gravitate toward one another, and we have lost sight of the sentiments that excite human beings to act and by which human beings judge their own and one another's conduct.[232]

Intellectually broad and culturally deep economists like John Maynard Keynes have noticed that ideas were in fact more important than economic interests in the making of history:

> [T]he ideas of economists and political philosophers, both when they are right and when they are wrong, are more powerful than it is commonly understood. Indeed, the world is ruled by little else . . . soon or late, it is ideas, not vested interests, which are dangerous for good or evil.[233]

Others have been intrigued by the possibility of harmonizing self-interest and social interest, which may seem to be contradictory, but only when we see them from a one-dimensional perspective. They are not contradictory in a multidimensional world, where self-interest prevails naturally in some dimensions while social interest prevails in others. John Stuart Mill, philosopher and economist of the nineteenth century, revealed the infinite ways in which social interest and self-interest can fuse to create a healthy, expansive society:

> I never, indeed, wavered in the conviction that happiness is the test of all rules of conduct, and the end of life. But I now thought that this end was only to be attained by not making it the direct end. Those

only are happy (I thought) who have their minds fixed on some object other than their own happiness; on the happiness of others, on the improvement of mankind, even on some art or pursuit, followed not as a means, but as itself an ideal end. Aiming just at something else, they find happiness by the way.[234]

Victor Frankl expressed the same idea after surviving Auschwitz:

For success, like happiness, cannot be pursued; it must ensue, and it only does so as the unintended side-effect of one's dedication to a cause greater than oneself or as the by-product of one's surrender to a person other than oneself. . . . Then you will live to see that in the long run—in the long run, I say!—success will follow you precisely because you had forgotten to think of it.[235]

Fyodor Dostoevsky said the same through one of his characters, "For the secret of man's being is not only to live but to have something to live for."[236]

The words of these authors express the wisdom that give multidimensional societies their success. They blend the satisfactions obtained from getting beyond oneself to work for a superior motive related to others. This wisdom, of course, can be gained and lost. And it can be gained or lost only at the individual level. That is the real secret that explains the formation of creative institutions. The seed of liberal democracy grows to fruition in environments in which people have complex objectives in life—excel in some pursuit, raise a family, help the community and their country—that exceed the desire to make money.

Mill's words are consistent with my analysis in this book and belie the notion about classical liberalism that it is the system invented to defend the interests of those who are devoid of social interests, those who think that only they have rights, who define as morally good anything that favors them economically and as immoral everything that dents their economic well-being. Liberal democracy asks sacrifices from individuals but provides enormous benefits in exchange—benefits that wildly exceed the economic dimension.

This is a truth that modern society seems to be forgetting. The cost of this neglect is becoming apparent. With the joy of communal life gone and with the one-dimensional pursuit of wealth replacing it, the logic of one-dimensionality, the kill-or-be-killed vision, has taken over everything, from business to politics. This cost explains the paradoxical

Table 2
Liberal and Illiberal Regimes

	Liberal Democracy	Illiberal Regimes
Individual		
Attitude in pursuing self-interest	Self-reliant	Dependent on others
Motivation	Self-interest and social interest	Self-interest exclusively
Values	Individualistic	Collective
Links to others	Cohesive	Divisive
Morality	Multidimensional	One-sided
Society		
Social field	Strong	Weak
Shape	Horizontal	Vertical
Dimensions	Multidimensional	One-dimensional
Role of the state	Service for the individual	Coercive
Definition of stability	Keep individual rights in place	Maintain a real or imagined status quo
Social stance to change	Flexible	Rigid

fact that the population of the United States is deeply unhappy while the country has never been as rich. The famous slogan "Make America Great Again" should refer to the recovery of the social interest that the American society has lost in the past several decades.

The realm of liberal democracy is *within the individual,* which is where the defense of liberal democracy should take place. This defense has to be based on values, not just on the idea that capitalism produces more wealth.

The Difference between Self-Interest and Social Interest

With time, the interaction between the shape of the state and the attitudes of individuals gives raise to national character. Table 2 compares the features of the two kinds of society we are discussing. The table has two parts. The first five rows compare the features of individual members of the two kinds of society in terms of their motivation, their attitude in pursuing their self-interest, their values, and the way they relate to each other. The second part compares features of the societies they create in terms of the strength of the social field, their shape, the number of dimensions of power, the role of the state, and the way they pursue stability.

The features of each of these types of societies are congruent. They are manifestations of the internal logic that gives shape to social life. The engine driving this logic is the attitude to freedom. People seeking stability of individual rights love freedom above everything else—not just for themselves but for everybody. For this reason, they are self-reliant. They do not want government interfering with the lives of others because they do not want it to interfere with theirs. They prefer to associate with others through horizontal relations built on cooperation. Cooperation develops social interest, which becomes social cohesion. When confronted with change, these individuals rely on themselves to cope with it as long as their freedoms and rights are kept in place.

Ultimately, values, or their absence or weak values, draw the line between healthy and sick individuals and societies. They are what make the difference in all dimensions of life, including economics. Values are what make the difference.

13

THE APPEAL
OF SLAVERY

*[F]or nothing has ever been more insupportable for man and a human
society than freedom.*

Fyodor Dostoevsky

THE AMBIGUITY OF LIBERALISM

If we assume that people have more than one motivation, we cannot
predict what they will do unless we know something about them that
goes beyond self-interest. This assumption refutes the pretension that
the social sciences are as exact as the physical sciences. But life is like
that. We cannot guess what a person or a society will do unless we
know the person or the society. And even if we know them, we can
make gross mistakes in predicting their behavior because they could
have hidden or changing priorities. Nobody, for example, suspected
that one issue, Brexit, could split Britain as deeply as it did and then
disappear as a factor of divisiveness so quickly.

This conclusion leaves some uncertainty. The only thing we can
tell regarding social behavior is that the future of individuals and the
societies they create is in their own hands. Depending on their attitude
toward social relations, they can be creative or destructive, they can
build humane societies or stagnate in divided communities, they can
strengthen institutions or corrupt them.

Such a conclusion may seem useless for people who want to reduce the diversity of human behavior to a simple equation and use it to predict an outcome. Such a prediction would be impressive but irrelevant. If the future could be known, then knowing it would be useless because there would be nothing that we could do to change it. It is precisely because we cannot know the future that we can do something about it.

This ambiguity is a great advantage for liberalism. However, it gives rise to a common argument against liberal democracy, centered not on cardinal sins like greed but on the problems that checks and balances may present in the midst of grave crises. This argument asserts that liberal democracy is unable to deal with such crises and that this inability means liberal democracy is unsustainable, not just during crises but generally.

This is an old criticism, and perhaps its best-known advocate is Carl Schmitt, a German jurist much interested in the political consequences of change. In the 1930s, Schmitt wrote a piece trying to justify Hitler's autocracy. Given the similarity of our times with his, he has been rediscovered recently and his works published by prestigious academic presses. His ideas have been used in academic environments to attack liberal democracy, as they were a century ago.

The Empty Container

Schmitt believed that liberalism is too weak to operate in the political world of the twentieth century and beyond, that there is a fundamental contradiction between the essential element of liberalism—its focus on diversity and individual rights—and the homogeneity that is needed for democracy to work.[237] According to him, a society can prioritize the rights of the individual or be managed as a coherent state, but not both. The diversity of liberalism eventually negates the governability of liberal regimes.

Because of its natural diversity, liberalism is, and has to be, an empty container. Because of its respect for freedom of thought, it must open itself to many different political ideas, some of them contradictory. It cannot have a unified sense of direction, especially if its ideas include those that can destroy democracy itself.[238]

This conceptual emptiness, Schmitt argued, weakens liberalism as a means of political order. People will not fight to advance the interests of an empty container. "In case of need, the political entity must demand the sacrifice of life. Such demand is in no way justifiable by the individualism of liberal thought."[239] The empty container of liberalism can produce, at best, an administrative state, a procedural system that works only in the most stable conditions. The arrival of doctrines aimed at destroying democracy, such as communism or later Nazi-fascism, would paralyze it.[240] How can liberalism work in crisis when it carries within it ideas and movements aimed at destroying it?

According to Schmitt, liberal societies have only two options when confronting modern forms of political disorder: they either surrender to chaotic revolution, which would mark their own end, or impose a dictatorship, which would negate their own liberal nature. The dictatorship could be temporary and could be called, as in Rome, a *state of exception*. But just the possibility of having to resort to a temporary dictatorship kills the fundamental idea of liberal democracy. In reality, said Schmitt, the sovereign would no longer be the population, as liberalism claims, but he who decides on the exception.[241] Liberalism would no longer exist. The regime would have become vertical, dependent on he who decides on the exception.[242]

In this way, Schmitt disqualified democracy because it cannot manage exceptional situations. He added that if liberal social orders are unable to manage borderline cases, they are unable to manage any case, because at any time it is clear that the true sovereign would not be the people but instead a hidden prince. The sovereignty of the hidden prince does not disappear just because he is not exercising his power in normal times. "Sometimes the people and sometimes the prince would rule, and that would be contrary to all reason and all law."[243] It seemed like checkmate.

THE GENIUS OF LIBERALISM

Contradictions

Is liberal democracy at the end of its effectiveness? Is Schmitt correct that democracy is not sustainable without resorting to authoritarianism? Not quite.

There are many ways of escaping Schmitt's trap once you realize that his is a one-dimensional construct. To be trapped in an unsolvable situation, the confrontation must be in a single dimension, or in multiple dimensions but with rigid comprehensive doctrines, which is really the same thing. In such conditions, you have only two choices: either you kill or you are killed.

In a world with many dimensions, however, compromise is always possible: you gain in some dimension, lose in others, break even in yet others, and so on. And the political world, even when understood in Schmitt's sense, is not one-dimensional. It has infinite dimensions, and there are infinite possibilities for compromise. What is needed is a disposition to compromise in those infinite dimensions, a possibility that Schmitt rules out because he does not consider the possibility of ceding in one dimension to gain in another. In reply to his argument, we can say that there is no contradiction between liberal individualism and the homogeneity needed for the functioning of democracy. That contradiction exists only in one-dimensional societies.

The only feature needed for a multidimensional society to work is the will to compromise, a common attribute of liberal democracies everywhere, which allows room for the infinite divergence of views among citizens. This attribute opens liberal democracy to a common criticism: that it lacks the necessary focus to resolve the complex problems of today's societies. Those who support this criticism ignore a simple, plain fact: liberalism is not a valueless container filled with contradictory ideas. It is built on an ethical vision of society, on a set of principles that gives clear direction to progress. It provides plenty to fight for. It contains all that is needed in a healthy institutional setting. Failing to see this is a typical mistake of the one-dimensional view of life.

Schmitt's theories, irrefutable when applied to one-dimensional societies like Weimar Germany, are easily refuted in the context of multidimensional societies of the twentieth century. Schmitt's theories were used to justify rule by decree in the Weimar Republic, which was a failure, and the rule of Hitler in the Third Reich, a genocidal and murderous failure. Although communists might recoil in horror to be included with Nazis in an analysis of Schmitt's ideas, they also lived by them. They did not copy them—the Soviet Union already existed when Schmitt published his writings—but Lenin and other communist leaders lived by the principles that inspired Schmitt's ideas.

Schmitt's theories fail because, even in vertical, one-dimensional societies, reality is full of contradictions. The art of living is precisely to reach equilibrium in the midst of so many contradictions—which help attain equilibrium by counterpoising one against the other. F. Scott Fitzgerald was describing reality when he wrote: "The test of a first-rate intelligence is the ability to hold two opposed ideas in the mind at the same time, and still retain the ability to function."[244] To be able to hold different and even contradictory ideas is one aspect of the genius of liberalism.

Uncertainty

But contradictions are not the only problem with one-dimensional theories of government. There is uncertainty, too, a problem that one-dimensional theories try to resolve with probabilistic methods that are, at best, childish and, at worst, dangerous for the false sense of security they breed. Such methods are good at predicting how many times a roulette ball will land on a certain number if it is played thousands of times, but they are not good at predicting a financial crisis that might devastate the world economy or the outcome of a roulette gamble played only once in history. The conceptual framework of the Soviet Union was consistent with Schmitt's logic, but it collapsed anyway and could not predict its own demise. In the real world, anything can happen. The future behavior of a society is impossible to predict.

Such a conclusion may seem useless for people wanting to reduce the wide diversity of human behavior to a simple equation and then use it to predict a deterministic outcome. But it is extremely useful to decide what kind of actions should be taken to develop a healthy society, and this is what really matters. What is needed is not a prediction of what is going to happen but a system designed to accommodate widely different potential events and to correct the course of an adjustment—and do whatever possible to make it work.

The Ability to Correct

The naked reasoning of Schmitt and his followers has another weakness that is intimately related to its incapacity to deal with uncertainty. Of course, reality does not conform to ideal scenarios. The waters of history are not crystal clear, and the currents of progress form whirlpools that can change the water's direction. This gives primary importance to the ability to correct.

William Morris, an English polymath of the nineteenth century, captured better than any one-dimensional thinker the true nature of history and the contradictions and uncertainties that permeate our lives:

> I . . . pondered how men fight and lose the battle, and the thing that
> they fought for comes about in spite of their defeat, and when it

comes turns out not to be what they meant, and other men have to fight for what they meant under another name. [245]

Morris's words summarize the history of the world. They portray the complexity of life, our inability to capture in a neat concept what we wish for, and our limited grasp of the effects of the interactions of the infinite dimensions of reality. They also portray how the loss of one battle may be offset by unexpected gains in other dimensions, and how desired outcomes have to be pursued again and again. They portray the confused nature of life and history. There is not a country that has not gone back and forth, sometimes contradicting the very principles it had sworn never to contradict.

The only way to manage a reality that is both contradictory and uncertain is to design a system that can correct its course, finding the right response by trial and error. This is precisely what liberal democracy does. The advantage of democracy is not that it produces the best policies from the start but that it has the ability to correct itself. As Viscount Bryce wrote:

> That a majority is always right, i.e. that every decision it arrives at by voting is wise, not even the most fervent democrat has ever maintained, seeing that popular government consists in the constant effort of a minority to turn itself by methods of persuasion into a majority which will then reverse the action or modify the decisions of the former majority. [246]

Karl Popper, the great philosopher, came to the same conclusion:

> What can be said . . . to be implied in the adoption of the democratic principle . . . is the conviction that the acceptance of even a bad policy in a democracy (as long as we can work for a peaceful change) is preferable to the submission to a tyranny, however wise or benevolent. [247]

This is the essence of flexibility. Different from the formal constructs of Marx, Schmitt, and other one-dimensional philosophers and social scientists, liberal democracy does not try to find the ultimate solution to a certain problem in one go. It relies on its flexibility to learn in an eternal search for improvement. It is a vessel, not a structure.

Vertical, rigid thought perceives flexibility as a fatal defect. In this vein, Wolfgang Streeck describes what he perceives as the failure of capitalism:

> Capitalism has always been an improbable social formation, full of conflicts and contradictions, therefore permanently unstable and in

flux, and highly conditional on historically contingent and precarious supportive as well as constraining events and institutions. . . . Motivating non-owners . . . to work hard and diligently in the interest of the owners . . . requires artful devices—sticks and carrots of the most diverse sorts that are never certain to function—that have to be continuously reinvented as capitalist progress continuously renders them obsolescent. . . . In fact, the history of modern capitalism can be written as a succession of crises that capitalism survived only at the price of deep transformations of its economic and social institutions, saving it from bankruptcy in foreseeable and often unintended ways.[248]

These words illustrate the stark difference between multidimensional and one-dimensional thought. Streeck seems to believe that the conflicts and contradictions of societies of the early twenty-first century are attributable not to reality but to capitalism itself. In fact, Streeck is almost repeating the observations that William Morris made about life and history, only attributing them to capitalism, not to life, and considering them not a wonderful feature of life but a crippling defect.

Second, Streeck implies that an alternative system that would eliminate the essence of capitalism—economic freedom—would eliminate conflicts and contradictions through the introduction of the rationalizing power of the state. This was the basic idea of the revolutionaries of more than a century ago. This is what Lenin thought. Of course, experience has shown that the economic power of the state does not eliminate conflicts but represses them and creates the conditions for abuse.

Third, Streeck deems capitalism's ability to adapt, by transforming economic and social institutions, to be a fatal defect rather than a manifestation of resilience in the face of radical change. Talking about the problem of enticing people to work diligently, he fails to see how this problem led to terror and corruption in communist countries, noting only that, in capitalism, solving it "requires artful devices—sticks and carrots of the most diverse sorts that are never certain to function—that have to be continuously reinvented as capitalist progress continuously renders them obsolescent." That is part of the genius of capitalism.

Rather than trying to make modern societies one-dimensional, we should reinforce the multidimensional nature of liberal democracy. Rather than polarization, we need tolerance; rather than political competition, we need to combine competition with political cooperation—the kind of cooperation that made possible the foundation of liberal democracy in the United States and elsewhere.

Such a change in perspective is required in the face of our contemporary crisis. But unfortunately we are seeing a renaissance of vertical ideas of government. For example, Francis Fukuyama has argued that the United States has fallen behind Germany, Japan, and Europe in general because its government lacks authority:

> The origins of the US approach lie in the historical sequence by which its three sets of institutions evolved. In countries such as France and Germany, law came first, followed by a modern state, and only later by democracy. In the United States, by contrast, a very deep tradition of English common law came first, followed by democracy, and only later by the development of a modern state. Although the last of these institutions was put into place during the Progressive Era and the New Deal, the American state has always remained weaker and less capable than its European or Asian counterparts. More important, American political culture since the founding has been built around distrust of executive authority.[249]

This paragraph is deeply disturbing. Democracy came to Germany in a permanent way only after the collapse of the autocratic Second Reich and the Nazi regime. It was under them that the German bureaucracy developed. So Fukuyama seems to be saying that these autocratic regimes were modern and effective states and that going through those stages provided the German state with an advantage the United States lacks.

In fact, as we have seen in previous chapters, we cannot say that "law" (in the sense given to this word in the twenty-first century) arrived in Germany before "modern" states and democracy. The Second Reich was deeply arbitrary, and the Nazi regime was entirely arbitrary. How can you say that the law was there unless you adopt the Nazi jurists' definition that the will of the führer was the law? Can we really believe that *not* having had a kaiser and a Hitler and their respective subservient bureaucracies has made the United States weaker and less capable than Germany?

According to Fukuyama, the problem with the American state is that "the United States has returned in certain ways to being a 'state of courts and parties,' that is, one in which the courts and the legislature have usurped many of the proper functions of the executive, making

the operation of the government as a whole both incoherent and inefficient."[250] He then directly attacks liberal democracy:

> [L]iberal democracy is almost universally associated with the market
> economies, which tend to produce winners and losers and amplify
> what James Madison termed the "different and unequal faculties of
> acquiring property." This type of economic inequality is not in itself
> a bad thing, insofar as it stimulates innovation and growth and occurs
> under conditions of equal access to the economic system. It becomes
> highly problematic, however, when the economic winners seek to
> convert their wealth into unequal political influence. They can do so
> by bribing a legislator or a bureaucrat, that is, on a transactional basis,
> or what is more damaging, by changing the institutional rules to favor
> themselves—for example, by closing off competition in markets they
> already dominate, tilting the playing field more steeply in their favor.[251]

This argument seems to coincide with mine regarding the dangers
of unifying political and economic power. But Fukuyama takes the
opposite direction when concluding his argument:

> Both processes lead to a reduction of bureaucratic autonomy, which in
> turn leads to rigid, rule-bound, uncreative and incoherent government.[252]

Together, these paragraphs suggest that winners and losers do not
exist in nonliberal regimes—as if people devoid of their rights, or worse,
sent to the gulag or to concentration camps, were not losers. They
also suggest that, while bureaucrats should be autonomous, free to regulate society, society should not be allowed to regulate bureaucracy.
In an oblique way, this assertion replaces the people with bureaucrats
as a nation's sovereign power. This independence of bureaucracy, of
course, does not exist in Germany or France, which are fully functional
democracies. Fukuyama's argument also gives the impression that the
market economy creates corruption among otherwise pristine legislators
and bureaucrats—something proved untrue by the terrible corruption
of communist regimes.

Finally, he cites an example of the backwardness of the United
States: how legal challenges and the need for approval from many different federal agencies delayed the dredging of Oakland Harbor, initially planned in 1970, by more than twenty years. As a comparison,
Fukuyama notes that a comparable expansion of the Port of Rotterdam,
in the Netherlands, was accomplished in a fraction of the time.

Comparing two political systems on the basis of the speed of execution of two single ports is, of course, superficial. Fukuyama gives the impression that "the conflicts that in Sweden or Japan would be solved through quiet consultations between interested parties in the bureaucracy are fought out through formal litigations in the U.S. court system."[253] This analysis ignores three facts: first, that while California was sinking in the swamp of legal challenge to the expansion of Oakland Harbor, it was leading the world with the connectivity revolution; second, that litigations are common in Europe, including Rotterdam[254]; and third, that ports in the Netherlands are managed, as is the system that keeps the sea away from the country, by decentralized local bodies that make their own decisions, apart from the country's central bureaucracy.

All these ideas romanticize authoritarian powers, giving the false impression that giving orders is superior as a method of governance to democracy, rights, and checks and balances. Guillaume-François Le Tronse, a French economist of the eighteenth century, thought that the French autocracy of those years was better than the nascent English democracy because things could be done faster—that is, it was more efficient to act on a vertical command without having to pay attention to people who thought differently:

> The situation in France . . . is infinitely better than in England, for here we can achieve reforms which change the state of the country in a flash whereas with the English such reforms can always be blocked by the party system.[255]

The argument for vertical government continues to be made today. Certainly, autocratic systems can be more "efficient" in the abstract. However, they have crippling problems. As we know well, the supposedly inefficient British system produced the greatest economic and political transformations of the eighteenth and nineteenth centuries—the industrial revolution and liberal democracy—while the supposedly efficient French system failed to produce them until a century later. Still, there is a strong current supporting the idea that centralizing economic and political power in a bureaucracy results in a more efficient society. It has been accompanied by a surge of intolerant vertical thinking that, even if coming from a different source, may combine with it in an explosive way.

THE BRILLIANCE OF THE FOUNDING FATHERS

British liberals, the Founding Fathers of the United States, and the shapers of the most developed societies were aware of the dangers of rigidity and one-dimensional thinking. They did not produce a plan, or a program, or a theory to attain the results they eventually attained. They did not prioritize finding solutions for every problem. They sought a political structure that would help them to reach truth gradually, by internalizing feedback and correcting their steps along the way. They knew that by dealing with contradictions and facing uncertainty they would make mistakes, and they opted for a political system that would allow them to correct these mistakes more easily. They constructed horizontal societies that became viable, even if challenged by innumerable contradictions, because of their multidimensionality.

Of course, the challenges that Schmitt, Fukuyama, and others saw in liberalism also existed in fascist and communist regimes. The difference is that authoritarian regimes only allow discussion of such problems among the elites. If ordinary people do not want to accommodate the wishes of the rulers, the solution is to keep them ignorant. As Schmitt wrote of communism, "The bourgeois is not to be educated, but eliminated." This, of course, was also true of the Nazi-fascist regimes.[256]

Defenders of authoritarianism should know that one-dimensional societies consistently fail, while those they believe have reached an impasse, liberal democracies, are highly successful. Liberal democracies do not break. Liberalism is not an empty box facilitating the discussion of problems or a political effluent of capitalism. It is a system of values that people have fought for again and again.

Liberalism leaves many knots untied. But this is precisely why it works. As the historian David Reynolds has noted:

> The contrast between Britain and Germany in the early 1930s is particularly marked. The German Depression proved the making of the Nazi Party as a political force; its rise to power was abetted by conservative elites who thought Hitler could be managed, and by the head of state President Paul Hindenburg, a retired field marshal and war hero who despised parliamentary politics. In Britain, however, the economic crisis resulted not in a government of the extreme right but in an all-party coalition forged with the encouragement of the head of the state.[257]

We know the history. Facing the same challenges, Germany became the slave of a single will, while Britain went into the uncertain world of balancing different parts of a coalition. Britain bet on finding solutions to the contradictions, not on suppressing them with dictatorship, while Germany believed in the absurd utopias offered by Hitler.

These experiences and others in history show that the people who followed the creators of liberal democracy—people like John Locke, Adam Smith, George Washington, Thomas Jefferson, Alexander Hamilton, James Madison, John Marshall, Edmund Burke, John Stuart Mill, Friedrich Hayek—were much wiser than those who followed Robespierre, George Danton, Jean-Paul Marat, Marx, Lenin, Hitler, Mussolini, and Carl Schmitt.

Marx and Schmitt and others sound sophisticated, while Adam Smith and Washington can sound simple. But the proponents of liberal democracy knew what they were talking about, not just from books but from their personal experience. They knew that life is multidimensional, which makes it impossible to make predictions, but they also knew that the mistakes made by reducing a complex world to one-dimensional reasoning are even worse. They understood that, while one cannot know the future, one can prepare for the future in weakness or in strength, and that the best way to do it is to keep the society multidimensional and promote self-reliance and respect for the rule of rights.

I believe that liberal democracy is the best system to face the challenges posed by the connectivity revolution. But lately it seems as if the world is taking the opposite direction, that of verticality, not because of any failure in liberal democracy but because liberal societies are weakening in their commitment to it. It is a commitment we need to reaffirm.

14

OUR 1776
MOMENT

*But when there are no shared goals or vision of the public good, is the
social contract any longer possible?*

Allan Bloom

WHAT IS TO BE DONE?

What kind of actions should we take to ease our adaptation to the world
that is emerging? And what kind of changes should be made to the
social order to frame such adaptation within a multidimensional society?
Seven important lessons from this book's review of history and the current crisis can help us to better adapt to the challenges I pose afterward.

Lesson 1: The Origin of Disruption

The ghosts that have returned from the past to disrupt our lives—gaps
in the distribution of income, financial crises, slow rates of economic
growth, divisiveness, the resistance to change, the use of hatred to unify
fragmented societies, the rise of authoritarian populist leaders, the fragmentation of the world order, the change of mood for the worse, and
the disenchantment with liberal democracy—are not evidence of the
failure of liberal democracy. Rather, they are the result of the processes
of change unleashed by the new connectivity revolution.

Lesson 2: The Origin of Conflict

Technological revolutions generate these problems mainly because different groups adjust to it at different speeds. Those left behind feel that this is a manifestation of unfairness embedded in the system. Depending on the size of the gap and the character of those affected, the perception of unfairness easily turns to hatred. People look for culprits in what is an impersonal process. They become prey to demagogues who fan the flames of these hatreds to grab power. If taken to extremes, this process can lead to chaos as intolerant coalitions face each other. There is nothing people fear more than chaos. In that situation, people easily accept tyranny.

Lesson 3: Reducing the Gap in the Speed of Adjustment

In the knowledge economy, you cannot produce without high levels of human capital. A healthy and educated labor force is critical to producing high added value. And unlike an industrial economy, a knowledge economy requires, first and foremost, investment in human capital, which is then used to produce wealth. In other words, health and education have become public goods whose provision benefits all in society. Education and health for all must be the concern of all, just like national defense and policing.

Any solution to the economic, social, and political problems posed by the technological revolution must address the fundamental problem of the transformation: reducing the inequality of the speed of adjustment of different groups. Society must invest heavily in its citizenry, creating strong human capital to help all citizens adjust harmoniously to the new circumstances. Many people see the problem of those left behind as a problem for them alone, so that their adaptation to the new world becomes a matter of solidarity having nothing to do with the economy. But as we saw in Chapter 4, the difficulty some people have in adapting is a problem for *everyone*: all society is affected by a reduction in the nation's capacity to grow. How this investment in human capital is carried out—by the public sector, the private sector, or a combination of the two—must be open for discussion, but it has to happen to secure the economic health of the United States.

Lesson 4: The Flexible Social Order

In the face of deep transformation, social order must be flexible, which can be attained only by giving priority to individual rights as a means of providing stability. As we have discussed throughout the book, the two features, individual rights and flexibility, reinforce each other, and the only social order that achieves this balance is liberal democracy. Certainly, many institutions may need changes because the relationships they channel are changing with the new technologies. But the basic principles of liberalism, democracy, and the rule of rights must be protected.

Lesson 5: The Multidimensional Society

Whatever the shape of new institutions in an emerging society, a strict separation must be kept between economic power and political power to create the umbrella of equal powers that gives life to a multidimensional society. In 1215, the lords who met King John of England in a meadow on the south bank of the Thames River knew the crucial importance of keeping these powers separated when they wrote Article 39 of the Magna Carta:

> We will sell to no man, we will not deny or defer to any man either Justice or Right.

These words have resounded throughout history, up to this moment, as the clearest enunciation of what a multidimensional society is: the strict separation between economic interests and judicial principles, which are the product of political power. It is the essence of the rule of rights.

Lesson 6: Dealing with the Decline of Social Cohesion

Threatening our ability to adjust to the challenges of the connectivity revolution is the tendency toward rigidity, which is a symptom of the weakening of social cohesion. Defending liberal democracy means more than simply advocating for free trade or prudent macroeconomic policies. The ability to deal harmoniously with the transformation crucially depends on developing a new kind of cohesion that is already contained in the basic conception of the nation but never fully applied in terms of the equality of all citizens regardless of their race, sex, or cultural origins.

Lesson 7: Rejecting the Search of Unity through Hatred

Finally, we must all be aware of the danger of hatred, no matter where it comes from and at whom it is aimed. Combating these attacks should not threaten freedom of speech but must counterbalance hatred with reasoned calls against hate speech and calls for compromise and cooperation.

How to Adapt?

Redefining What Makes America Great

Donald Trump's slogan "Make America Great Again" is based on nostalgia for something that the country is supposed to have lost. The slogan can be interpreted in different ways, depending on what is meant by the word *great*. Trump seems to believe that the United States was great because it was rich in a purely monetary way. He also seems to think that what defined economic greatness was specific industrial activities the United States had when it had no rival in the world, not the ecosystem that produced the successful economy he would like to bring back—even if the goods and services that the old successful economy produced can no longer create the wealth that other, newer products can create. It makes much more sense to train people who used to produce air conditioners to produce software rather than bring back the production of air conditioners from the countries that can produce them at a much lower cost than can American workers.

More important, the word *great* should refer to something much more significant than money. And there is a real nostalgia for something that US culture is in danger of losing completely as a result of the pursuit of money alone. In his *Alienated America: Why Some Places Thrive while Others Collapse,* Timothy Carney concludes that the greatness of America is not associated with money but with communal life.[258]

> The materialistic view of the American Dream . . . misses the point. The worst analyses assume that *wealth* or the *opportunity* for wealth is the American Dream. . . . But maybe the things we think *accompany* the American dream are the things that really *are* the American Dream. What if the T-ball game, the standing-room-only high school concert, the parish potluck, and decorating the community hall for a wedding—what if those activities are not the dressings around the American Dream, but what if they are the American Dream?[259]

Carney's question is rhetorical. His implicit answer is a resounding yes. Communal life generates support, creativity, a sense of responsibility, desire for growth, role models—features needed to adjust to existing and new circumstances. Even economic success in the midst of change is linked to this sense of community, which is another name for social interest. Carney shows how this sense of community has been lost in the places that feel the American Dream is over. This weakening of social interest at all levels of society is a worrying development. It is the kind of decay that leads to a crack-up that, as F. Scott Fitzgerald wrote in words I quoted in Chapter 10, "happens almost without your knowing but is realized suddenly indeed."

On the 150th anniversary of the Declaration of Independence, Calvin Coolidge said:

> We live in an age of science and of abounding accumulation of material things. These did not create our Declaration [of Independence]. Our Declaration created them. The things of the spirit come first. Unless we cling to that, all of our material prosperity, overwhelming though it may appear, will turn to a barren scepter in our grasp. [260]

Coolidge's "things of the spirit" are moral principles expressed by the Golden Rule—do unto others what you want others to do unto you. It has been an American ideal for two and a half centuries. But there are other dimensions to a multidimensional society that define the happiness of its citizens, including *meaning,* which is closely related to social interest.

The US diplomat Richard Holbrooke wrote the following words in 2008:

> Yesterday I went to the final performance of the revival of *South Pacific* at Lincoln Center [in New York City]. A fantastic production, which I found immensely moving. Men were crying, myself included. I tried to understand why that show had such an enormous emotional impact on us. For me it was the combination of the beauty of the show and its music, and the capturing in that show of so many moments in American history, the show itself opening in New York at the height of New York's greatness, 1949, the theme—Americans at war in a distant land or islands in the South Pacific—the sense of loss of American optimism and our feeling that we could do anything. The contrast with today—it was very powerful, and I kept thinking of where we were today, our nation, our lack of confidence in our own ability to lead compared to where we were in 1949 when it came out, evoking an era only five years or seven years earlier, when we had gone to the most distant corners of the globe and saved civilization.[261]

These words are just another symptom of the crack-up. Holbrooke lamented not the loss of wealth (the United States is much wealthier today than in the 1940s) or the loss of power (the United States is still the most powerful country in the world), but the loss of a sense of meaning that has existed throughout the history of the United States. There is no single meaning for everyone, but there has been a specific meaning that all Americans shared in feeling that the United States is a free society in which everybody can pursue excellence in whatever activity they please—serving in the armed forces, perhaps, or manufacturing the best product in the world, or producing the best art in the country.

Individual aspirations, although disparate, are coherent in their national pride, in the search for excellence that is needed to meet them. They are essential to produce the material, intellectual, and spiritual accomplishments, not just in the United States but in all liberal democracies. They are essential to generate the self-satisfaction that is the fuel that propels those accomplishments. And they merge social interest and self-interest in the search for happiness.

As I mentioned earlier, Adam Smith, John Stuart Mill, Victor Frankl, and Fyodor Dostoevsky all see the meaning of life as a means to happiness. The dedication of life to something bigger than oneself is an essential ingredient in the organization of an efficient and humane society, not just because it introduces multidimensionality but also because it gives an ethical sense to the production of excellence.

A fully meaningful liberal democracy has companies that are proud of what they produce. High quality has been a trademark of proud capitalist firms. This pride is being lost as many companies act to produce the highest possible returns for their shareholders in the short term, often at the expense of excellence. This difference, subtle as it might seem, turns the world of commerce into a one-dimensional one, with negative results in economic and ethical terms. This sense of meaning is being lost in the United States, partly because of the now popular belief that the only purpose of people, and of companies, is to make money in the short term. Arising out of this dangerous belief is a willingness to forgive anything of a president if the economy is doing fine.

In his book *Obliquity: Why Our Goals Are Best Achieved Indirectly,* John Kay illustrated this shift in objectives by examining Boeing:

> Boeing created the most commercially successful aircraft company, not through love of profit but through love of planes. . . . Yet, it took only ten years for Boeing to prove me wrong in asserting that its market position in civil aviation was impregnable. A decisive shift in corporate culture followed the acquisition of the company's chief US rival, McDonnell Douglas. The new CEO, Phil Condit, explained

that the company's previous preoccupation with meeting "technological challenges of supreme magnitude" would have to change. Directness would have to displace obliquity: "We are going into a value based environment where unit cost, return on investment, shareholder return are the measure by which you'll be judged. That's a big shift."[262]

As Kay noted, Boeing stock, which increased from $32 to $59 when Condit took over with these new ideas, fell to $34 by the time of his forced resignation in 2003, when Boeing's order book had fallen behind Airbus. Kay wrote his book in 2011 and thus could not see the much worse effects that the new management doctrine had on Boeing in 2019 and 2020.

Shifting the objectives of companies in the direction of maximizing just one indicator, profits, negatively affects creativity in an economy increasingly dependent on innovation.[263] It also negatively affects ethical conduct, as we know from several highly visible cases, including the behavior of financial companies during the 2008 crisis; the case of Volkswagen, which cheated in official environmental tests; Theranos, which cheated customers and shareholders into believing it had invented a machine to test blood with very small samples; and Boeing, which designed a defective plane and then concealed this fact from regulators and customers at the eventual cost of 345 lives. These companies and many others shifted their priority from a passion for excellence (while providing adequate returns to shareholders) to the maximization of returns to shareholders.

Keeping Government under Control

The American tradition of small government is based on three factors: first, that big government easily becomes incompetent, tyrannical, or both; second, that undesirably high taxes are needed to keep a large government in place; and third, that bureaucracies tend to grow uncontrollably as they increase their own power. Inventing new roles for themselves, the belief is, bureaucracies become useless and expensive. Ronald Reagan encapsulated this view of bureaucracy in his quote, "The most terrifying words in the English language are: I'm from the government and I'm here to help." As a result of this resistance to big bureaucracies, even Roosevelt's New Deal and Lyndon Johnson's Great Society remained substantially smaller in proportion to the economy than comparable government programs in European countries.

Ideally, government must be kept to a size compatible with what is demanded from it. As Hayek said, we "should make as much use as possible of the spontaneous forces of society, and resort as little as possible to coercion."[264] The challenge faced by American society in this respect is to attain this objective in a new world that seems to be demanding more rather than less government intervention in the economy as a result of the increasing complexity of economic, political, and social interrelationships. Such complexity is partly attributable to technological transformation. Yet it is mainly the result of three other changes that have taken place in the last hundred years.

First is the gradual crowding of urban areas, which creates more and more complex relations between individuals. As a rule, private organizations say that regulations have become excessive, and thus we need less, not more of them. They tend to attribute this explosion of regulations to the government. Yet the private sector is an inexhaustible source of detailed and exasperating regulations, even in private environments in which we interact with each other, as in, say, clubs and condominiums. Many government-created regulations are established by popular demand, such as those meant to restrict the noise of airplane engines or the times of delivery of trucks in cities, the ban on construction of oil platforms in the ocean, or the amount of pollution that cars are permitted to release into the atmosphere.

A second reason for the increase in the size of government is the growing complexity of the impact of productive activities on individuals, which in turn results in higher demand for regulations regarding safety and environmental protection. These are the regulations that private organizations oppose the most, demanding either their elimination or their conversion into self-regulation—a system in which the regulated design and impose the regulations on themselves. Their main argument for self-regulation is that mature productive sectors have a vested interest in regulating themselves effectively because if they damage their customers, they lose their patronage. This argument has been used to promote the total lack of regulation as well. While it seems to make sense, it has not worked in practice. In many cases, it is not regulation at all.

The argument may be reasonable if we are talking about a restaurant that serves bad food or an airline whose planes don't arrive on time. It is not reasonable, however, if we are talking about an airline that doesn't adequately maintain its aircraft. In these cases, self-regulation not only sounds unreasonable, it fails, as the cases I mentioned above illustrate. The arguments for government regulation will become stronger as the economy moves toward automatic equipment, such as driverless cars.

The third reason why governments are tending to grow is the redefinition of activities considered public goods to include investment in human capital. This redefinition has taken place over the last century and was motivated first by solidarity and lately by the realization that investment in human capital is essential for economic growth and development.

Certainly, the private sector should play a key role in the provision of the health and education now essential to compete and cooperate in the international chains of supply of knowledge. Yet the magnitude of the effort needed to integrate those left behind into the new society of knowledge and keep the country competitive makes the participation of federal, state, and local governments essential.

These three factors will likely increase the size of government. Many are uncomfortable with this conclusion, but most alternatives fail to produce solutions that would reduce regulation if public demand does not diminish. Certainly, energetic efforts to reduce regulation through its rationalization must be made from time to time to cut the excess that bureaucracy tends to produce. But pretending that government will not grow prevents us from discussing one of the biggest challenges of the current transformation: to find how to keep government under the democratic control of citizens and respecting the rule of rights while substantial government action is required. This is a real challenge while support for vertical solutions to the current problems of adjustment is on the rise.

Achieving this equilibrium will be difficult because it must exist between those who think that the government is essentially bad and those who believe that an authoritarian government is needed. In fact, government intervention is not good or bad per se. It depends on its nature and implementation.

Biting the Bullet

The fate of the housing program was a stark warning in this respect. Starting in the early 1990s, administrations of the two main American political parties embarked on a policy aimed at financing housing for people who had been left behind by the new knowledge economy. As the return on innovation and knowledge increased, the incomes of the unskilled stagnated, and income inequality widened. The government did not try to help improve incomes by enhancing skills. Rather, the idea was that, if the government could not increase incomes, it could at least help those left behind to get a home—without seriously taking into consideration their limited ability to pay.[265] Taking this route meant that they were not biting the bullet. They were not confronting the real problem.

In 1995, Bill Clinton set a goal to increase the home ownership rate from 62.9 percent to 67.5 percent.[266] George W. Bush made the so-called home ownership society a centerpiece of his political platform. The two administrations took many actions to attain these objectives. First, they greatly facilitated the development of low-cost housing and its financing, going well beyond prudent practices. The housing and financial authorities looked the other way regarding compliance with prudential regulations. But they did even more. They actually pushed the financial institutions to lend to people who could not possibly repay.

Second, the housing effort was combined with an independent process of financial deregulation that had already started. In 1999, Congress abolished the 1933 Glass-Steagall Act, which banned the use of the funds of commercial banks to speculate in securities. From that year on, banks could use the deposits from the population to take risks in apparently highly profitable, speculative operations that turned out to lead to failures in a highly volatile market. The use of bank deposits for speculation greatly increased the funds available for housing financing.

Third, the economic authorities created a political environment that encouraged the Federal Reserve (the Fed) to engage in highly expansionary monetary policies, which flooded the market with credits. Starting in 1987, when Alan Greenspan became the chair of the Fed, the strange idea arose that stock prices growing faster than the economy would keep the economy growing as well. The Greenspan Fed kept the stock market booming. He was so successful pushing up the market that people characterized his policies as the Greenspan Put—a put was understood as an implicit guarantee that if there was a fall in the stock prices, the Fed would do whatever was needed to reverse it. Low interest rate policies did not spur real economic growth. Instead, the Fed became a serial bubble generator. It allowed financial firms to take excessive risks in the stock market, housing, housing derivatives, commodities, and

FIGURE 9
Serial Bubbles since 1987

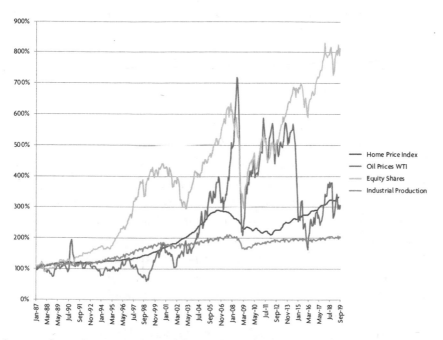

Sources and notes: Housing, S&P/Case-Shiller U.S. National Home Price Index and the rest International Financial Statistics of the International Monetary Fund. WTI refers to West Texas Intermediate (oil prices).

other assets. The price of assets grew much faster than the economy, increasing the risks of investing in them. The ample liquidity provided by lax Fed policies and regulations magnified those risks.

After 1999, housing prices soared while the median real household income declined for five straight years. [267] As shown in Figure 9, expansionary monetary policies affected not just housing prices but also the price of oil and especially the price of equities. Since 1987, the Fed found itself tied to the Greenspan Put—first expanding the money supply to increase stock prices and thus creating a bubble; then, when the bubble burst, as it did in 2000 and 2008, doing the same to minimize the fallout; then, to recover the previous price level; then, when the price increases weakened, political pressure became unbearable, until a second bubble burst; and so on. The graph shows very clearly that the amazingly high rates of growth of stock prices had nothing to do with the increase in production, shown in the graph by the industrial production index. The rationale given today to justify the huge increases in prices, which had taken place since 2009 while production was not increasing as fast, is that investors looked ahead, knowing that production and earnings would increase quickly in the future. This is what they said at the time of the dot.coms before 2000 and in the subsequent boom that led to the 2008 recession crisis. At the time of this writing, the third bubble in stock prices is fluctuating in reaction to the coronavirus pandemic.

These housing programs led to a terrible financial crisis and the Great Recession. The cost of the policy excesses was staggering. Yet not one of the actions taken by the government in the housing credit programs addressed the underlying problem of the transformation—the lack of skills in the human capital for people left behind. The main effects of government action were to delay the solution of the underlying problem and to waste enormous quantities of money.

The enormous transfers of money from the middle and working classes to Wall Street financiers produced no good effect at all. People did not get more houses, the poor got houses that they lost a few years later, and the country's productivity did not increase. As Paul Volker said in 2009, there was little evidence that the innovations displayed with great fanfare in the financial markets had had any visible effect on the productivity of the economy.[268] By the second quarter of 2016, the home ownership rate, which had peaked at 69 percent in 2004–2006, had fallen back to 62.3 percent, below that of 1995, when the housing bubble began. It was the lowest rate since the index was first estimated in 1965.[269] In fact, the country and the world had enormous emotional and monetary losses as a result of the housing boom and bust, and the similar booms and busts that affected the stock exchange and the commodities markets.

But the damage was much worse than that. The method used by the government to save the endangered financial institutions did not follow the protocols established by the Federal Deposit Insurance Corporation (FDIC), which first separates the executives and owners of these institutions and only then transfers the resources needed to recapitalize them. In this crisis, the transfers from the government refloated not just the institutions but their owners as well, in quantities that dwarf the gross domestic product (GDP) of several American states. This was a direct transfer of wealth to these individuals paid by the taxpayer.

This established a terrible precedent as people gained or retained incredible riches not through economic performance but by political means. It was the negation of all that capitalism and liberal democracy are about. In fact, the procedures were very similar to the scandal-ridden processes used in emerging economies to recapitalize their banking systems and their shareholders. Simon Johnson and James Kwak summarized the situation in this way:

> Today, however, it is clear that Wall Street did not end. While some fabled institutions have vanished, the survivors have survived larger, more profitable, and even more powerful. The vague expectation that the government would bail out major financial institutions when necessary has become official policy. The connections between Wall Street and Washington have become stronger. A Democratic administration has done everything in its power to restore a private, profitable financial sector. A casual observer would be forgiven for thinking that Washington has behaved like an emerging market government in the 1990s—using public resources to protect a handful of large banks with strong political connections. Whether this was due to political capture or to unbiased economic policy making, the results were the same: Wall Street only became stronger as a result of the financial crisis. [270]

In the epilogue to his book *Getting Off Track: How Government Actions and Interventions Caused, Prolonged and Worsened the Financial Crisis,* economist John B. Taylor wrote the following:

> In this book I have provided empirical evidence that government actions and interventions caused, prolonged, and worsened the financial crisis. They caused it by deviating from historical precedents and principles for setting interest rates that had worked well for twenty years. . . . They made it worse by supporting certain financial institutions and their creditors but not others in an ad hoc way, without a clear and understandable framework. Although other factors were certain to play, those government actions should be first on the list of answers to the question of what went wrong. [271]

Taylor, who was undersecretary of the treasury and a member of the Council of Economic Advisers in three administrations (both Democratic and Republican), detailed some implications from his analysis. The most important was that "policy makers should rethink the idea that frequent and large government interventions are the only answer to our current economic problems. Such a philosophy could take us further off track and, according to the analysis of this book, could make things worse rather than better." [272]

It would be naïve to believe that the gigantic bailout did not translate into giving the bankers political power over their regulators and over their customers. This concentration of political power in an economic sector is clearly dangerous for democracy and true liberal capitalism. Politics becomes the road to economic success. Notice that this unholy mixture is not a problem of income or wealth distribution. You do not have to be part of the richest 1 percent to control the flows of funds between the government and the banks. *It is a problem of political connections.* It is a problem in the intersection between the public and the private sectors. And it is many orders of magnitude more dangerous than the general income distribution problem.

In his book *Crashed: How a Decade of Financial Crises Changed the World,* Adam Tooze discusses how politics is invading the regulation of the increasingly complex systems in the current economy:

> There are ways of describing the operations of these systems that void the presence of politics. But if a history such as this has any purpose, it is to reveal the poverty of such accounts. Political choice, ideology and agency are everywhere across this narrative with highly consequential results, not merely as disturbing factors but as vital reactions to the huge volatility and contingency generated by the malfunctioning of the giant "systems" and "machines" and apparatuses of financial engineering. [273]

The negative effects of the financial collapse went well beyond economic losses. For many people, including many of the young, the crisis and its solution destroyed the faith they had in capitalism and liberal democracy. This was like breaking a spell. The impact of this catastrophe on the prestige of the liberal social order was much smaller in magnitude than that of the Great Depression. Yet it was sufficient to prompt people to look at capitalism and liberal democracy as outdated, corrupt systems and to open themselves to the appeal of other systems. It is no coincidence that two of the most radical candidates for the 2020 Democratic presidential nomination, Bernie Sanders and Elizabeth Warren, used the financial crisis and its resolution as evidences of capitalism gone wrong.[274]

The primary cause of the fury of the popular response to the crisis was not the financial failure itself. People accept mistakes and errors, but they do not accept manipulations that amount to fraud, which then enjoys impunity. This rejection then turned into cynicism. And this cynicism is the worst enemy of liberal democracy. This is the kind of cynicism that existed in the 1920s and 1930s. This cynicism would only increase with another crash and another bailout of the financial system.

The financial crash and the cases of Boeing, Theranos, Volkswagen, and similar recent scandals show the need to revise all the mechanisms of regulation, and particularly those that involve the interface between the private and the public sectors, because experience has shown quite clearly that the danger of collusion and capture is very real. It has also shown that self-regulation cannot be trusted to keep political and economic power apart.

The housing disaster also showed that ignoring change and trying to circumvent it is terribly expensive. The money lost in the attempt to give houses to those left behind—which even if successful would not have solved their real problem—would have been more than enough to invest in the improvement of their education and health. Education is expensive, but ignorance is more so.

Embracing Change

It is impossible to foresee the consequences of these changes, but we can identify two directions in which they are pushing us: toward globalization and toward the knowledge economy.

Globalization has been widely demonized, even by people who support it in their actions and their purchases and who benefit financially from it. As in the times that preceded the French Revolution, people want to return to a time of perceived greatness, while continuing to enjoy the means provided by the technology and commercial relations they reject in abstract. Like Peter the Great, they want the fruits of modernity without making the changes required to obtain them.

They refuse to recognize that today countries have become so intertwined that the individual nation-states can no longer determine their own destiny without considering what the other nation-states will do. Of course, they can isolate themselves from the other nation-states, but isolation has grave consequences. It would cut their economic growth, exposing them to internal political turmoil. Also, isolation would weaken their ability to make defensive military treaties. It would invite aggression.

On the other hand, trying to form alliances with other nation-states would impair their political independence. Their citizens would lose sovereignty. Doing nothing would let the problem grow and invite disaster, very much as resistance to change in pre-Nazi Germany and tsarist Russia led to divisiveness, chaos, and tyranny. There is only so much change that a social order can resist before breaking apart. And technology relentlessly leads to globalization through communications, international supply chains, unified financial markets, and the new global culture.

Of course, the rejection of globalization in the long term would lead to a rejection of the knowledge economy, which feeds itself from the creativity that sprouts from diversity and the free exchange of information and ideas. Countries wishing to remain developed must adapt in some way to globalization.

Fortunately, new technologies facilitate integration to the global realities without requiring geographical, political, or military integration. The idea that economic and cultural integration requires political integration is a one-dimensional notion, an ember from the fires that moved the nineteenth century toward the formation of empires, toward trade and military wars, and toward chaos and revolution. It is a leftover of the times when modern globalization did not exist, when communications could be managed only under the power of a political authority, when the lines of production had to be built in a single place because they could not be established in different parts of the country or the world. Of course, the idea that the integration is possible only through one common political authority naturally leads to a union of political and economic authority. It is a Napoleonic idea, not unlike the ideas of Germany of the Second Reich.

This vertical idea recently became popular, however, when Britain decided to leave the European Union (EU) while still trying to keep access to the Common Market. People of all convictions thought it was logical that the EU refused to provide access to its market to a country that refused to be part of it politically. The irrationality of their idea was exposed by the fact that they did not think Canada should become a member of the EU to have access to its markets.

The problems posed by commercial globalization are real, but the most effective way to confront them is to take advantage of the technological revolution to unify the world economically without relinquishing political and cultural sovereignty. Otherwise, because the integration cannot be stopped, the result would be one-dimensional, the strong taking advantage of the weak, with unthinkable consequences. The historical model should be the Hanseatic League, not a Napoleonic dream of politically unified continents.[275]

The COVID-19 pandemic has been as traumatic as World War I and the Great Depression combined in terms of bringing forth the subjacent conflicts in society, thus worsening the pressures that had been stressing the social order in the previous decades. The impact of the pandemic has been extremely asymmetric in geographical, racial, and social terms and has accentuated the already existing discontent in these respects. Moreover, people more fully integrated to the new technologies, those who can work at a distance, have fared much better than those who need physical presence to be effective. These two classes of people, those who can work at home and those who cannot, do not always coincide with socioeconomic classes. Medical personnel, who tend to earn substantial incomes, have to be in place to work, while some people doing simple administrative chores with much lower salaries may work from afar. Yet, in the overall picture, poor people tend to be both in the groups that have to be in place and in those that lost their jobs when lockdowns were imposed. Thus, if anything, the pandemic turned all the existing problems worse.

The pandemic has added a new argument to those who suggest that globalization should be backtracked: that it facilitates the transmission of plagues and leads not just to loss of life but also to economic breakdowns. But such a suggestion is very superficial. To really stop pandemic waves, the world would have to go back to a level of isolation never attained in history. The Black Death arrived in Europe in the fourteenth century, killing about twenty million people, about one-third of the population of the continent, within five years. It stayed there, striking from time to time until at least the London Plague of 1665–1666. This pandemic, the worst in history, took place even though the world was hardly globalized. The same can be said of the Justinian Plague, which started in AD 541 and killed approximately fifty million people over the next two centuries. Reducing trade to the number of people and packages that walked the Silk Route in the thirteenth century would leave a hugely impoverished world, incapable of sustaining today's population, and still would not stop the contagion of a potential pandemic.

The drastic contraction experienced by economies all over the world as a result of their isolation from each other is clear evidence of how deeply modern production depends on the global chains of supply. The idea that countries can attain self-sufficiency was never true. It is less so today, when production requires so many different inputs coming from so many different kinds of expertise. Trying to go back to the primitive autarky of the medieval feuds would be a catastrophic return to the past that would not resolve any problem because any potential pandemics would find ways to expand through the walls of the feudal principalities—as happened in the Middle Ages. Trying to do that would be similar to what the United States tried to do regarding the serious conflicts raging all over the world at the end of World War I, when it stepped out of the League of Nations. As we discuss in the next subsection, isolating itself from the rest of the world did not exclude the country from paying a terrible price for these conflicts in World War II. Certainly, international institutions are difficult to organize and manage. Yet it is better to invest in their development than to ignore the problems that require their existence to be solved.

The Open Society

In June 2017, Graham Allison published an article in *Foreign Policy* entitled "The Thucydides Trap." In it, he wrote, "When one great power threatens to displace another, war is always the result—but it doesn't have to be."[276] Thucydides, in his *History of the Peloponnesian War,* written at the end of the fifth century BC, examined the rise of Athens while Sparta declined as the dominant military power in ancient Greece. Graham notes that in the past five hundred years, sixteen rising powers have challenged ruling ones, and twelve of those confrontations ended in war. Today, an ascendant power, China, is challenging the United States. The challenge has already led to a commercial war and some saber rattling.

The current situation is much more complex than this, however. China is not the only rising power. Russia has recovered from the collapse of the Soviet Union and is again flexing its muscles internationally. Rogue states and terrorist groups are threatening world peace, creating platforms where the great powers jostle in an increasingly violent international scenario. The institutional setting for international relations established by the United States at the end of World War II is disintegrating in a way that is not just accepted by the United States but actively promoted by it. The world at large seems to be drifting into a primeval chaos in which might is right.

This dramatic reversal of the American attitude toward international order augurs the return of another ghost from the past. Before World War II, the United States, a nation of immigrants, turned its back on the world and pursued the path of isolationism. It is amazing how many people have forgotten how damaging this set of policies was for the United States and for the world. In the late 1940s, the statesman Dean Acheson noted that the isolationism and economic protectionism that prevailed prior to the war had led to the "derangement of the international economy," which in turn became a major cause of widespread economic nationalism, reduced cooperation, radical populism, and global conflict. He warned that if these conditions remained in place, the United States would be forced to adopt a managed, autarkic economic regime that "would completely change our Constitution, our relations to property, human liberty, our very conception of law."[277]

Acheson was one of the architects of the foreign policy that gave shape to postwar US hegemony, which followed the abandonment of prewar isolationism. That policy served the United States, and the world, extremely well. In a globalized economy, an internationally engaged United States is more important than ever. But one of the forces of divisiveness plaguing the country today is the myth that returning to isolationism will "make America great again."

The twentieth century was the US century. By design, however, the United States was never alone at the peak of its power. Since the beginning, the US government leveraged the country's power with the participation of others. In this way, the source of the country's ascendancy was not just the enormous economic and military dominance that it accumulated through the century, but also the wide network of alliances it built all over the world after World War II. The country's soft power, the idea that Americans represented the ideals of liberal democracy, would never betray their allies, and would always be reasonable, was even more powerful than its weapons. Countries liked to be on the side of the United States.

The network of alliances was solidified by the aid that the United States provided to its former enemies and allies at the end of World War II. This international engagement established the United States as the undisputable leader of liberal democracies. Never before had one victorious power turned to help its defeated enemies as the United States did with Germany and Japan while also helping its former allies to rebuild.

After the disastrous experiences of the 1920s and 1930s, when countries subordinated their trade policies to domestic political objectives, the United States established an international institutional setting that clearly separated trade from political issues. In the 1920s, countries looked to protectionism and created a weak, fragmented world that collapsed under the divisive forces of the Great Depression, but the new American order established a network of free trade that unified the world in a prolonged boom that created the prosperous world of the late twentieth century.

While separated from politics, free trade created the economic environment necessary for progress that facilitated the political and military agreements. As a result, the United States presented its enemies with a formidable alliance that not only protected the Western world and liberal democracy but also helped create more opportunities for multidimensionality in each participating country. The focus abroad helped the focus within and aided in the avoidance of one-dimensional societies. Countries that isolated themselves economically from the rest of the world, on the other hand, were forced to subordinate their economy to political power, a recipe for the creation of a one-dimensional society.

Keeping borders open for the flow of knowledge and participating in global networks of production and information are essential to maintain US influence, as is its ability to coordinate complex tasks at a distance. China may have a larger population and a dynamic and technologically advanced economy, but the United States has an overwhelming advantage in terms of technology and reach around the world. Both countries depend on having extended connections abroad, so it is essential for the United States to keep and fortify the networks it created after World War II.

The Trump administration weakened this power substantially. In an incredible move, in 2017, it pulled the United States out of the Trans-Pacific Partnership (TPP), a trade network of twelve countries on the Pacific Rim, which would have surrounded China with a solid trade alliance. With this move, the United States let China off the hook, allowing it to seek economic agreements with many of the countries that had already decided to become part of the group organized by the United States. As an economist at the Asian Development Bank told the *New York Times,* "The US has lost its leadership role, and China is quickly replacing it."[278]

This is just one manifestation of a new trend. The United States has opted for increasingly protectionist trade policies not just with China but also with allies that had formed the core of Pax Americana. Protectionism proclaims that the United States will work and fight only for its immediate economic interests, even if that means leaving aside agreements of mutual interest with close allies. The Trump administration has given other signals that it intends to withdraw from its role as leader of the free world, helping to create an everything-allowed environment that favors rogue states and terrorist groups. This was the environment that populists of yesteryear created, resulting in grave international conflicts that eventually dragged the United States into two world wars and many other local conflicts. If American foreign policy is not changed, the risk that these conflicts will return remains high. The risk that the United States might move toward one-dimensionality would remain high as well.

E Pluribus Unum

A country cannot act in all dimensions if it does not pursue its own unity as a priority. This requires putting a price on unity so that, as they make major decisions, politicians weigh the attainment of narrowly defined goals against the cost of damaging the country's unity. The current price must be very high because unity is desperately needed.

This price of unity, a notional conception, has an anchor in reality. The costs associated with rigid positions and fanatical comprehensive doctrines are extremely high. Huge problems that concern everybody cannot even be discussed properly and objectively because political parties battle on all possible fronts—from abortion rights issues to the need for investment in human capital, to the defense policies in the Middle East, and to the confrontations with China—with the same intensity, not allowing agreement in any essential area. If the divisiveness problem is not solved, the costs in terms of stagnation will rapidly escalate because the main political parties already promise to nullify anything that the other party has done in government—a strategy that began with Trump's promise to undo everything that Barack Obama had done during his administration. The next time Democrats are in power, they will undo many things that Trump has done. This is a recipe for a lethal tit-for-tat that would further destroy the country's ability to function politically.

At this point, it is necessary to distinguish clearly between two interpretations of Carl Schmitt's criticism of liberalism discussed in the last chapter. His arguments are invalid in terms of predicting the inevitable failure of liberal democracy. A modern democracy is sufficiently complex to allow a conflict in one dimension to negotiate with conflict in another dimension. In such societies, if there is a will, there is a way to keep liberal democracy in place.

However, Schmitt's reasoning is right if it is used to describe the conditions under which liberal democracy would inevitably fail. Liberal democracy became strong through the centuries not because the system, once established, could not fail but because these societies kept alive the spirit that turned them multidimensional. If that spirit fails, liberal democracy will fail as well. The difference between these interpretations is like saying that all planes will inevitably crash or that if one particular plane runs out of gas it must crash.

Schmitt clearly identified the condition that can kill liberal democracy: divisiveness. When taken to extremes, divisiveness results in social and political chaos. This is what killed democracy in interwar Italy and in the Weimar Republic, and it is what destroyed the possibility of creating democracy in Russia, China, and so many other places.

George Washington worried about this possibility. He was not the brightest of the Founding Fathers, yet he occupies an unparalleled place in the history of the country. Curiously, he was not subject to envy in his time. His colleagues gave him his exalted position from the very beginning. He occupied this place not because he was intelligent, which he was, or courageous, which he also was, but because he was wise. His peers recognized him as irreplaceable in the foundation of the new country.

His wisdom can be found in his decisions, in his mediations among his fellow Founding Fathers, and in his Farewell Address, which Alexander Hamilton and James Madison drafted for him. In this address, Washington chose divisiveness as the most important danger to the country:

> Interwoven as is the love of liberty with every ligament of your hearts, no recommendation of mine is necessary to fortify or confirm the attachment. The unity of government which constitutes you one people is also now dear to you. It is justly so, for it is a main pillar in the edifice of your real independence, the support of your tranquility at home, your peace abroad; of your safety; of your prosperity; of that very liberty which you so highly prize. But as it is easy to foresee that, from different causes and from different quarters, much pains will be taken, many artifices employed to weaken in your minds the conviction of this truth; as this is the point in your political fortress against which the batteries of internal and external enemies will be most constantly and actively (though often covertly and insidiously) directed, it is of infinite moment that you should properly estimate the immense value of your national union to your collective and

individual happiness; that you should cherish a cordial, habitual, and immovable attachment to it; accustoming yourselves to think and speak of it as of the palladium of your political safety and prosperity; watching for its preservation with jealous anxiety; discountenancing whatever may suggest even a suspicion that it can in any event be abandoned; and indignantly frowning upon the first dawning of every attempt to alienate any portion of our country from the rest, or to enfeeble the sacred ties which now link together the various parts.[279]

What Washington described as the main danger is what is happening today. For the country to survive as the great power it is, unity must be attained—although not at the cost of the rights of groups or individuals.

THE DAWN OF CHAOS?

The 2020 Election

As this book went to print, Joe Biden was declared the winner of the 2020 US presidential election. The sitting president, Donald Trump, refused to concede, claiming fraud with no evidence and mounting a smear campaign aimed at delegitimizing the election with propaganda rather than the long-standing traditions of the US electoral process. As usual, the language he used was marked by hatred.

Fortunately, the results were clear enough to discourage a direct challenge. But rejecting the electoral process without evidence was in itself a challenge to the institutional foundations of liberal democracy, especially when the president had a history of disrespect for those foundations and had continually attempted, while in office, to overstep limitations to presidential power established by the Constitution.

Anticipating that Trump's legal actions would produce nothing material, former president George W. Bush congratulated Biden and his running mate, Kamala Harris, with these words:

> The American people can have confidence that this election was fundamentally fair. Its integrity will be upheld and its outcome is clear.[280]

Refusing to concede without a solid legal basis was the last and most damaging of Trump's attempts to corrode the institutional setting of the United States for the sake of imposing his will. Sneering at institutions and disobeying their directives create the impression among many citizens that those institutions no longer work, leading to delegitimization and, potentially, their fall.

Mitt Romney, prominent Republican and former presidential candidate, summarized the environment that Trump helped to create during his mandate with these words:

> The rabid attacks kindle the conspiracy mongers and the haters who take the small and predictable step from intemperate word to dangerous action. The world is watching America with abject horror. More consequently, our children are watching. Many Americans are frightened for our country, so divided, so angry, so mean, so violent. It is time to lower the heat. The leaders must tone it down, leaders from the top and leaders of all stripes. Parents, bosses, reporters, columnists, professors, union chiefs, everyone. The consequence of the crescendo of anger leads to a very bad place. No sane person can want that.[281]

Yet Trump was not the only factor contributing to the deterioration of the American institutional setting. Urban violence is probably the most spectacular symptom of a breakdown of social order and, beginning in the late spring of 2020, the United States experienced increasingly violent confrontations in an increasing number of cities. As in the interwar years in Europe, fringes on both the left and the right resorted to violence, sometimes lethal and often in paramilitary garb. Fortunately, they did not, at least up to now, reach the condition that would make them truly dangerous to the survival of liberal institutions: they were not officially linked to any of the major political parties. The violence has been perpetuated by extremists. Ominously, however, unlike the German and Italian strife of the 1920s and 1930s, these latest violent conflicts feature a lot of guns.

In this age of comprehensive coalitions, these extreme reactions betray a fundamental, two-sided division over a broad range of issues, from matters of identity to opposing beliefs about how the social order of the country should be shaped. As history continues, the country's new president and his administration will face many difficult tasks, among them redefining what makes America great, keeping government under control, embracing change while focusing on helping people to face the emergence of the knowledge society, combatting racism, and integrating the country with the rest of the world while crafting a humane approach to immigration.

Two Wrongs Do Not Make a Right

By definition, authoritarian leaders legitimate authoritarianism. Donald Trump used the power of the presidency to impose his will on important issues that should have been met with bipartisan effort. Democrats will be tempted to counter Trumpism with similar methods. But such an approach would be counterproductive and could put the country on a path toward chaos and tyranny. Were Democrats to try to impose their will in the same way, they would, firstly, lose legitimacy in the fight against the radical right; secondly, fail to pass sustainable legislation if, as appears to be the case, the Senate remains majority Republican; and, thirdly, face the prospect of the fragmentation of their own party. After all, seventy million people voted for Trump, nearly 50 percent of all votes cast. The real lesson of Trump's demise should be that imposed change is not sustainable in a society based on the rule of rights—as long as society respects that rule.

Comprehensive doctrines easily turn unreasonable and threaten both sides. The coalition that dethroned Trump was strong because it had a specific objective of unifying the Democratic party and the country via the electoral process—an objective that had top priority for people all over society. It is highly unlikely, however, that the majority of Americans would risk a breakdown of institutional order for the sake of a series of single-issue objectives that do not have priority for the population at large. A breakdown in unity risks confrontation between different groups within each comprehensive coalition, which in turn would lead to fragmentation in both parties, and the risk of increasing chaos.

As Kevin Stevens remarked postelection in the *Dublin Review of Books*:

> So the dangers that led to his election in 2016 remain: the very real threats of fragmentation and division, in which social and political constituencies—from conservative state legislatures to progressive city governments, from street protest groups to armed militias—occupy a self-defined moral high ground and, under pressure, can and do reject any authority but their own. In such an environment, national political discourse, cheapened by social media, becomes ragged and hostile, and analysis becomes less and less thoughtful. More and more we hear the language of civil conflict, and not just on the fringes. And not just words. In the first nine months of 2020, Americans bought seventeen million guns, more than for any single full year on record. The American schism is not a rhetorical exercise.[282]

Healing the Wounds

In his victory speech, Joe Biden promised to heal the country's wounds, giving priority to the restoration of unity that George Washington warned was fundamental to the country. This is not a task solely for government. It is for the population as a whole. However, it will not take place automatically. A new civic leadership is needed.

There are many in the United States, both Republican and Democrat, with liberal democratic convictions. They are probably the majority. Many of them, however, have allowed themselves to be pushed into a one-dimensional world that has given them false objectives and a false sense of identity. Differences of opinion are not bad at all—in fact they are good, if both sides respect democracy and the rule of rights. But that respect is diminishing. Political parties have defined their identity in terms of defeating the other on every issue, trapping themselves in a one-dimensional world. Their identity should be defined first by being American and then, secondarily, by their belief in a particular ideology—if they wish.

Because of the excesses of the Trump administration, many observers associate threats to liberal, democratic order with the Republican party. Certainly, the party did close to nothing to stop the dangers posed by Trump. Yet among Democrats there are similar threats, which will likely surface as individual groups that formed the coalition that defeated Trump exert pressure to impose a narrowly conceived social order. Historically, the inclination toward authoritarian and one-dimensional regimes is not confined to the right.

What is needed now is the formation of blocs inside each party aimed at keeping the country united, which should seek shared decisions and policies to attain this objective. Keep the United States united, or something to this effect, must be a bipartisan slogan. Those who inject hatred must be pushed to the edges of society, which is where they belong in accordance with their numbers.

If nothing of the sort is done, divisiveness will worsen. The current two-sided division is unlikely to remain as is. The two main blocs are likely to split into smaller blocs, and these into even smaller ones as internal party conflicts expose differences. Such a pattern would accelerate the risk of chaos and weaken defenders of liberal democracy, support of which needs to be a central objective cutting across all political parties.

Certainly, the country needs to address the issue of racism, the cause of much national tension. Yet what is at stake in the diffuse conflicts now besieging the country goes beyond race. The United States and the rest of the world are facing a fundamental choice between liberal democracy and some form of illiberal regime that, by definition, would be tyrannical. All issues must be seen within this framework. No solution to the world's problems will be permanent if it is imposed by one half of the population on the other half. Imposition is inimical to liberal democracy.

THE CRUX OF THE MATTER

My constant theme in this book has been that liberal democracy must be reasserted and that such reassertion will not happen automatically. The will to sustain it must be reawakened. And the institutional setting must be adapted to the new relationships of a more connected world. In order to be defended successfully, liberal democracy must evolve to channel the relationships of a society based on knowledge networks.

The task of the Founding Fathers is not finished. As the historian Joseph Ellis has written of them:

> They could imagine a nation-size republic, which nobody else had ever done before.
> They could imagine the separation of church and state, which nobody else had ever done before.
> They could imagine a government based on checks and balances that prohibit any form of dictatorship at the presidential level. Nobody had ever done that before.
> They could imagine power flowing from the people upwards, rather than from God downward.
> All those unbelievable acts of imagination. The most creative political group in American history. We'll never replicate that.
> But they could not imagine a biracial society.[283]

We have imagined a multicultural society, but we still haven't learned to make it work. Racial tribalism continues to afflict the world. Racism and discrimination against the "other" (racially, religiously, or culturally) are observable in all societies—developed, developing, underdeveloped. Genocides have taken place all over the world and at all times. Yet technology and social, economic, and political events are pushing us all closer to each other. This is the great challenge of today. The greatness of the Founding Fathers is that, even if they were thinking only of their own tribe, and even if some of them, as slave owners, were hypocritical, they, along with many others in other countries, invented the only vehicle, liberal democracy, that can help us to deal in a humane way with the complex interrelationships brought about by connectivity and globalization. That was their great accomplishment. Now it is our turn to make sure that achievement is sustained. It is our 1776 moment.

BIBLIOGRAPHY

Abramovitz, Alan I. *The Disappearing Center: Engaged Citizens, Polarization and American Democracy*. New Haven, CT: Yale University Press, 2010.

Acemoglu, Daron, and James A. Robinson. *Why Nations Fail: The Origins of Power, Prosperity, and Poverty*. New York: Crown, 2012.

Addison, Paul. *No Turning Back: The Peacetime Revolution of Post-War Britain*. Oxford: Oxford University Press, 2010.

Aganbegyan, Abel. *Inside Perestroika: The Future of the Soviet Economy*. New York: Harper and Row, 1990.

Alexievich, Svetlana. *Secondhand Time: The Last of the Soviets, an Oral History*. New York: Random House, 2016.

Allen, Robert C. *The British Industrial Revolution in Global Perspective*. Cambridge: Cambridge University Press, 2009.

Applebaum, Anne. *Gulag: A History*. London: Penguin, 2003.

Applebaum, Anne. *Red Famine: Stalin's War on Ukraine*. New York: Anchor Books, 2018.

Arendt, Hannah. *The Origins of Totalitarianism*. New York: Harcourt Brace Jovanovich, 1973 [1948].

Arnot, Bob. *Controlling Soviet Labor: Experimental Change from Brezhnev to Gorbachev*. Armonk, New York: M. E. Sharpe, 1988.

Aron, Raymond. *The Opium of the Intellectuals*. New Brunswick, NJ: Transaction, 2009 [1955].

Aslund, Anders. *Gorbachev's Struggle for Economic Reform*. Ithaca, NY: Cornell University Press, 1989.

Baldwin, Richard. *The Great Convergence: Information Technology and the New Globalization*. Cambridge, MA: Harvard University Press, 2016.

Banfield, Edward C. *The Moral Basis of a Backward Society*. New York: Free Press, 1958.

Bankier, David. *The Germans and the Final Solution: Public Opinion under Nazism*. Oxford: Blackwell, 1996.

Barraclough, Geoffrey. *The Origins of Modern Germany*. New York: W. W. Norton & Co., 1984.

Beckert, Jens. *Imagined Futures: Fictional Expectations and Capitalism Dynamics*. Cambridge, MA: Harvard University Press, 2016.

Bernanke, Ben S. *Essays on the Great Depression*. Princeton, NJ: Princeton University Press, 2000.

Bernstein, Michael A. *The Great Depression: Delayed Recovery and Economic Change in America, 1929–1939*. Cambridge: Cambridge University Press, 1987.

Bingham, Tom. *The Rule of Law*. London: Allen Lane, 2010.

Blackbourn, David. *History of Germany, 1780–1918: The Long Nineteenth Century*. Oxford: Blackwell Publishing, 2003.

Blackbourn, David, and Geoff Eley. *The Peculiarities of German History: Bourgeois Society and Politics in Nineteenth Century Germany*. Oxford: Oxford University Press, 1984.

Borgese, G. A. *Goliath: The March of Fascism*. New York: Viking Press, 1938. Reprinted by Kessinger Legacy Reprints.

Buckley, F. H. *The Once and Future King: The Rise of Crown Government in America*. New York: Encounter Books, 2014.

Bullock, Alan. *Hitler and Stalin: Parallel Lives*. New York: Alfred A. Knopf, 1992.

Bullock, Alan. *Hitler: A Study in Tyranny*. New York: Harper Perennial, 1962.

Burke, Edmund. *Reflections on the Revolution in France*. Indianapolis, IN: Hackett Publishing Company, 1987.

Burleigh, Thomas. *The Third Reich: A New History*. New York: Hill and Wang, 2000.

Burnham, James. *The Machiavellians: Defenders of Freedom: A Defense of Political Truth against Wishful Thinking*. Washington, DC: Gateway Editions, 1943.

Bryce, James Viscount. *Modern Democracies*. New York: MacMillan, 1921. Kindle.

Cannadine, David. *The Decline and Fall of the British Aristocracy*. New Haven, CT: Yale University Press, 1990.

Carney, Timothy. *Alienated America: Why Some Places Thrive while Others Collapse*. New York: Harper, 2019.

Cashman, Sean Dennis. *America in the Gilded Age: America from the Death of Lincoln to the Rise of Theodore Roosevelt*. 3rd ed. New York: New York University Press, 1993. Kindle.

Chandler, Alfred D. *The Visible Hand: The Managerial Revolution in American Business*. Cambridge, MA: Harvard University Press, 1977. Kindle.

Chartier, Roger. *The Cultural Origins of the French Revolution*. Durham, NC: Duke University Press, 1991.

Clark, Christopher. *Iron Kingdom: The Rise and Downfall of Prussia, 1600–1947*. London: Penguin, 2007.

Clark, Christopher. *Sleepwalkers: How Europe Went to War in 1914*. London: Penguin, 2012.

Clark, Gregory. *A Farewell to Alms: A Brief Economic History of the World*. Princeton, NJ: Princeton University Press, 2007.

Clark, Ronald W. *Lenin: A Biography*. New York: Harper and Row, 1990.

Clover, Charles. *Black Wind, White Snow: The Rise of Russia's New Nationalism*. New Haven, CT: Yale University Press, 2016.

Cohen, Stephen F. *Bukharin and the Bolshevik Revolution: A Political Biography, 1888–1938*. New York: Oxford University Press, 1980.

Conquest, Robert. *The Great Terror: A Reassessment*. New York: Oxford University Press, 2008 [1990].

Conquest, Robert. *The Harvest of Sorrow: Soviet Collectivization and the Terror-Famine*. New York: Oxford University Press, 1986.

Courtois, Stéphane, Nicolas Werth, Jean-Louis Panné, Andrzej Paczkowski, Karel Bartosek, and Jean-Louis Margolin. *The Black Book of Communism: Crimes, Terror, Repression*. Cambridge, MA: Harvard University Press, 1999.

Dangerfield, George. *The Strange Death of Liberal England*. Stanford, CA: Stanford University Press, 1997 [1935].

Davies, R. W. *The Soviet Collective Farm, 1929–1930*. London: Macmillan, 1980.

Davies, R. W. *The Soviet Economy in Turmoil, 1929–1930*. Cambridge, MA: Harvard University Press, 1989.

Davies, R. W., ed. *From Tsarism to the New Economic Policy: Continuity and Change in the Economy of the USSR*. Ithaca, NY: Cornell University Press, 1990.

De Filippi, Primavera, and Aaron Wright. *Blockchain and the Law: The Rule of Code*. Cambridge, MA: Harvard University Press, 2018.

d'Encausse, Hélène Carrère. *Lenin: Revolution and Power*. London: Longman, 1982.

d'Encausse, Hélène Carrère. *Stalin: Order through Terror*. London: Longman, 1981.

Doder, Dusko. *Shadows and Whispers: Power Politics inside the Kremlin from Brezhnev to Gorbachev*. New York: Penguin, 1988.

Dolot, Miron. *Execution by Hunger: The Hidden Holocaust*. New York: W. W. Norton, 1987.

Durant, Will. *The Life of Greece: The Story of Civilization, Part II.* New York: Simon and Schuster, 1966 [1939].

Eichengreen, Barry. *Golden Fetters: The Gold Standard and the Great Depression, 1919–1939.* New York: Oxford University Press, 1995.

Ellis, Joseph J. *American Sphinx: The Character of Thomas Jefferson.* New York: Vintage, 1996.

Ellis, Joseph J. *Founding Brothers: The Revolutionary Generation.* New York: Vintage, 2000.

Ferguson, Niall. *Empire: The Rise and Demise of the British World Order and Lessons for Global Power.* New York: Basic Books, 2002.

Fischer, Fritz. *Germany's Aims in the First World War.* New York: W. W. Norton, 1967 [1961].

Ford, Martin. *Rise of the Robots: Technology and the Threat of a Jobless Future.* New York: Basic Books, 2015.

Frankl, Victor. *Man's Search for Meaning.* Boston: Beacon Press, 2006 [1959]. Kindle.

Fraser, Antonia. *Perilous Question: Reform or Revolution? Britain on the Brink, 1832.* New York: Public Affairs, 2013.

Fried, Johannes. *The Middle Ages.* Cambridge, MA: Harvard University Press, 2015. Kindle.

Fritz, Stephen G. *Ostkrieg: Hitler's War of Extermination in the East.* Lexington, KY: University Press of Kentucky, 2011. Kindle.

Fritzsche, Peter. *Germans into Nazis.* Cambridge, MA: Harvard University Press, 1998.

Galli, Carlo. *Janus's Gaze: Essays on Carl Schmitt.* Durham, NC: Duke University Press, 2015.

Gatrell, Peter. *The Tsarist Economy, 1850–1917.* London: Batsford, 1986.

Girard, René. *Violence and the Sacred.* New York: Continuum, 2005 [1972].

Gorbachev, Mikhail. *Perestroika: New Thinking for Our Country and the World.* New York: Harper and Row, 1988.

Gordon, Robert J. *The Rise and Fall of American Growth: The U.S. Standard of Living since the Civil War.* Princeton, NJ: Princeton University Press, 2016.

Haffner, Sebastian. *The Ailing Empire: Germany from Bismarck to Hitler.* New York: Fromm International Publishing Corporation, 1989.

Hayek, F. A. *The Collected Works of Friedrich August Hayek.* Vol. 1, *The Fatal Conceit: The Errors of Socialism.* London: Routledge, 1992.

Hayek, F. A. *The Constitution of Liberty*. Chicago: University of Chicago Press, 1960.

Hayek, F. A. *The Road to Serfdom*. Chicago: University of Chicago Press, 2007 [1944].

Heiber, Helmut. *The Weimar Republic*. Oxford: Blackwell, 1993.

Heiden, Konrad. *The Fuhrer*. Edison, NJ: Castle Books, 2002 [1944].

Heiden, Konrad. *The New Inquisition*. New York: Starling Press and Alliance Book Corporation, 1939.

Hidalgo, Cesar. *Why Information Grows: The Evolution of Order, from Atoms to Economies*. New York: Basic Books, 2015. Kindle.

Hilberg, Raul. *The Destruction of the European Jews*. New York: Holmes and Meier, 1985.

Hilberg, Raul. *Perpetrators, Victims, Bystanders: The Jewish Catastrophe, 1933–1945*. New York: Harper Perennial, 1992.

Hillman, Arye. *Markets and Politicians: Politicized Economic Choice*. Boston: Kluwer Academic Publishers, 1991.

Hillman, Arye, and Branko Milanovic. *The Transition from Socialism in Eastern Europe: Domestic Restructuring and Foreign Trade*. Washington, DC: World Bank, 1992.

Hinds, Manuel. *Issues in the Introduction of Market Forces in Eastern Europe*. Washington, DC: World Bank, 1990. http://documents.worldbank.org/curated/en/723021468915008930/Issues-in-the-introduction-of-market-forces-in-Eastern-European-socialist-economies.

Hinds, Manuel. "Markets and Ownership in Socialist Countries in Transition." In *Markets and Politicians: Politicized Economic Choice*, edited by Arye Hillman, 137–168. Boston: Kluwer Academic Publishers, 1991.

Hinds, Manuel. "Policies to Overcome the Transformation Crisis: The Case of Russia." In *Overcoming the Transformation Crisis: Lessons for the Successor States of the Soviet Union*, edited by Horst Siebert, 285–304. Tübingen: J. C. B. Mohr, 1993.

Hinds, Manuel. "Policy Effectiveness in Reforming Socialist Economies." In *The Transition from Socialism in Eastern Europe: Domestic Restructuring and Foreign Trade*, edited by Arye Hillman and Branko Milanovic, 13–39. Washington, DC: World Bank, 1992.

Hinds, Manuel. *The Triumph of the Flexible Society: The Connectivity Revolution and Resistance to Change*. Westport, CT: Praeger, 2003.

Hitler, Adolf. *Mein Kampf*. London: Hurst and Blackett, 1939.

Hofstadter, Richard. *The Age of Reform: From Bryan to F.D.R.* New York: Vintage, 1955. Kindle.

Huff, Toby E. *Intellectual Curiosity and the Scientific Revolution: A Global Perspective.* Cambridge: Cambridge University Press, 2003.

Hunt, Tristram. *Ten Cities That Made an Empire.* London: Allen Lane, 2014.

Johnson, Paul. *A History of the American People.* New York: HarperCollins, 1997.

Johnson, Simon, and James Kwak. *13 Bankers: The Wall Street Takeover and the Next Financial Meltdown.* New York: Vintage, 2010.

Jones, Ronald W. *Globalization and the Theory of Input Trade.* Cambridge, MA: MIT Press, 2000.

Judson, Pieter. *The Habsburg Empire: A New History.* Cambridge, MA: Harvard University Press, 2016.

Kagan, Robert. *The Jungle Grows Back: America and Our Imperiled World.* New York: Alfred A. Knopf, 2018.

Kagan, Robert. "The Strongmen Strike Back." *Washington Post*, March 14, 2019.

Kay, John. *Obliquity: Why Our Goals Are Best Achieved Indirectly.* New York: Penguin, 2011.

Keegan, John. *The First World War.* New York: Random House, 1998.

Kennedy, Ellen. *Constitutional Failure: Carl Schmitt in Weimar.* Durham, NC: Duke University Press, 2004. Kindle.

Kershaw, Ian. *The End: The Defiance and Destruction of Hitler's Germany, 1944–1945.* New York: Penguin, 2011.

Kershaw, Ian. *To Hell and Back: Europe 1914–1949.* New York: Viking, 2015.

Kershaw, Ian. *Hitler: 1989–1936 Hubris.* New York: Norton, 1998.

Kershaw, Ian. *The "Hitler Myth": Image and Reality in the Third Reich.* Oxford: Oxford University Press, 1987.

Keynes, John Maynard. *The General Theory of Employment, Interest, and Money.* New York: Harcourt, Brace & World, Inc., 1964 [1936].

Khrushchev, Nikita. *Khrushchev Remembers: The Glasnost Tapes.* New York: Little Brown and Co., 1990.

Kindleberger, Charles. *The World in Depression, 1929–1939.* Berkeley: University of California Press, 1986.

Kotkin, Stephen. *Stalin: Waiting for Hitler, 1929–1941.* New York: Penguin, 2018.

Kotkin, Stephen. *Steeltown, USSR: Soviet Society in the Gorbachev Era*. Berkeley: University of California Press, 1991.

Kuromiya, Hiroaki. *Stalin's Industrial Revolution: Politics and Workers, 1928–1932*. Cambridge: Cambridge University Press, 1990.

Kuznets, Simon. "Economic Growth and Income Inequality." *American Economic Review*, 45, no. 1 (March 1955): 1–28.

Landes, David. *The Unbound Prometheus: Technological Change and Industrial Development in Western Europe from 1750 to the Present*. Cambridge: Cambridge University Press, 1969.

Landes, David. *The Wealth and Poverty of Nations*. New York: W. W. Norton, 1998.

Laqueur, Walter. *Stalin: The Glasnost Revelations*. New York: Scribner, 1990.

Lefebvre, Georges. *The Coming of the French Revolution*. Princeton, NJ: Princeton University Press, 1989.

Lenin, Vladimir Ilyich, *The Lenin Anthology*, edited by Robert C. Tucker. New York: W. W. Norton, 1975.

Levy, Leonard W. *Jefferson and Civil Liberties: The Darker Side*. Chicago: Elephant Paperbacks, 1963.

Lincoln, W. Bruce. *The Great Reforms: Autocracy, Bureaucracy, and the Politics of Change in Imperial Russia*. Dekalb, IL: Northern Illinois University Press, 1990.

Lincoln, W. Bruce. *The Romanovs: Autocrats of All the Russias*. New York: Anchor Books, 1981.

Lincoln, W. Bruce. *In the Vanguard of Reform: Russia's Enlightened Bureaucrats, 1825–1861*. Dekalb, IL: Northern Illinois University Press, 1982.

Lindberg, David C. *The Beginnings of Western Science: The European Scientific Tradition in Philosophical, Religious, and Institutional Context, Prehistory to A.D. 1450*, 2nd ed. Chicago: University of Chicago Press, 2007.

Lucas, Robert E., Jr. *Lectures on Economic Growth*. Cambridge, MA: Harvard University Press, 2002.

Luce, Edward. *The Retreat of Western Liberalism*. London: Little, Brown, and Co., 2017.

Lukianoff, Greg, and Jonathan Haidt. *The Coddling of the American Mind: How Good Intentions and Bad Ideas Are Setting Up a Generation for Failure*. New York: Penguin, 2018.

Madariaga, Isabel de. *Russia in the Age of Catherine the Great*. New Haven, CT: Yale University Press, 1981.

Magnusson, Lars. *An Economic History of Sweden*. London: Routledge, 2000.

Marquand, David. *Britain since 1918: The Strange Career of British Democracy*. London: Weidenfeld & Nicolson, 2008.

Mason, Paul. *Post-Capitalism: A Guide to Our Future*. New York: Penguin, 2015. Kindle.

Mathias, Peter. *The First Industrial Nation: An Economic History of Britain, 1700–1914*. London: Methuen & Co. Ltd., 1969.

Mayer, Arno. *The Persistence of the Old Regime: Europe to the Great War*. New York: Pantheon Books, 1981.

Mayer, Milton. *They Thought They Were Free: The Germans, 1933–45*. Chicago: University of Chicago Press, 1955.

Mazower, Mark. *Dark Continent: Europe's Twentieth Century*. New York: Alfred A. Knopf, 1999.

Medvedev, Roy. *Let History Judge: The Origins and Consequences of Stalinism*. New York: Columbia University Press, 1989.

Milanovic, Branko. *Worlds Apart: Measuring International and Global Inequality*. Princeton, NJ: Princeton University Press, 2011. Kindle.

Mill, John Stuart. *Considerations on Representative Government*. Amherst, NY: Prometheus Books, 1991 [1861].

Mishra, Pankaj. *Age of Anger: A History of the Present*. New York: Farrar, Straus and Giroux, 2017.

Mokyr, Joel. *The Enlightened Economy: Britain and the Industrial Revolution 1700–1850*. New York: Penguin, 2011 [2009]. Kindle.

Mombauer, Anikka. *The Origins of the First World War: Controversies and Consensus*. London: Routledge, 2013 [2002]. Kindle.

Murray, Charles, *Coming Apart: The State of White America, 1960–2010*. New York: Crown Forum, 2013. Kindle.

Mussolini, Benito. *My Rise and Fall*. New York: Da Capo Press, 1998.

Norman, Kajsa. *Sweden's Dark Soul: The Unraveling of a Utopia*. London: Hurst & Company, 2018.

North, Douglas. *Institutions, Institutional Change and Economic Performance*. Cambridge: Cambridge University Press, 1990.

North, Douglas. *Structure and Change in Economic History*. New York: W.W. Norton & Co., 1981.

North, Douglas, and Robert Paul Thomas. *The Rise of the Western World: A New Economic History*. Cambridge: Cambridge University Press, 1973.

North, Douglas, and Barry R. Weingast. "Constitutions and Commitment: The Evolution of Institutional Governing Public Choice in Seventeenth Century England." *The Journal of Economic History*, 49, no. 4 (December 1989): 803–832.

Nove, Alec. *An Economic History of the Soviet Union*. London: Penguin, 1989.

Oxenstierna, Susanne. *From Labour Shortage to Unemployment?: The Soviet Labour Market in the 1980s*. Stockholm: University of Stockholm, 1990.

Palmer, R. R. *Twelve Who Ruled: The Year of Terror in the French Republic*. Princeton, NJ: Princeton University Press, 2005 [1941]. Kindle.

Parente, Stephen L., and Edward C. Prescott. *Barriers to Riches*. Cambridge, MA: MIT Press, 2000.

Piketty, Thomas. *Capital in the Twenty-First Century*. Cambridge, MA: Harvard University Press, 2014. Kindle.

Pipes, Richard. *The Russian Revolution*. New York: Alfred A. Knopf, 1990.

Pipes, Richard. *Russia under the Old Regime*. New York: Charles Scribner's Sons, 1974.

Prigogine, Ilya, and Isabelle Stengers. *Order Out of Chaos: Man's New Dialogue with Nature*. New York: Bantam Books, 1984.

Putnam, Robert D. *Bowling Alone: The Collapse and Revival of American Community*. New York: Simon & Schuster, 2000.

Putnam, Robert D. *Our Kids: The American Dream in Crisis*. New York: Simon & Schuster, 2015. Kindle.

Rajan, Raghuram G. *Fault Lines: How Hidden Fractures Still Threaten the World Economy*. Princeton, NJ: Princeton University Press, 2010.

Rawls, John. *A Theory of Justice*. Cambridge, MA: Belknap, 1999 [1971].

Rawls, John. *Political Liberalism*. New York: Columbia University Press, 1993. Kindle.

Renwick, Chris. *Bread for All: The Origins of the Welfare State*. London: Allen Lane, 2017.

Riemen, Rob. *To Fight against This Age: On Fascism and Humanism*. New York: W. W. Norton & Company, 2018. Kindle.

Röhl, John C. G. *Kaiser Wilhelm II, 1859–1941: A Concise Life*. Cambridge: Cambridge University Press, 2014.

Rosenfeld, Sam. *The Polarizers: Postwar Architects of Our Partisan Era.* Chicago: University of Chicago Press, 2017.

Runciman, David. *How Democracy Ends.* New York: Basic Books, 2018.

Sabine, George H. *A History of Political Theory.* New York: Holt, Rinehart and Winston, 1961 [1937].

Sacks, Jonathan. *Not in God's Name: Confronting Religious Violence.* London: Hodder & Stoughton, 2015.

Salisbury, Harrison E. *Black Night, White Snow: Russia's Revolutions 1905–1917.* New York: Da Capo Press, 1977.

Sanandaji, Nima. *Debunking Utopia: Exposing the Myth of Nordic Socialism.* Washington, DC: WND Books, 2016.

Schall, Carly Elizabeth. *The Rise and Fall of the Miraculous Welfare Machine: Immigration and Social Democracy in Twentieth-Century Sweden.* Ithaca, NY: Cornell University Press, 2016.

Schama, Simon. *Citizens: A Chronicle of the French Revolution.* New York: Vintage Books, 1990.

Schlesinger, Arthur M. *The Age of Jackson.* New York: Little, Brown and Co., 1945.

Schlesinger, Arthur M. *The Coming of the New Deal: 1933–1935, The Age of Roosevelt, Volume II.* New York: Houghton Mifflin, 2003 [1958].

Schlesinger, Arthur M. *The Crisis of the Old Order: 1919–1933, The Age of Roosevelt, Volume I.* New York: Houghton Mifflin, 2003 [1957].

Schlesinger, Arthur M. *The Politics of Upheaval: 1935–1936, The Age of Roosevelt: Volume III.* New York: Houghton Mifflin, 2003 [1960].

Schmidt, Carl T. *The Corporate State in Action: Italy under Fascism.* Oxford: Oxford University Press, 1939. Kindle.

Schmitt, Carl. *The Concept of the Political.* Expanded ed. Chicago: University of Chicago Press, 2007 [1932]. Kindle.

Schmitt, Carl. *Constitutional Theory.* Durham, NC: Duke University Press, 2008 [1928]. Kindle.

Schmitt, Carl. *The Crisis of Parliamentary Democracy.* Cambridge, MA: MIT Press, 2001 [1923].

Schmitt, Carl. *Dictatorship.* Cambridge: Polity Press, 2014 [1921]. Kindle.

Schmitt, Carl. *Land and Sea: A World Historical Meditation.* Candor, NY: Telos Press Publishing, 2015 [1942]. Kindle.

Schmitt, Carl. *Legality and Legitimacy*. Durham, NC: Duke University Press, 2004 [1932]. Kindle.

Schmitt, Carl. *Political Romanticism*. Cambridge, MA: MIT Press, 2001 [1919].

Schmitt, Carl. *Political Theology: Four Chapters on the Concept of Sovereignty*. Chicago: University of Chicago Press, 2005 [1922].

Schulze, Hagen. *The Course of German Nationalism: From Frederick the Great to Bismarck, 1763–1867*. Cambridge: Cambridge University Press, 1991.

Schumpeter, Joseph. *Business Cycles: A Theoretical, Historical and Statistical Analysis of the Capitalist Process*, 2 Vols. Philadelphia: Porcupine Press, 1989 [1939].

Schumpeter, Joseph A. *Capitalism, Socialism and Democracy*. New York: Harper Torchbooks, 1975 [1942].

Scruton, Roger. *Conservatism*. London: Profile Books, 2017.

Scurr, Ruth. *Fatal Purity: Robespierre and the French Revolution*. New York: Metropolitan Books, 2006.

Sellars, John, ed. *The Routledge Handbook of the Stoic Tradition*. Abingdon-on-Thames: Routledge, 2016. Kindle.

Seymour, Richard. *The Twittering Machine*. London: Indigo Press, 2019.

Shirer, William. *The Rise and Fall of the Third Reich: A History of Nazi Germany*. New York: Fawcett Crest, 1983.

Shlaes, Amity. *Coolidge*. New York: Harper Perennial, 2013.

Shlaes, Amity. *The Forgotten Man: A New History of the Great Depression*. New York: Harper Collins Publishers, 2007.

Smith, Hedrick. *The New Russians*. New York: Random House, 1990. Kindle.

Smith, Hedrick. *The Russians*. New York: Ballantine Books, 1976.

Smith, Vernon L., and Bart J. Wilson. *Humanomics: Moral Sentiments and the Wealth of Nations for the Twenty-First Century*. Cambridge, MA: Cambridge University Press, 2019.

Stiglitz, Joseph E. *The Price of Inequality: How Today's Divided Society Endangers Our Future*. New York: W. W. Norton & Company, 2012.

Strachey, John. *The End of Empire*. London: Victor Gollancz Ltd, 1961.

Streeck, Wolfgang. *How Will Capitalism End?: Essays on a Failing System*. London: Verso, 2016. Kindle.

Theriault, Sean M. *The Gingrich Senators: The Role of Partisan Warfare in Congress*. New York: Oxford University Press, 2013.

Tocqueville, Alexis de. *The Ancien Régime and the French Revolution.* London: Penguin, 2008 [1856]. Kindle.

Tocqueville, Alexis de. *Democracy in America.* Toronto: HarperCollins, 2014. Kindle.

Tooze, Adam. *Crashed: How a Decade of Financial Crises Changed the World.* New York: Viking, 2018.

Toynbee, Arnold. *A Study of History.* Abridgement in two volumes by D. C. Somervell. New York: Oxford University Press, 1957.

Tucker, Robert C. *The Marx-Engels Reader.* New York: W. W. Norton and Company, 1978.

Tucker, Robert C. *Stalin as Revolutionary: A Study in History and Personality.* New York: W. W. Norton and Company, 1974.

Tucker, Robert C. *Stalin in Power: The Revolution from Above, 1928–1941.* New York: W. W. Norton and Company, 1990.

Turner, Henry Ashby, Jr. *German Big Business and the Rise of Hitler.* New York: Oxford University Press, 1985.

Van Zanden, J. L. "Tracing the Beginning of the Kuznets Curve: Western Europe during the Early Modern Period." *Economic History Review*, 48, no. 4 (1995): 643–664.

Wallerstein, Immanuel, Randall Collins, Michael Mann, Georgie Derluguian, and Craig Calhoun. *Does Capitalism Have a Future?* New York: Oxford University Press, 2013. Kindle.

Wiener, Norbert. *Cybernetics: Or Control and Communication in the Animal and the Machine.* Cambridge, MA: MIT Press, 1961 [1948].

Wiener, Norbert. *The Human Use of Human Beings: Cybernetics and Society.* London: Free Association Books, 1989 [1950].

Wilkerson, Isabel. *The Warmth of Other Suns: The Epic Story of America's Great Migration.* New York: Vintage, 2010.

Witoszek, Nina, and Lars Tragardh, eds. *Culture and Crisis: The Case of Germany and Sweden.* New York: Berghahn Books, 2002.

Wood, Gordon S. *The Radicalism of the American Revolution.* New York: Vintage, 1993.

ENDNOTES

1. Letter from John Adams to John Whitney, June 7, 1826, https://founders. archives.gov/documents/Adams/99-02-02-8023.

2. Quoted by Amity Shlaes, *The Forgotten Man: A New History of the Great Depression* (New York: Harper Collins Publishers, 2007), 341.

3. John Maynard Keynes, *The Tract on Monetary Reform* (London: MacMillan and Co., 1924), http://delong.typepad.com/keynes-1923-a-tract-on-monetary-reform.pdf.

4. See Michael Pearson, *The Sealed Train* (New York: Putnam, 1975), 62.

5. Stéphane Courtois, Nicolas Werth, Jean-Louise Panné, Andrzej Paczkowski, Karel Bartosek, and Jean-Louis Margolin, *The Black Book of Communism: Crimes, Terror, Repression* (Cambridge, MA: Harvard University Press, 1999), 4–14.

6. See "Would-be autocrats are using covid-19 as an excuse to grab power," *Economist,* April 23, 2020, https://www.economist.com/international/2020/04/23/would-be-autocrats-are-using-covid-19-as-an-excuse-to-grab-more-power.

7. Klaus Schwab, *The Fourth Industrial Revolution* (Cologny: World Economic Forum, 2016).

8. John Rawls, *Political Liberalism,* expanded ed. (New York: Columbia University Press, 2011), 164–175, Kindle.

9. A Georgetown University poll found that, asked how close the country is to the "edge of civil war"—with 0 being not close at all and 100 being time to get the "go bag"—the average response was 67.3. See Adam K. Raymond, "How Close Is the U.S. to Civl War?," *Intelligencer, New York Magazine,* October 24, 2019, https://nymag.com/intelligencer/2019/10/americans-say-u-s-is-two-thirds-of-the-way-to-civil-war.html. See also Robin Wright, "Is America Headed for a New Kind of Civil War?", *New Yorker,* August 14, 2017, https://www.newyorker.com/news/news-desk/is-america-headed-for-a-new-kind-of-civil-war.

10. See Dan Roberts and Ryan Felton, "Trump and Clinton's Free Trade Retreat: A Pivotal Moment for the World's Economic Future," *Guardian,* August 20, 2016; and Shawn Donnan, "Hillary Clinton's Awkward History on Trade Policy," *Financial Times,* September 28, 2016.

11. See Charles P. Kindleberger, *The World in Depression, 1929–1939* (Berkeley: University of California Press, 1986 [1973]); and Douglas A. Irwin, *Clashing*

Over Commerce: A History of US Trade Policy (Chicago: University of Chicago Press, 2017).

12. See Primavera De Filippi and Aaron Wright, *Blockchain and the Law: The Rule of Code* (Cambridge, MA: Harvard University Press, 2018).

13. Robert Kagan, *The Jungle Grows Back: America and Our Imperiled World* (New York: Alfred A. Knopf, 2018), loc. 379, Kindle.

14. Stefan Zweig, *The World of Yesterday* (Lincoln: University of Nebraska Press, 1963 [1943]), 1–4.

15. Jonathan Rauch, "How American Politics Became So Insane," *Atlantic,* July/August 2016, http://www.theatlantic.com/magazine/archive/2016/07/how-american-politics-went-insane/485570/.

16. Peggy Noonan, "That Moment When 2016 Hits You," *Wall Street Journal,* April 21, 2016, http://www.wsj.com/articles/that-moment-when-2016-hits-you-1461281849?tesla=y.

17. Walter Lippmann, *A New Social Order* (New York: John Day Pamphlets, 1933).

18. Wolfgang Streeck, *How Will Capitalism End?: Essays on a Failing System* (London: Verso, 2016), loc. 867–1294, Kindle.

19. Mark Mazower, "Ideas that Fed the Beast of Fascism Flourish Today: The Crisis of Political Institutions Provides Striking Parallels with the 1930s," *Financial Times,* November 6, 2016, https://www.ft.com/content/599fbbfc-a412-11e6-8898-79a99e2a4de6.

20. F. Cambó, *Les Dictadures* (Paris: Libraries Felix Alcan, 1930), 98, quoted in Mark Mazower, *Dark Continent: Europe's Twentieth Century* (New York: Alfred A. Knopf, 1999). Cambó's book was initially published in Catalan in the 1920s.

21. Emilio Gentile, "Fascism in Power: The Totalitarian Experiment," in *Liberal and Fascist Italy, Short Oxford History of Italy,* ed. Adrian Lyttelton (Oxford: Oxford University Press, 2002), loc. 1982–1985, Kindle.

22. Adolf Hitler, *Mein Kampf* (London: Hurst and Blackett, Ltd, 1939), 102.

23. Albert Speer, *Inside the Third Reich* (New York: Macmillan, 1970), 17.

24. Milton Mayer, *They Thought They Were Free: The Germans, 1933–45* (Chicago: University of Chicago Press, 2017 [1955]), loc. 1478, Kindle.

25. Rob Riemen, *To Fight against This Age: On Fascism and Humanism* (New York: W. W. Norton & Company, 2018), loc. 25–36, Kindle.

26. See David Frum, "The Great Republican Revolt," *Atlantic,* January/February 2016, http://www.theatlantic.com/magazine/archive/2016/01/the-great-republican-revolt/419118/.

27. "Fear, Anger and Hatred: The Rise of Germany's New Right," *Der Spiegel,* December 11, 2015, http://www.spiegel.de/international/germany/refugee-crisis-drives-rise-of-new-right-wing-in-germany-a-1067384.html.

28. Quoted in "Fear, Anger and Hatred: The Rise of Germany's New Right," *Der Spiegel,* December 11, 2015, http://www.spiegel.de/international/germany/refugee-crisis-drives-rise-of-new-right-wing-in-germany-a-1067384.html.

29. For an analysis of how populism is growing on both the left and the right in the United States, see Benjy Sarlin, *The United States of Trump,* NBC News, June 20, 2016, http://www.nbcnews.com/specials/donald-trump-republican-party.

30. Simon Schama, *Citizens: A Chronicle of the French Revolution* (New York: Vintage Books, 1990), 860.

31. Joseph A. Schumpeter, *Capitalism, Socialism and Democracy* (New York: Harper Torchbooks, 1975 [1942]).

32. Joseph E. Stiglitz, "Of the 1%, By the 1%, For the 1%," *Vanity Fair,* March 31, 2011, https://www.vanityfair.com/news/2011/05/top-one-percent-201105 and Joseph Stiglitz, *The Price of Inequality: How Today's Divided Society Endangers Our Future* (New York: W. W. Norton & Company, 2012).

33. John Van Reenen, "Increasing Differences between Firms: Market Power and the Macro-Economy," July 29, 2018, http://online.wsj.com/public/resources/documents/van_reenen_paper0824.pdf.

34. Kuznets estimated that income inequalities had widened from 1780 to 1850 in England; from 1870 on in the United States; and from the 1840s to the 1890s in Germany. He put the phase of narrowing inequality at about the last quarter of the nineteenth century for England and about World War I in the United States and Germany. See Simon Kuznets, "Economic Growth and Income Inequality," *American Economic Review,* 45, no. 1 (March 1955): 1–28.

35. International dollars have been adjusted to compensate for purchasing parity geographically and over time. A negative number means that the income of the relevant country is higher than that of the United Kingdom.

36. See Richard Baldwin, *The Great Convergence: Information Technology and the New Globalization* (Cambridge, MA: Harvard University Press, 2016), 54–63, Kindle; Robert E. Lucas Jr., "The Industrial Revolution: Past and Future" in his *Lectures on Economic Growth* (Cambridge, MA: Harvard University Press, 2002), 171–172.

37. Robert C. Allen, an Oxford professor, validated Kuznets's hypothesis with English data. He found that the output per worker went up faster than wages from 1800 to 1840, while in the next sixty years, to 1900, wages grew faster than output per worker. This increased inequality first and then decreased it, just as Kuznets had believed. Starting in 1900, another cycle developed, leading first to an increase in inequality and then to a decrease in such inequality. The existence of more than one cycle is explained by the emergence of two cycles of innovation during the industrial revolution. See R. C. Allen, "Engels' Pause: Technical Change, Capital Accumulation, and Inequality in the British Industrial Revolution," *Exploring Economic History* (2009), doi:10.1016/j.eeh.2009.04.004. In a 1995 paper, J. L. van Zanden validated Kuznets's hypothesis in various processes of innovation that took place between the late sixteenth and the twentieth century in many cities and regions in Europe. He found that, in all cases, there was an increase in inequality that was followed by an opposite increase in equality, exactly as Kuznets had predicted. See J. L. van Zanden, "Tracing the Beginning of the Kuznets Curve: Western Europe during the Early Modern Period," *Economic History Review,* 48, no. 4 (1995): 643–664.

38. See Thomas Piketty, *Capital in the Twenty-First Century* (Cambridge, MA: Harvard University Press. 2014), Kindle.

39. Thomas Piketty, *Capital in the Twenty-First Century* (Cambridge, MA: Harvard University Press. 2014), loc. 4562, Kindle.

40. "Forbes Billionaires: Full List of the 500 Richest People in the World 2016," *Forbes,* August 7, 2016, http://www.forbes.com/sites/kerenblankfeld/2016/03/01/forbes-billionaires-full-list-of-the-500-richest-people-in-the-world-2016/#5b9fdf146c24.

41. See Robert Watts, "The Rich List: At Last, the Self-Made Triumph over Old Money," *Sunday Times,* May 13, 2018, https://www.thetimes.co.uk/edition/news/sunday-times-rich-list-2018-at-last-the-self-made-triumph-over-old-money-0qx8tqvjp; Robert Watts, "30 Years of the Sunday Times Rich List: How Britain Has Changed," *Sunday Times,* May 6, 2018, https://www.thetimes.co.uk/edition/rich-list/sunday-times-rich-list-30-years-how-britain-has-changed-d8krmwps2.

42. David Autor, *Skills, Education, and the Rise of Earnings Inequality among the "Other 99%",* SNS Seminar, Stockholm, August 28, 2015,

https://hceconomics.uchicago.edu/sites/default/files/file_uploads/autor_2015
_presentation.pdf.

43. Schumpeter believed that creative destruction was the essential fact of
    capitalism because he thought that "[c]apitalism . . . is by nature a form
    or method of economic change and not only never is but never can be
    stationary." Joseph A. Schumpeter, *Capitalism, Socialism and Democracy*
    (New York: Harper Torchbooks, 1975 [1942]), loc. 1700–1714, Kindle.

44. Melissa S. Kearney, Brad Hershbein, and Elisa Jácome, "Profiles of
    Change: Employment, Earnings and Occupations from 1990–2013,"
    Hamilton Project, 2015, http://www.hamiltonproject.org/assets/legacy/
    files/downloads_and_links/Employment_Earnings_Occupations_
    Changes_1990-2013_FINAL_1.pdf.

45. "Working It: Across the Rich World, an Extraordinary Jobs Boom Is Under
    Way," *Economist,* May 23, 2019, https://www.economist.com/briefing/
    2019/05/23/across-the-rich-world-an-extraordinary-jobs-boom-is-
    under-way.

46. "Working It," *Economist.*

47. "Working It," *Economist.*

48. Michael A. Bernstein, *The Great Depression: Delayed Recovery and Economic
    Change in America, 1929–1939* (Cambridge: Cambridge University Press, 1987).

49. Data for the United States and Europe from United States Census, Histor-
    ical Poverty Tables, People, http://www.census.gov/hhes/www/poverty/
    data/historical/people.html.

50. In East Asia, poverty fell by 91.6 percent; in South Asia, it fell by 83.2
    percent; in Sub-Saharan Africa, by 8.8 percent; in Latin America, by 60.3
    percent; and in the Middle East and North Africa, by 46.2 percent. Maxim
    Pinkovsky and Xavier Sala-i-Martin, *Parametric Estimations of the World
    Distribution of Income,* Working Paper 15433, National Bureau of Economic
    Research, http://www.nber.org/papers/w15433.pdf.

51. See, for example, Matt Ridley, *The Rational Optimist: How Prosperity
    Evolves (P.S.),* (New York: HarperCollins, 2010); and Peter Diamantis and
    Steven Kotler, *Abundance: The Future Is Better than You Think* (New York:
    Free Press, 2012).

52. Time Staff, "Here's Donald Trump's Presidential Announcement Speech,"
    Time, June 16, 2015, https://time.com/3923128/donald-trump-
    announcement-speech/.

53. F. A. Hayek, *The Road to Serfdom* (Chicago: University of Chicago Press, 2007 [1944]), 61.

54. See Hannah Arendt, *The Origins of Totalitarianism* (New York: Harcourt Brace Jovanovich, 1973 [1948]); F. A. Hayek, "Chapter 12," in *The Road to Serfdom* (Chicago: University of Chicago Press, 2007 [1944]), 181–192; and "Susan Sontag Provokes Debate on Communism," *New York Times*, February 27, 1982, https://archive.nytimes.com/www.nytimes.com/books/00/03/12/specials/sontag-communism.html. The point is also discussed in many other serious books, including Stéphane Courtois, Nicolas Werth, Jean-Louis Panné, Andrzej Paczkowski, Karel Bartosek, and Jean-Louis Margolin, *The Black Book of Communism: Crimes, Terror, Repression* (Cambridge, MA: Harvard University Press, 1999).

55. Catherine the Great, quoted by Isabel de Madariaga, in *Russia in the Age of Catherine the Great* (New Haven, CT: Yale University Press, 1981), 580.

56. G. A. Borgese, *Goliath: The March of Fascism* (New York: Viking, 1938), reprinted by Kessinger Legacy Reprints, 479.

57. Quoted in Ian Kershaw, *The End: The Defiance and Destruction of Hitler's Germany, 1944–1945* (New York: Penguin, 2011), 9.

58. Alan Bullock, *Hitler: A Study in Tyranny*, abridged ed. (New York: Harper Perennial, 1992), 53.

59. Edmund Burke, *Reflections on the Revolution in France* (Indianapolis, IN: Hackett Publishing Company, 1987), 33.

60. Quoted in Robert D. Lachlin, *A New Chicago Edition of Schmitt's Seminal Work*, H-Net Reviews, October 2007, http://www.h-net.org/reviews/showpdf.php?id=13761. Schmitt also wrote several Nazi laws himself and produced several theories defending the legality and legitimacy of the Nazi regime.

61. Maunz stated this in "Gestalt und Recht der Polizei," quoted by Hannah Arendt, *Eichmann in Jerusalem: A Report on the Banality of Evil* (New York: Penguin, 2006, [1963]), loc. 726, Kindle.

62. Sophocles, *Antigone*, translated by R. C. Jebb, http://classics.mit.edu/Sophocles/antigone.html.

63. See George H. Sabine, *A History of Political Theory* (New York: Holt, Rinehart and Winston, 1961 [1937]), 597–617; and Will Durant, *The Story of Philosophy* (New York: Washington Square Press, 1926), 258.

64. A more modern version of Hume's skepticism is provided by postmodernism, a philosophical school born during the second part the twentieth century. Jacques Derrida thought that all texts conveyed hidden prejudices

that were slyly transferred to the reader or listener. For this reason, there is no absolute truth, only different perspectives of reality. Because of this, all texts should be "deconstructed" to understand the particular prejudices that they conceal. Michel Foucault thought that language is an instrument of power and therefore asserting that there is a specific truth is tantamount to an assertion of power. Thus, postmodernism challenges the idea of truth, much more than an absolute set of values. For a brief discussion of these ideas, see Lee McIntyre, *Post-Truth* (Cambridge, MA: MIT Press, 2018), loc. 1930–2230, Kindle.

65. Edward C. Banfield, *The Moral Basis of a Backward Society* (New York: Free Press, 1958), 19.

66. Banfield, *The Moral Basis of a Backward Society,* 17.

67. Robert D. Putnam, *Making Democracy Work: Civic Traditions in Modern Italy,* (Princeton, NJ: Princeton University Press, 1993), loc. 4257–4269, Kindle. Emphasis in original.

68. The discussion of the history of tsarist Russia is based primarily on Richard Pipes, *Russia under the Old Regime* (New York: Charles Scribner's Sons, 1974); W. Bruce Lincoln, *The Romanovs: Autocrats of All Russias* (New York: Anchor Books, 1981); and George Vernadsky, *A History of Russia,* 6th rev. ed. (New Haven, CT: Yale University Press, 1961).

69. The system under which Ivan Moneybags thrived, known as tax farming, also existed in some countries in Western Europe. Tax farmers collected the taxes in France, and some famous characters, such as the chemist Lavoisier, were among their ranks. Their illegitimacy in the eyes of the population was one of the causes of the revolution. They survived even longer in Italy. No Western tax farmer, however, enjoyed a monopoly such as the one granted to the Muscovite princes. Most important, they could not become the owners of the localities that did not pay their taxes.

70. Toby E. Huff, *The Rise of Early Modern Science: Islam, China and the West,* 2nd ed. (Cambridge: Cambridge University Press, 2003 [1993]), 251.

71. See Will and Ariel Durant, *Rousseau and Revolution* (New York: Simon & Schuster, 1967), 20–26.

72. See Durant, *Rousseau and Revolution,* 25.

73. There were some exceptions to this policy. The most important was the charter that the crown issued for trading with India.

74. See Schama, *Citizens,* 83–85; and Durant, *Rousseau and Revolution,* 858–859.

75. See Schama, *Citizens,* 85–86.

76. See Schama, *Citizens*, 87.

77. See Alexis de Tocqueville, *The Ancien Régime and the French Revolution* (New York: Penguin, 2008 [1856]).

78. See Tom Bingham, *The Rule of Law* (London: Allen Lane, 2010), 11–12.

79. Sir James Clarke Holt, quoted by Bingham, *The Rule of Law*, 12.

80. "Habeas Corpus Act 1679" *Wikipedia*, April 3, 2020, http://en.wikipedia. org/wiki/Habeas_Corpus_Act_1679.

81. "Magna Carta," *Wikipedia*, April 21, 2020, http://en.wikipedia.org/wiki/ Magna_Carta.

82. Bingham, *The Rule of Law*, 16.

83. Ron Harris, "Could the Crown Credibly Commit to Respect Its Charters?," in *Questioning Credible Commitment: Perspectives on the Rise of Financial Capitalism*, ed. D'Maris Coffman, Adrian Leonard, and Larry Neal (Cambridge: Cambridge University Press, 2013), loc. 1014-1025, Kindle.

84. See *"Case of Proclamations," Wikipedia*, February 5, 2020, http://en.wikipedia. org/wiki/Case_of_Proclamations#cite_note-bailii.org-3.

85. Bingham, *The Rule of Law*, 24.

86. See Antonia Fraser, *Perilous Question, Reform or Revolution?: Britain on the Brink, 1832* (New York: Public Affairs, 2013).

87. Walter F. Willcox, ed., "International Migrations," *National Bureau of Economic Research*, 1931, http://www.nber.org/chapters/c5108.pdf.

88. John Strachey, *The End of Empire*, 2nd ed. (London: Victor Gollancz Ltd., 1961), 40.

89. Walpole most likely overestimated the victims in 3 million. Modern calculations put them at 1.2 million. See Tristram Hunt, *Ten Cities That Made an Empire* (London: Allen Lane, 2014), 194.

90. See Hunt, *Ten Cities That Made an Empire*, 235–238.

91. Niall Ferguson, *Empire: The Rise and Demise of the British World Order and Lessons for Global Power* (New York: Basic Books, 2002), 277.

92. Quoted by Hunt, *Ten Cities That Made an Empire*, 195.

93. Ferguson, *Empire*, 278–284.

94. See Hannah Arendt, *The Origins of Totalitarianism* (New York: Harcourt Brace Jovanovich, 1973 [1948]).

95. Quoted by Alexis de Tocqueville, *The Ancien Régime and the Revolution* (New York: Penguin, 2008 [1856]), 23, Kindle.

96. Ian Kershaw, *The End: The Defiance and Destruction of Hitler's Germany, 1944–1945* (New York: Penguin, 2011), 400 (his emphasis).

97. Alexis de Tocqueville, *Democracy in America* (Toronto, Canada: HarperCollins, 2014), loc. 6413, Kindle.

98. de Tocqueville, *Democracy in America*, loc. 6456–6464.

99. de Tocqueville, *Democracy in America*, loc. 6109–6125.

100. Joseph J. Ellis, *American Sphinx: The Character of Thomas Jefferson* (New York: Random House, 1998), loc. 5282, Kindle.

101. Thomas Jefferson, *Notes on the State of Virginia* (Digireads.com, 2010, [1782]), loc. 3497, Kindle.

102. Jefferson, *Notes on the State of Virginia*, 3476.

103. Data on wealth estimated by Roger Ransom and Richard Sutch, quoted in Samuel H. Williamson and Louis P. Cain, "Measuring Slavery in 2016 Dollars," MeasuringWorth.com, http://www.measuringworth.com/slavery.php#text21.

104. Estimates by Ransom and Sutch, quoted in Williamson and Cain, "Measuring Slavery in 2016 Dollars."

105. Sean Dennis Cashman, *America in the Gilded Age: America from the Death of Lincoln to the Rise of Theodore Roosevelt*, 3rd ed. (New York: New York University Press, 1993), loc. 3941-4098, Kindle.

106. Abraham Lincoln, "House Divided Speech," *Abraham Lincoln Online.org*, http://www.abrahamlincolnonline.org/lincoln/speeches/house.htm.

107. Isabel Wilkerson, *The Warmth of Other Suns: The Epic Story of America's Great Migration* (New York: Vintage Books, 2011), loc. 262–270, Kindle.

108. For the migration and the conditions of life of African Americans in the South that prevailed in the years that preceded it, see Isabel Wilkerson, *The Warmth of Other Suns: The Epic Story of America's Great Migration* (New York: Vintage Books, 2011).

109. Paul Johnson, *A History of the American People* (New York: HarperCollins, 1997), 349.

110. Johnson, *A History of the American People*, 349.

111. Johnson, *A History of the American People*, 350–351.

112. Alexis de Tocqueville, *Democracy in America* (Toronto, Canada: HarperCollins, 2014), loc. 6110-6129, Kindle.

113. de Tocqueville, *Democracy in America*, loc. 6104.

114. C. Vann Woodward in *The National Experience* (1981), quoted in Sean Dennis Cashman, *America in the Gilded Age: America from the Death of Lincoln to the Rise of Theodore Roosevelt*, 3rd ed. (New York: New York University Press, 1993), loc. 5331, Kindle.

115. All quotations from Richard Hofstadter, *The Age of Reform: From Bryan to F.D.R.* (New York: Vintage, 1955), loc. 999–1251, Kindle.

116. Sean Dennis Cashman, *America in the Gilded Age: America from the Death of Lincoln to the Rise of Theodore Roosevelt*, 3rd ed. (New York: New York University Press, 1993), loc. 1012, Kindle.

117. Cashman, *America in the Gilded Age*, loc. 1092.

118. Cashman, *America in the Gilded Age,* loc. 1923.

119. Cashman, *America in the Gilded Age*, loc. 1943.

120. Ron Chernow, *Titan: The Life of John D. Rockefeller* (New York: Vintage, 2004), 439.

121. "McClure's Magazine," *Pressinamerica*, 2009, http://pressinamerica.pbworks.com/w/page/18360223/McClure%27s%20Magazine.

122. See Ida Tarbell, *All in the Day's Work* (New York: Macmillan, 1939), 280. Questia. https://www.questia.com/read/2891372/all-in-the-day-s-work-an-autobiography.

123. Ron Chernow, *The House of Morgan: An American Banking Dynasty and the Rise of Modern Finance* (New York: Grove Press, 1990), 130–132.

124. Chernow, *The House of Morgan,* 132.

125. The most important excerpts of the speech can be read at http://germanhistorydocs.ghi-dc.org/pdf/eng/1_C_NS_Bismarck.pdf.

126. David Blackbourn and Geoff Eley, *The Peculiarities of German History: Bourgeois Society and Politics in Nineteenth Century Germany* (Oxford: Oxford University Press, 1984), 108–109.

127. Ralf Dahrendorf, quoted in Henry Ashby Turner Jr., *German Big Business and the Rise of Hitler* (New York: Oxford University Press, 1985), 4.

128. Fritz Fischer, *Germany's Aims in the First World War* (New York: W. W. Norton & Company, Inc, 1967 [1961]), 3.

129. Fischer, *Germany's Aims in the First World War*, 7.

130. The development and popularization of the concept of Volk are attributed to Ernst Moritz Arndt (1796–1860) and his disciple Friedrich Ludwig Jahn (1778–1852). The first defined Volk in opposition to French liberal ideas in a pamphlet he published in 1808 (*Reden an die deutsche Nation*); the second followed with a book in 1810 (*Deutsches Volkstum*), in which he denigrated the Gypsies and the Jews as *bodiless airy phantoms* for being Volks without a state. See Lucy Davidowicz, *The War against the Jews* (New York: Bantam Books, 1986), 26–27. For the burning of books, see Paul Johnson, *Modern Times* (New York: Harper Perennial, 1992), 118.

George L. Mosse provides a comprehensive history of the Volk movement in his *The Crisis of German Ideology: Intellectual Origins of the Third Reich* (New York: Howard Fertig, 1964).

131. For the esoteric connections of Volk culture and anti-Semitism, see Nicholas Goodrick-Clarke, *The Occult Roots of Nazism: Secret Aryan Cults and Their Influence on Nazi Ideology* (New York: New York University Press, 1992); and Lucy Davidowicz, *The War against the Jews* (New York: Bantam Books, 1986), 8–10.

132. George L. Mosse, *The Crisis of German Ideology: Intellectual Origins of the Third Reich* (New York: Howard Fertig, 1964), 19–24.

133. See William L. Shirer, *The Rise and Fall of the Third Reich* (New York: Fawcett Crest, 1992), 152–162.

134. See Fischer, *Germany's Aims in the First World War*, 11.

135. See Fischer, *Germany's Aims in the First World War*.

136. See "World War I Casualties," *Wikipedia*, May 8, 2020, http://en.wikipedia.org/wiki/World_War_I_casualties.

137. Theobald von Bethmann-Hollweg, quoted in Arno Mayer, *The Persistence of the Old Regime: Europe to the Great War* (New York: Pantheon Books, 1981), 318.

138. See Mayer, *The Persistence of the Old Regime*, 319.

139. Based on the existence of these conditions, Fritz Fischer, a German historian, explained in the 1960s why the German ruling classes found it worthwhile to ignite the powder keg of World War I. In the process, he presented damning evidence that destroyed the myth of sleepwalking. See Fritz Fischer, *Germany's Aims in the First World War* (New York: W. W. Norton & Company, 1967 [1961]). Fischer's evidence has never been challenged. Criticisms have focused on saying that Germany's enemies were also aggressive, that they had created huge empires that left Germany out, and that this had prompted Germany's response. These assertions may be true, but they do not address Fischer's point. They only suggest that Germany was not the only power bent on invading other countries, something that was obviously true. Germany's ambitions collided with the ambitions of its enemies. For Germany, the fact that its rivals had arrived earlier to colonial lands was not relevant. They were ready to create their colonies in Europe.

140. Pieter M. Judson, *The Habsburg Empire: A New History* (Cambridge, MA: Harvard University Press, 2016), 383–384.

141. Richard Pipes, *The Russian Revolution* (New York: Knopf, 1990), 196.

142. Pipes, *The Russian Revolution*, 209.

143. Mayer, *The Persistence of the Old Regime*, 322.

144. In World War I, the German armies went deeper into southern Russia than in World War II. See Pipes, *The Russian Revolution*, 595.

145. Sebastian Haffner, *Failure of a Revolution: Germany 1918–1919* (Chicago: Banner Press, 1986), 37–41.

146. See Phillip Cagan, "The Monetary Dynamics of Hyperinflation," in *Studies in the Quantity Theory of Money*, ed. Milton Friedman (Chicago: University of Chicago Press, 1956).

147. Neumann, Franz, *Behemoth: The Structure and Practice of National Socialism, 1933–1944* (Oxford University Press, Oxford, 1944), 23–24, www.unz.org/Pub/NeumannFranz-1942.

148. See Samuel W. Mitcham Jr., *Why Hitler?: The Genesis of the Nazi Reich* (Westport, CT: Praeger, 1996).

149. William L. Shirer, *The Rise and Fall of the Third Reich* (New York: Fawcett Crest, 1992), 320.

150. Quoted in Arthur M. Schlesinger, *The Age of Roosevelt*, vol. 2, *The Coming of the New Deal: 1933–1935* (New York: Houghton Mifflin, 2003 [1958]), 115.

151. Schlesinger, *The Coming of the New Deal*, 179.

152. See Amity Shlaes, *The Forgotten Man: A New History of the Great Depression* (New York: Harper Collins, 2007), 214–245; Schlesinger, *The Coming of the New Deal*, 87–176.

153. See Schlesinger, *The Coming of the New Deal*, 92–94.

154. Quoted in Schlesinger, *The Coming of the New Deal*, 90.

155. Adam Smith, *Wealth of Nations* (Amherst, NY: Prometheus, 1991), 137.

156. Michael A. Bernstein, *The Great Depression: Delayed Recovery and Economic Change in America, 1929–1939* (Cambridge: Cambridge University Press, 1987), 194–195.

157. Bernstein, *The Great Depression*, 194–195.

158. General Hugh S. Johnson, quoted in Schlesinger, *The Coming of the New Deal*, 114–115.

159. See Michael Hannon, "Clarence Darrow and the National Recovery Review Board" (Minneapolis, MN: University of Minnesota Law Library, 2010), http://moses.law.umn.edu/darrow/trialpdfs/National_Recovery_Review_Board.pdf. See also Lowell B. Mason, "*Darrow v. Johnson*," *North American Review*, 238, no. 6 (December 1934): 524–532.

160. Schlesinger, *The Coming of the New Deal*, 131.

161. General Hugh S. Johnson, quoted in Schlesinger, *The Coming of the New Deal*, 131–133.

162. For the relations between Henry Ford and the NRA, see Sidney Fine, "The Ford Motor Company and the NRA," *Business History Review*, 32, no. 4 (Winter 1958): 353–385; Burton W. Folsom, *Michigan Resists the New Deal*, Mackinac Center for Public Policy, March 2, 1998.

163. Schlesinger, *The Coming of the New Deal*, 160.

164. The book was Fausto Pitigliani, *The Italian Corporative State* (New York: Macmillan, 1934), xi, http://www.questia.com/read/28552779/the-italian-corporative-state.

165. James Q. Whitman, "Of Corporatism, Fascism, and the First New Deal," *American Journal of Comparative Law*, 39 no. 747 (1991): 747, https://digitalcommons.law.yale.edu/cgi/viewcontent.cgi?httpsredir=1&article=1656&context=fss_papers.

166. Whitman, "Of Corporatism, Fascism, and the First New Deal," 766.

167. See Amity Shlaes, *The Forgotten Man: A New History of the Great Depression*, (New York: Harper Collins Publishers, 2007), 242–243.

168. Julia Kagan, "Unemployment Compensation," *Investopedia*, https://www.investopedia.com/terms/u/unemployment-compensation.asp. A general criticism of Marxism about the welfare state can be found in Karl Marx and Friedrich Engels, "Address of the Central Committee to the Communist League," in *The Marx-Engels Reader*, edited by Robert C. Tucker (New York: Norton, 1978), 501–511. In it, Marx and Engels use the same argument: that welfare measures would prevent the revolution desired by the communists.

169. Roosevelt had enough votes to attempt to bypass the Supreme Court by changing the Constitution. However, he insisted that the Constitution did not need to be amended but interpreted in a way more adapted to the modern times. See Keith E. Whittington, *Political Foundations of Judicial Supremacy: The Presidency, the Supreme Court, and Constitutional Leadership in U.S. History* (Princeton, NJ: Princeton University Press, 2007), 48, http://www.questia.com/read/120603071/political-foundations-of-judicial-supremacy-the.

170. See Shlaes, *The Forgotten Man*, 305–317.

171. Schumpeter, *Business Cycles: A Theoretical, Historical and Statistical Analysis of the Capitalist Process*, 2 vols. (Philadelphia: Porcupine Press, 1989, [1939]), 419.

172. Whitman, "Of Corporatism, Fascism, and the First New Deal," 748.

173. Bernstein, *The Great Depression*, 203.

174. Most scholars have focused their attention on macroeconomic variables, such as fiscal deficits, exchange rate regimes, monetary policies, and banking system instability, in their analyses of the Great Depression. Many of them think that Roosevelt's policies in this respect were positive, especially the depreciation of the dollar. Certainly, these variables were quite important, but even if the positive effect of these macro policies is taken as a given, it is still true that the United States did not recover from the Depression until the beginning of World War II.

175. Shlaes, *The Forgotten Man*, 341.

176. See Russell D. Renka, "Party Control of the Presidency and Congress, 1933-2010," *Southeast Missouri State University*, https://cstl-cla.semo.edu/rdrenka/ui320-75/presandcongress.asp.

177. Shlaes, *The Forgotten Man*, 209.

178. *Schechter Poultry Corp. v. United States*, 295 U.S. 495, 528.

179. See Carly Elizabeth Schall, *The Rise and Fall of the Miraculous Welfare Machine: Immigration and Social Democracy in Twentieth-Century Sweden* (Ithaca, NY: Cornell University Press, 2016).

180. Lars Magnusson, *An Economic History of Sweden* (London: Routledge, 2000), 185.

181. Magnusson, *An Economic History of Sweden*, 186–187.

182. Magnusson, *An Economic History of Sweden*, 235; Kajsa Norman, *Sweden's Dark Soul: The Unraveling of a Utopia* (London: Hurst & Company, 2018), loc. 1699, Kindle.

183. See Norman, *Sweden's Dark Soul*, loc. 1709.

184. Norman, *Sweden's Dark Soul*, loc. 1719–1762.

185. See Norman, *Sweden's Dark Soul*, loc. 1730-1762.

186. Bengt Furaker, "The Swedish Wage-Earner Funds and Economic Democracy: Is There Something to Be Learned from Them?" (Newbury Park, CA: Sage, 2015), https://socav.gu.se/digitalAssets/1557/1557499_transfer_-european-review-of-labour-and-research-151217.pdf.

187. Furaker, "The Swedish Wage-Earner Funds and Economic Democracy."

188. See Magnus Isberg and Hans Hegeland, "The Development of Constitutional Law in Sweden," in *The Constitution of Sweden: The Fundamental Laws and the Riksdag Act* (Stockholm: Sveriges Riksdag, 2016), 17.

189. See Nima Sanandaji, *Debunking Utopia: Exposing the Myth of Nordic Socialism* (Washington, DC: WND Books, 2016), loc. 1107–1242, Kindle.

190. See Norman, *Sweden's Dark Soul*, loc. 1709; Andreas Borgh, "The Rise, Fall and Revival of the Swedish Welfare State: What Are the Policy Lessons from Sweden?," Research Institute of Industrial Economics, *IFN Working Paper No. 873*, 2011, Stockholm.

191. The reforms listed in the next paragraphs are taken from a much longer list published in an appendix of Andreas Borgh's "The Rise, Fall and Revival of the Swedish Welfare State: What Are the Policy Lessons from Sweden?," Research Institute of Industrial Economics, *IFN Working Paper No. 873*, 2011, Stockholm.

192. IMF WEO Data.

193. Lars Lokke Rasmussen, quoted in "Danish PM in US: Denmark Is Not Socialist," *Local DK*, November 1, 2015.

194. Maddison Project Database 2018, Groningen Growth and Development Centre, https://www.rug.nl/ggdc/historicaldevelopment/maddison/releases/maddison-project-database-2018.

195. See Markus Jantti, Eva Sierminksa, and Tim Smeeding, *The Joint Distribution of Household Income and Wealth: Evidence from the Luxembourg Wealth Study*, OEDC Social, Employment and Migration Social Papers, 65, OECD, 2008, http://www.oecd.org/social/soc/40774821.pdf.

196. For a detailed discussion of the central role of the principal-agent problem in turning socialism (communism) unworkable, see Manuel Hinds, "Markets and Ownership in Socialist Countries in Transition," in *Markets and Politicians: Politicized Economic Choice*, ed. Arye Hillman (Boston: Kluwer Academic Publishers, 1991); Manuel Hinds, "Policy Effectiveness in Reforming Socialist Economies," in *The Transition from Socialism in Eastern Europe: Domestic Restructuring and Foreign Trade*, ed. Arye Hillman and Branko Milanovic (Washington, DC: World Bank, 1992); and Manuel Hinds, "Policies to Overcome the Transformation Crisis: The Case of Russia," in *Overcoming the Transformation Crisis: Lessons for the Successor States of the Soviet Union*, ed. Horst Siebert (Tübingen: J. C. B. Mohr, 1993).

197. Alec Nove, *An Economic History of the Soviet Union* (London: Penguin, 1989), 57.

198. Paul R. Gregory and Robert C. Stuart, *Soviet Economic Structure and Performance*, 3rd ed, (New York: Harper and Row, 1986), 58; Alec Nove, *An Economic History of the Soviet Union* (London: Penguin) 1989), 84.

199. Lenin, quoted by Roy Medvedev, *Let History Judge: The Origins and Consequences of Stalinism* (New York: Columbia University Press, 1989), 643.

200. See Trotsky, *Military Writings and Speeches: The Intelligentsia and Power*, quoted in Philip Pomper, *Lenin, Trotsky and Stalin* (New York: Columbia University Press, 1990), 359.

201. See Stephen F. Cohen, *Bukharin and the Bolshevik Revolution: A Political Biography, 1888–1938* (New York: Oxford University Press, 1980), 139–143.

202. Quoted in Cohen, *Bukharin and the Bolshevik Revolution*, 92. Bukharin was condemned to death and shot in 1937. For a list of all the relatives that were also killed or imprisoned because of their relationship with him, see Robert Conquest, *The Great Terror: A Reassessment* (New York: Oxford University Press, 2008 [1990]), 395–396.

203. Quoted in Robert Conquest, *The Harvest of Sorrow: Soviet Collectivization and the Terror-Famine* (New York: Oxford University Press, 1986), 24. Zinoviev was killed in 1937, in his cell. He was to be executed in the prison's yard, but he went to his knees and cried so loudly that the officer in charge decided to kill him right there to avoid disturbing the other prisoners.

204. See Lewis Siegelbaum, *Militarization of Labor*, Seventeen Moments in Soviet History, http://soviethistory.msu.edu/1921-2/militarization-of-labor/, which is an online archive of primary sources, and Richard Pipes, *The Russian Revolution* (New York: Alfred A. Knopf, 1990), 856.

205. Cohen, *Bukharin and the Bolshevik Revolution*, 107–125.

206. The six persons were Zinoviev, Kamenev, Bukharin, Pyatakov, Trotsky, and Stalin. The first four were tried and shot under Stalin's orders during the Great Terror of the late 1930s. Trotsky was assassinated, also under Stalin's instructions, in Mexico in 1940. The "testament" is included in Robert C. Tucker, *The Lenin Anthology* (New York: W. W. Norton, 1975), 725–728.

207. The corruption that pervaded the Soviet Union in its last several decades has been documented extensively in books and newspaper articles. For a general view, see, for example, Vladimir Shlapentokh, *Public and Private Life of the Soviet People: Changing Values in Post-Stalinist Russia* (New York: Oxford University Press, 1989), especially pages 203–216; Hedrick Smith, *The New Russians* (New York: Ballantine Books, 1976); and Dusko Doder, *Shadows and Whispers: Power Politics inside the Kremlin from Brezhnev to Gorbachev* (New York: Penguin, 1988).

208. Stanley Baldwin in 1925, quoted in David Marquand, *Britain since 1918: The Strange Career of British Democracy* (London: Weidenfeld and Nicolson, 2008).

209. George Dangerfield, *The Strange Death of Liberal England* (Stanford, CA: Stanford University Press, 1997), 354.

210. Norbert Wiener, *Cybernetics: Or Control and Communications in the Animal and the Machine* (Cambridge, MA: MIT Press, 1965 [1948]).

211. Norbert Wiener in 1949, quoted in John Markoff, "In 1949, He Imagined an Age of Robots," *New York Times*, May 20, 2013, http://www.nytimes.com/2013/05/21/science/mit-scholars-1949-essay-on-machine-age-is-found.html.

212. Sir Alfred Ewing in his address to the British Association for the Advancement of Science, reported in the *Times*, September 1, 1932, and quoted in Arnold Toynbee, *A Study of History*, Abridgement, 2 vols., by D. C. Somervell, Vol. 1 (New York: Oxford University Press, 1957), 206–207.

213. Toynbee, *A Study of History*, 208.

214. F. Scott Fitzgerald, "The Crack-Up," *Esquire* (1936); http://www.esquire.com/news-politics/a4310/the-crack-up/.

215. See, for example, Jochen Bittner, "How the Far Right Conquered Sweden," *New York Times,* September 6, 2018, https://www.nytimes.com/2018/09/06/opinion/how-the-far-right-conquered-sweden.html.

216. Hendrik Willem van Loos, introduction to Konrad Heiden, *The New Inquisition* (New York: Starling Press and Alliance Book Corporation, 1939).

217. F. A. Hayek, *The Road to Serfdom* (Chicago: University of Chicago Press, 2007 [1944]), 72.

218. Hayek, *The Road to Serfdom,* 71.

219. Hayek, *The Road to Serfdom,* 71–72.

220. Quoted in Bertrand Russell, *History of Western Philosophy* (London: Routledge, 2004 [1946]), loc. 15120, Kindle.

221. Many other thinkers have proposed that the impulses of people are not one-dimensional. David Hume, for example, believed that people acted on many different motivations and that, among these, egoistic motivations were not particularly prominent. See George H. Sabine, *A History of Political Theory* (New York: Holt, Rinehart and Winston, 1961 [1937]), 602.

222. Adam Smith wrote an entire book discussing the importance of what today we associate with empathy in motivating human behavior. He did not integrate this analysis, however, with that of the better-known *The Wealth of Nations*. See Adam Smith, *The Theory of Moral Sentiments*, copyright Jonathan Bennett, 2017, https://www.earlymoderntexts.com/assets/pdfs/smith1759.pdf.

223. Alfred Adler, *The Individual Psychology of Alfred Adler: A Systematic Presentation in Selections from His Writings*, ed. Heinz Ansbacher and Rowena Ansbacher (New York: Harper Torchbooks, 1964), 175.

224. In this point, Adler comes very close to the ideas developed later by Victor Frankl in *Man's Search for Meaning* (New York: Beacon Press, 2006).

225. Alfred Adler, *The Individual Psychology of Alfred Adler*, 155–156.

226. Alfred Adler, *The Individual Psychology of Alfred Adler*, 135. In this definition, he quoted an unnamed English author.

227. Alfred Adler, *The Individual Psychology of Alfred Adler*, 270–271.

228. Lenin in an article written for *Krasnyi Mech (The Red Sword)*, a weekly published by the *Cheka*, the original KGB. Quoted in Ronald W. Clark, *Lenin: A Biography* (New York: Harper and Row, 1990), 378.

229. Adam Smith, *The Theory of Moral Sentiments* (Kansas City, MO: Digireads, 2018), Kindle, loc. 9.

230. Vernon L. Smith and Bart J. Wilson, *Humanomics: Moral Sentiments and the Wealth of Nations for the Twenty-First Century* (Cambridge: Cambridge University Press, 2019).

231. Smith and Wilson, *Humanomics*, loc. 284, Kindle.

232. Smith and Wilson, *Humanomics*, loc. 312–321, Kindle.

233. John Maynard Keynes, *The General Theory of Employment, Interest, and Money* (New York: Harcourt, Brace & World, Inc., 1964 [1936]), 384.

234. John Stuart Mill, *Autobiography* (London: Penguin, 1989), 117.

235. Victor Frankl, *Man's Search for Meaning* (Boston: Beacon Press, 2006 [1959]), loc. 75, Kindle.

236. Fyodor Dostoevsky, *The Brothers Karamazov* (New York: Barnes and Noble, 1995 [1880]), 234.

237. Carl Schmitt, *The Crisis of Parliamentary Democracy* (Cambridge, MA: MIT Press, 2001 [1923]), 17.

238. Schmitt, *The Crisis of Parliamentary Democracy*, 24.

239. Carl Schmitt, *The Concept of the Political*, expanded ed. (Chicago: University of Chicago Press, 2007 [1932]), loc. 1450, Kindle.

240. See Carlo Galli, *Janus's Gaze: Essays on Carl Schmitt* (Durham, NC: Duke University Press, 2015), loc. 1090–1102, Kindle.

241. Carl Schmitt, *Political Theology: Four Chapters on the Concept of Sovereignty,* (Chicago: University of Chicago Press, 2005 [1922]), 5.

242. Schmitt, *Political Theology*, 5–7.

243. Schmitt, *Political Theology*, 5–7.

244. F. Scott Fitzgerald, "The Crack-Up," *Esquire* (1936), http://www.esquire. com/news-politics/a4310/the-crack-up/.

245. William Morris, Chapter IV, in *A Dream of John Ball*, 1866, https://www. marxists.org/archive/morris/works/1886/johnball/chapters/chapter4.htm.

246. James Viscount Bryce, *Modern Democracies* (New York: MacMillan, 2013 [1921]), loc. 14510–14513, Kindle.

247. Karl R. Popper, *The Open Society and Its Enemies, 1 Plato* (Princeton, NJ: Princeton University Press, 1966), 124–125.

248. Wolfgang Streeck, *How Will Capitalism End?: Essays on a Failing System*, (London: Verso, 2016), loc. 98–114, 138, Kindle.

249. Francis Fukuyama, "America in Decay: The Sources of Political Dysfunction," *Foreign Affairs*, 93, no. 5 (September/October): 5–26.

250. Fukuyama, "America in Decay," 11.

251. Fukuyama, "America in Decay," 10.

252. Fukuyama, "America in Decay," 11.

253. Fukuyama, "America in Decay," 13.

254. The example is the judgment that the district court of Rotterdam passed on a dispute about the way in which the Port of Rotterdam Authority developed the Second Massvlakte in September 2014. See the Port of Rotterdam online site, https://www.portofrotterdam.com/en/news-and-press-releases/ district-court-rejects-ect-claims-against-port-authority.

255. Quoted by Alexis de Tocqueville, *The Ancien Régime and the Revolution* (London: Penguin Classics, 2008), loc. 2730, Kindle.

256. Schmitt, *The Crisis of Parliamentary Democracy*, 64.

257. David Reynolds, *The Long Shadow: The Legacies of the Great War in the Twentieth Century* (New York: W. W. Norton & Company, 2015), 69.

258. Timothy Carney, *Alienated America: Why Some Places Thrive while Others Collapse* (New York: Harper, 2019), loc. 98-108, Kindle.

259. Carney, *Alienated America*, loc. 98.

260. Address at the celebration of the 150th anniversary of the Declaration of Independence in Philadelphia, Pennsylvania, July 5, 1926, http://www. presidency.ucsb.edu/ws/?pid=408.

261. Richard Holbrooke, quoted in George Packer, "The Longest Wars: Richard Holbrooke and the Decline of American Power," *Foreign Affairs*, 90, no. 3 (May/June 2019), https://www.foreignaffairs.com/articles/ 2019-04-16/longest-wars.

262. John Kay, *Obliquity: Why Our Goals Are Best Achieved Indirectly* (New York: Penguin, 2011), loc. 293–324, Kindle.

263. Kay, *Obliquity*.

264. F. A. Hayek, *The Road to Serfdom* (Chicago: University of Chicago Press, 2007 [1944]), 71.

265. Raghuram G. Rajan, *Fault Lines: How Hidden Fractures Still Threaten the World Economy* (Princeton, NJ: Princeton University Press, 2010), 31.

266. Simon Johnson and James Kwak, *13 Bankers: The Wall Street Takeover and the Next Financial Meltdown* (New York: Vintage, 2010), 112.

267. Johnson and Kwak, *13 Bankers*, 112.

268. Bethany McLean and Joe Nocera, *All the Devils Are Here: The Hidden History of the Financial Crisis* (New York: Penguin, 2010), loc. 6847, Kindle.

269. Samantha Sharf, "Sorry Trump, The Lowest Homeownership Rate in 51 Years Isn't Tragic but Inventory Woes Might Be," *Forbes*, August 8, 2016, http://www.forbes.com/sites/samanthasharf/2016/08/08/sorry-trump-the-lowest-homeownership-rate-in-51-years-isnt-tragic-but-inventory-woes-might-be/#51fd99120dfc.

270. Johnson and Kwak, *13 Bankers*, 155–156.

271. John B. Taylor, *Getting Off Track: How Government Actions and Interventions Caused, Prolonged, and Worsened the Financial Crisis* (Stanford, CA: Hoover Institution Press, 2009), loc. 478, Kindle.

272. Taylor, *Getting Off Track*, loc. 482.

273. Adam Tooze, *Crashed: How a Decade of Financial Crises Changed the World*, (New York: Viking, 2018), 614–615.

274. See, for example, Elizabeth Warren, "The Coming Economic Crash—and How to Stop It," Team Warren, *Medium*, https://medium.com/@teamwarren/the-coming-economic-crash-and-how-to-stop-it-355703da148b; and Bernie Sanders on financial regulation, FeelTheBern.org, https://feelthebern.org/bernie-sanders-on-financial-regulation/.

275. For a more complete discussion of this point, see Manuel Hinds, *The Triumph of the Flexible Society: The Connectivity Revolution and Resistance to Change* (Westport, CT: Praeger, 2003).

276. Graham Allison, "The Thucydides Trap: When One Great Power Threatens to Displace Another, War Is Almost Always the Result—But It Doesn't Have to Be," *Foreign Policy.com*, https://foreignpolicy.com/2017/06/09/the-thucydides-trap/.

277. Dean Acheson, quoted in Robert Kagan, *The Jungle Grows Back: America and Our Imperiled World* (New York: Alfred A. Knopf, 2018), loc. 404, Kindle.

278. Alexandra Stevenson and Motoko Rich, "Trans-Pacific Trade Partners Are Moving On, without the U.S.," *New York Times*, November 11, 2017.

279. Washington's Farewell Address 1796, https://avalon.law.yale.edu/18th_century/washing.asp.

280. Maggie Haberman et al, "Republicans Are Split Over Whether to Call the Election Over," *New York Times*, accessed November 9, 2020, https://www.nytimes.com/live/2020/11/08/us/trump-biden?action=click&module=Spotlight&pgtype=Homepage#republicans-are-split-over-whether-to-call-the-election-over.

281. Martin Pengelly, "Mitt Romney Decries US Politics: 'The World is Watching with Abject Horror'," *Guardian*, October 13, 2020, https://www.theguardian.com/us-news/2020/oct/13/mitt-romney-abject-horror-us-politics-trump-biden.

282. Kevin Stevens, "A Difficult Healing," *Dublin Review of Books*, no. 127, November 7, 2020, https://www.drb.ie/blog/comment/2020/11/07/a-difficult-healing.

283. Joseph J. Ellis, quoted in Jude Sheerin, "Should Washington and Jefferson Monuments Come Down?" *BBC News*, August 18, 2017, https://www.bbc.com/news/world-us-canada-40978515.

Epigraph Sources

Introduction

Thomas Paine, "The American Crisis," December 23, 1776.

Part I

Schmitt, Carl, *The Crisis of Parliamentary Democracy* (Cambridge, MA: MIT Press, 2001 [1923]), 17.

Chapter 1

Eric Hoffer, *The Ordeal of Change* (Titusville, NJ: Hopewell Publications, 2006 [1963]), 3, 6.

Chapter 2

Detlev J. K. Peukert, *The Weimar Republic* (New York: Hill and Wang, 1993), 282.

Chapter 3

Quoted by Will Durant in *The Story of Philosophy* (New York, Simon and Schuster, 1953), 100.

Chapter 4

Étienne de la Boétie, *Discourse on Voluntary Servitude*, 1548, http://www.constitution.org/la_boetie/serv_vol.htm.

Chapter 5

These are the final words in Keynes's *The General Theory of Employment, Interest, and Money*, (New York: Harcourt, Brace & World, Inc., 1964 [1936]), 384.

Part II

William Faulkner, *Requiem for a Nun* (Vintage International, New York, 2012 [1951]).

Chapter 6

Karl R. Popper, *The Open Society and Its Enemies, 1 Plato* (Princeton, NJ: Princeton University Press, 1966), 111.

Chapter 7

1. Simon Schama, *Citizens: A Chronicle of the French Revolution* (New York: Vintage Books, 1990), 185.

Chapter 8

Karl R. Popper, *The Open Society and Its Enemies, 1 Plato* (Princeton, NJ: Princeton University Press, 1966), 200–201.

Chapter 9

1. Paul Celan, quoted by Neil MacGregor in *Germany: Memories of a Nation* (New York: Penguin, 2014), 491.
2. *Schechter Poultry Corp. v. United States*, 295 U.S. 495, 528.

Chapter 10

Nina Witoszek, "Moral Community and the Crisis of the Enlightenment: Sweden and Germany in the 1920s and 1930s," *Culture and Crisis: The Case of Germany and Sweden*, ed. Nina Witoszek and Lars Tragardh (New York: Berghahn Books, 2002), 65.

Part III

Quoted in Charles Murray, *Coming Apart: The State of White America, 1960–2010* (New York: Crown Forum, 2013), loc. 2132, Kindle.

Chapter 11

Ilya Prigogine and Isabelle Stengers, *Order out of Chaos: Man's New Dialogue with Nature* (New York: Bantam Books, 1984).

Chapter 12

Quoted in James Burnham, *The Machiavellians: Defenders of Freedom: A Defense of Political Truth against Wishful Thinking* (Washington, DC: Gateway Editions, 1943), 111–113.

Chapter 13

Dostoevsky, *The Brothers Karamazov*, 232.

Chapter 14

Allan Bloom, *The Closing of the American Mind* (New York: Simon & Schuster, 1987), 27.

ACKNOWLEDGMENTS

I am indebted to three people for the publication of this book. My friend Michael O'Malley, former editor at Yale University Press, made two key contributions. He suggested I update and expand a book I had written ten years before on the impact of technological revolutions on the social order, and that suggestion led to my writing *In Defense of Liberal Democracy*. Michael put me in touch with Susan Ginsburg, of Writers House. Susan became my literary agent at a time when very few people in the publishing industry believed that the world was heading for a crisis of values. She gave me valuable advice and connected me to an excellent publisher, Imagine Books, which was willing to invest in a book offering an unconventional approach to current problems. My editor there, Kevin Stevens, flawlessly did what a great editor should do: help me write the best book I could.

I also want to thank several people who read the manuscript and gave me ideas to improve it. They include Millard Long, Fernando Saldanha, Gabriela Calderón de Burgos, and Julian Altamirano.

INDEX

A

AAA (Agricultural Adjustment Act), 168–70, 173–74
abortion, 24
absolute power, 15, 104–105, 110, 128, 147, 183, 198, 224
Acheson, Dean, 267
Afghanistan, 13
Africa, 13, 126
African Americans, 91, 132–33, 136
Agricultural Adjustment Act. *See* AAA
agricultural workers, 18, 43–44, 197
Airbnb, 213
Airbus, 255
Allied powers, 160
Allison, Graham, 266
Amalgamated Clothing Workers, 171
American Revolution, 3, 71
Ancien Régime, 112,
Andropov, Yuri, 200–202, 205–6
anticompetitive practices, 169
anti-Semitism, 36, 41, 216
Arendt, Hannah, 67, 127
aristocracy, 112, 118, 120–22, 128, 131
assassination, political, 188
Australia, 18, 58, 71, 124, 152
Austro-Hungarian Empire, 11, 154
authoritarianism, 36–38, 40, 72–73, 219, 239, 247

B

Baldwin, Stanley, 207
Baruch, Bernard, 170
Bavaria, 150, 161
Bentham, Jeremy, 223
Bethmann-Hollweg, Theobald von, 155
Biden, Joe, 271, 274
Bismarck, Otto von, 12, 145,

147–48, 152
Black Death, 265
Bolshevik Revolution, 72, 103, 157, 161, 194, 196
bourgeoisie, 13, 34, 105, 122, 217, 219
Brezhnev, Leonid, 198
Britain. *See* United Kingdom
British constitution, 71
Bukharin, Nikolai, 194–97, 305
Bullock, Alan, 69
Bundesrat, 146
bureaucracy, 101, 111, 115, 124, 127, 245–46, 255, 257
Burke, Edmund, 248
Bush, George W., 258, 271

C

Calhoun, John C., 137
Cambodia, 13, 15, 184
Canada, 18, 58, 71, 124, 152, 264
capital, 19, 52–53, 133, 139, 180, 192, 194, 200, 224
capitalism, 12, 14, 21–22, 31–32, 42, 44, 52–53, 146, 149, 180, 192, 195, 223–24, 242–43
    modern, 19, 177, 232, 243
capitalism and liberal democracy, 12–13, 20, 32, 42, 44, 215, 260, 262
Carnegie, Andrew, 46
Central Powers, 11, 154
Centralverband Deutscher Industrieller. *See* CVDI.
China, 13, 15, 27–28, 34, 45–46, 67, 87, 106, 125, 144, 266, 268–70
Churchill, Winston, 177
city-states, 107–8
Civilian Conservation Corps (CCC), 175
civilization, 137, 151, 207, 215–16
civil rights, 22

civil war, 14, 25, 120, 122
    American Civil War, 4, 71, 133,
        136–37, 139
climate change, 28
Cold War, 183–84
communism, 12–13, 15, 20, 23–24,
    31–32, 66–67, 78, 80, 164, 168,
    184, 194–97, 204–6, 247
communists, 14, 34, 36, 67, 70, 72, 74,
    128, 157, 161, 163–64, 166, 177,
    194, 197–98, 204–5, 231, 240
community, 5, 45, 88, 98–99, 103,
    105, 138, 221, 234, 237, 252
competition, 35–37, 51, 55, 98, 107,
    131, 155, 243
        economic, 13, 26, 45–46, 141–42,
            149, 169–71, 173, 245
Confucius, 38
Congress, US, 134–35, 138, 142, 167,
    173, 176, 179, 258, 273
connectivity revolution, 6, 16–17, 20,
    43, 52, 56, 59, 61, 184, 211–13,
    216, 246, 248, 249, 251
Constitution, US, 71, 132, 134–35,
    137–38, 178, 181–82, 267
Coolidge, Calvin, 253
Corn Laws, 121
coronavirus. See pandemic
corruption, 12, 32, 37, 39, 126, 132,
    194–95, 199–202, 204, 226–27,
    243, 245
COVID-19. See pandemic
Cromwell, Oliver, 71
CVDI (Centralverband Deutscher Indus-
    trieller), 147, 149
Czechoslovakia, 166, 198

D

Daimler Benz, 148
Darcy, Edward, 119
Darrow, Clarence, 174

Declaration of Independence, 3, 253
democracy, 2–6, 12–16, 22–23,
    31–33, 40, 42, 63, 71–72, 79, 81,
    83–84, 90–91, 116–17, 126–28,
    150, 152, 162–65, 218–20,
    234–36, 238–40, 242–51, 262,
    266–71, 274–76
        constitutional, 160
        modern, 71, 116, 269
        parliamentary, 39, 160
Democratic-Republican Party, 133
Denmark, 189–90
depression, economic, 4, 5, 12, 29, 142
discrimination, 65, 127, 130, 133, 136,
    216–17, 275
diversity, 75, 83, 106–7, 238, 241, 264
divisiveness, 13, 15, 21–23, 34, 42,
    61–62, 65, 73–74, 100, 108,
    145–46, 153, 164, 215–17, 219,
    222, 231, 249, 264, 270
Douglas, Stephen, 135

E

Eastern Europe, 13, 32, 68, 155, 191
East India Company, 124–25
economic cycles, 60, 177
economic freedom, 112–13, 189–90,
    226, 232, 243
economic growth, 26, 111, 249,
    257–58, 263
economic interests, 232–33, 251, 268
economic policies, 112, 179, 181, 220
economic power, 55, 80, 82, 98, 100,
    105–7, 143, 147–48, 170, 172,
    189, 225, 243, 245, 251, 263
economic problems, 59, 62, 87, 113
economics, 7, 82, 106–7, 180, 193,
    206, 232, 236
economies, 17–19, 41, 43, 45, 55–57,
    59–60, 62–63, 79–80, 82, 89,
    112–13, 147, 149, 188–89, 212–13

American, 25, 44, 58, 143–44,
　167, 169–71, 180, 254–60
capitalist, 32, 56, 224
German, 147, 149, 156, 162–63
industrial, 19, 52, 131
knowledge, 214, 250, 257, 263–64
socialist, 56, 191–93, 200
Soviet, 194, 196, 200–205
education, 45–47, 55, 62–63, 78, 90,
　156, 214–15, 250, 257, 263
Eichmann, Adolf, 87
election, 2020 presidential, 271-75
El Salvador, 15
emigration, 124
employment, 4, 18, 21–22, 44, 55, 58,
　63, 80, 143, 159, 213
industrial, 194
employment creation, 56, 180
energy, 16, 79
Engels, Friedrich, 22
England, 112, 116–26, 131, 207–8,
　246, 251
Entente powers, 154
equilibrium, 43–44, 62–63, 76–77, 106,
　128, 195, 212, 216, 219, 233, 240
Estates General, 115
Europe, 11, 18–20, 23, 29, 30, 39, 80,
　103–8, 110, 155–56, 158
European Union (EU), 30, 264

F

fascism, 32, 39, 67, 80, 179
FBI (Federal Bureau of Investigation), 38
FDIC (Federal Deposit Insurance
　Corporation), 260
Federal Bureau of Investigation. *See* FBI
Federal Deposit Insurance Corporation.
　See FDIC
federal government, US, 25, 136, 138,
　143–44, 153, 178
Federal Reserve, 258

feudalism, 72, 107, 113–14, 151, 167
financial crises, 18, 59–61, 139, 142,
　183, 241, 249, 260–62
financial markets, 19, 58, 260, 264
First World War. *See* World War I
Founding Fathers, 2–7, 15, 247, 270–72
France, 49–50, 72–73, 108–16, 127,
　129, 145–46, 152, 154, 184
freedom
individual, 77
intellectual, 107
of thought, 108, 238
political, 79–81, 153
free trade, 21, 25–26, 104, 113, 157,
　196, 268
French Revolution, 42, 70–73, 109,
　115–16, 127–28, 263
French society, 109–11, 113–116

G

GDP (Gross Domestic Product), 60,
　188, 260
genocide, 32, 65–67, 87, 231, 275
Gentile, Emilio, 33
German industries, 142, 148–9, 152
German states, 146–47, 161, 165
Germany, 11–12, 14, 34, 49–50, 69–
　70, 72–73, 122, 129–30, 140–41,
　145–57, 159–66, 230–31, 247–48
Gilded Age, 46–47, 55, 129, 141,
　153, 159
Glass-Steagall Act, 258
globalization, 21, 25, 46, 60–61, 263–65
Glorious Revolution, 71, 119
Golden Horde, 96
Gorbachev, Mikhail, 196, 198, 200,
　202, 204–7
government intervention, 55, 79, 187,
　256–57, 261
government regulation, 111, 171–72,
　256–57

Great Depression, 4, 26, 59, 163, 16771, 173–74, 178–82
Great Recession, 22, 56–59, 62, 159, 260
Great Terror, 195, 197, 301
Greenspan, Alan, 258
Greenspan Put, 258–59
Gross Domestic Product. *See* GDP

H

Hamilton, Alexander, 232, 248, 270
Hanseatic League, 264
Harris, Kamala, 271
Hayek, Friedrich A., 66–67, 220–21, 248, 256
Hillman, Sidney, 171
Hindenburg, Paul, 247
Hitler, Adolf, 12–14, 34–35, 37, 41, 67–70, 72–74, 84, 128, 152, 163–66, 228, 230–31, 247–48
Hong Kong, 125
Hoover, Herbert, 26
housing bubble, US, 259–60
Huff, Toby E., 106
Hughes, Charles Evan, 178
human capital, 54, 59, 63, 90, 159, 178, 185, 213–14, 250, 260
    investment in, 182, 214, 250, 257, 269
Hungary, 15, 37, 166, 198
hyperinflation, 162

I

illiberal regimes, 33, 235
immigration, 36, 39, 64–65, 217, 219, 272
imperialism, 32, 124–27, 155, 157
income concentration, 21–22
income distribution, 15, 23, 44, 46–47, 49–50, 52–53, 55, 60, 63, 139, 183, 258, 262

India, 124–25
individualism, 168, 240
industrial economy, 19, 52, 131, 250
industrialists, 131, 141, 144, 148
industrialization, 18–19, 45, 80, 127, 131, 133, 147, 149, 151, 183
industrial revolution, 3–4, 6–7, 16–20, 49–52, 59, 61–62, 70–71, 80, 108, 116–17, 120, 129–31, 148–49, 153–57, 179, 183–84, 212–16
inequality, 44–47, 49, 51–55, 184
infrastructure, 133
injustice, 133, 139
innovation, 16–17, 45, 47–49, 52, 78, 171, 185, 245, 255, 257
instability, economic, 14–15, 21–22, 158
institutions, 3, 5–7, 27–28, 33, 71, 76–77, 108, 150, 169, 182, 218–21, 223–33, 243–44, 260
    liberal, 219, 221, 225–27
Ireland, 122–23
isolationism, 27, 267
Italy, 33, 88–89, 154, 165, 168, 175–76, 182, 227

J

Jackson, Andrew, 133–34, 138
Jaenecke, Heinrich, 69
Japan, 184, 213, 244, 246
Jefferson, Thomas, 131–32, 232, 248
Jews, 13, 34–36, 41–42, 65–66, 74, 84, 141, 151, 218–19, 230
Jim Crow, 136
Johnson, Hugh S., 170, 172, 174–176
Johnson, Lyndon, 255
justice, 85–86, 118, 122, 132, 251

K

King Charles I, 71, 118–20
King Henry I, 117

King Henry III, 118
King Louis XIV, 72, 108, 110–13, 115, 128
King Louis XV, 112–13
King Louis XVI, 109, 112–15, 127
knowledge economy. *See* economies, knowledge
Kuznets, Simon, 47, 49, 52, 58
Kuznets curve, 47–52, 58, 63

L

labor market, 56–58, 187
Lenin, Vladimir, 11–14, 34, 68, 70, 72, 103, 194, 196–98, 228, 231, 240, 248
liberalism, 125, 190–91, 220, 237–41, 247
Lincoln, Abraham, 1–4, 135–36
Lloyd, Henry Demarest, 142
Ludendorff, Erich, 160

M

Madison, James, 245, 248, 270
Magna Carta, 117–19, 251
Mao Zedong, 34, 67–68, 70, 72, 128
market economies, 189,200, 245
markets, 89, 129, 139–40, 142, 169–70, 175, 180, 223–25, 258, 264
    black, 194, 200, 203–5
    financial, 19, 260, 264
market theory, 223, 225–26
Marx, Karl, 12, 21–23, 47, 190–91, 222–25, 227–28, 242, 248
Mississippi River, 137–38
Missouri Compromise, 135
Mongol empire, 96, 98–100, 104
monopolies, 99, 111, 114, 119, 125, 129, 142–44, 174
    state-sponsored, 112
Morgenthau, Henry, Jr., 4, 181
Morgan, J. P., 46, 143–44, 171

Morris, William, 241–43
muckrakers, 143–44
multidimensional societies, 81- 84, 87, 90, 104–8, 110, 120–22, 124, 128–30, 136, 139, 192, 218, 221, 234, 240, 248–49, 251, 253
Munich, 161
Mussolini, Benito, 12–14, 34, 41, 72, 157, 165, 173, 175–76, 248

N

National Industrial Recovery Act, 167, 170, 173, 176
National Recovery Administration. *See* NRA
Native Americans, 91, 137–39
Nazism, 13–14, 34, 41, 65–67, 72–73, 84, 87, 89, 163–67, 207, 217–18, 230–31, 244
NEP (New Economic Policy), 196
Netherlands, 49, 108, 245–46
New Deal, 4, 177–181
    First, 26, 162, 167–72, 177–80
    Second, 177–78, 180
New Economic Policy. *See* NEP
New York (City), 253
Nietzsche, Friedrich, 23, 151, 222, 224
nobility, 101–3, 108–10, 112–15, 127
Nordic welfare state, 184, 189–90
Notes on the State of Virginia, 131–32
NRA (National Recovery Administration), 26, 162, 167–77, 180
Nuremberg Laws, 84–86

O

OECD (Organisation for Economic Co-operation and Development), 58
ownership
    private, 12, 104, 168, 192–93, 202, 204
    state, 13

P

pandemic, COVID-19 or coronavirus, 5, 15, 22, 28, 30, 40–41, 44, 59–61, 260, 265–66
Paris, 72, 114
Parliament, British, 71, 119
Pax Americana, 268
peasants, Russian, 72, 100, 102–3, 166, 194, 196
peers, 112, 117–18, 121
perestroika, 196, 202, 206
physiocrats, 112–14
Piketty, Thomas, 52–53
political parties, 137, 140, 147–48, 165, 273–74
political power, 55, 79–82, 100, 105–7, 120–22, 124, 143, 147–49, 188, 191, 224–25, 246, 251, 262, 268
political systems, 3, 107, 116, 246–47
populists, 32–33, 37–42, 139–41, 151, 217, 219, 249, 269
poverty, 18, 30, 44–46, 60–61, 66–67, 70, 73–74, 133, 143, 189–90
price competition, 167, 174
price controls, 111–12, 114
price fixing, 167, 170, 175
prices, 19, 59, 102, 111, 114, 116, 121, 139–40, 147–49, 162, 167–71, 173–75, 259
principalities, 99, 104–5, 107–8, 266
production, industrial, 19, 194, 259
production quotas, 169–71
products, agricultural, 111, 140, 174, 196
progressives, 24, 109, 143, 169, 171
property rights, 98, 189–90
prosperity, 97, 130, 270–71
protectionism, 79, 148, 267–68
protest, 113, 143, 188, 196
Prussia, 145–46, 150
public domain, 32

Public Works Administration (PWA), 167, 174
PWA. *See* Public Works Administration

Q

Queen Elizabeth I, 119, 124

R

racism, 87, 138, 216, 272, 275
railroads, 139, 141
recessions, 56–57, 142, 158
regulations, 26, 106–7, 112, 114, 187, 256–59, 262–63
Reichstag, 84, 146–47, 160, 163, 165
rights, 33, 87, 91, 98, 105, 117–23, 126–27, 185–86, 221, 232, 234, 245–46
    individual, 4, 6, 77–79, 81–86, 145, 150, 221, 236, 238, 250–51
    property, 189–90
    rule of, 63, 83–84, 87, 90–91, 107, 116–17, 123–24, 127, 165, 187–88, 191, 220, 232, 248, 251, 257, 274
robber barons, 46, 141–44, 148, 153, 171
Rockefeller, John D., 46, 141–42, 171
Roman Empire, 104
Romney, Mitt, 272
Roosevelt, Franklin Delano, 4, 167, 173, 175–82
Roosevelt, Theodore, 55, 143–44, 169
Rotterdam, 245–46, 308
Royal Navy, 123–25
Russia, 11, 27, 29, 40, 67, 69–71, 95–107, 152–54, 156–57, 160–61, 182, 195–96, 205, 266
Russian Revolution, 70, 72, 98, 103

S

Schmitt, Carl, 84, 182, 238–41, 247–48
Schumpeter, Joseph, 43, 56, 178
Scott, Dred, 134–35
SDP. *See* Social Democratic Party
Second Reich, 12, 72, 146, 152–53, 161–63, 244, 264
self-determination, 105
self-interest, 90, 192, 200, 224–27, 229–33, 235–37, 254
serfdom, 72, 101–3
Servicemen's Readjustment Act, 182
Sherman Act, 142, 144
slavery, 36, 97, 101–3, 130–37, 216, 223, 229–30, 237
Smith, Adam, 227, 232–33, 248, 254
social change, 75, 77, 150, 215
Social Democratic Party, 147–49, 160, 187–88
social interest, 33, 83, 87–90, 97, 105, 169, 192, 219, 226–30, 232–36, 252–54
socialism, 12–13, 40, 123–24, 148, 150–53, 166, 184, 186–93, 195, 197, 199–202
social order, 2–7, 15–17, 19–20, 23, 35, 40, 42–43, 63, 68, 70–71, 73, 75–76, 81, 83, 97, 100, 102–3, 112, 184, 190, 218–19, 223, 250–51
societies
    capitalist, 150, 192
    communist, 67, 204
    creative, 89, 219, 232
    destructive, 89–90
    developing, 87–88, 226
    divisive, 35, 145
    free, 89, 97, 254
    horizontal, 19, 82, 87, 137, 247
    liberal, 35, 232–33, 239, 248

    vertical, 82–83, 97, 110, 122, 130, 152
Soviet Union, 13–14, 20, 22, 32, 34, 66–68, 95–96, 184, 191, 193–206, 231, 240–41
Stalin, Josef, 13, 34, 67–68, 70, 194, 196–98, 202, 228, 231
Standard Oil, 141–44
Supreme Court, US, 65, 134–35, 138, 173, 176–77, 181–82
Sweden, 49–50, 90, 184–91
Switzerland, 71, 108

T

Taney, Roger, 134–35
Tarbell, Ida, 143–44
taxes, 28, 45, 90, 98–99, 104–5, 114–16, 125, 178–80, 187
technological revolution, 5–6, 16–17, 20, 23, 26, 54, 58, 73, 139, 169, 208, 212, 220, 250, 264
terror, 12, 68, 115, 166, 191, 193–200, 202, 226–27, 231, 243
Tocqueville, Alexis de, 130–31, 138–39
TPP (Trans-Pacific Partnership), 25, 268
trade, 19, 28, 67, 96, 112, 124–25, 141–42, 174, 176, 194
    free, 21, 25–27, 104, 121, 157, 196, 251, 268
Trans-Pacific Partnership. *See* TPP
Triple Entente. *See* Entente Powers
Trotsky, Leon, 194–96
Trump, Donald, 15, 25–26, 36–37, 39, 42, 64–65, 217, 252, 271–74
Trump administration, 27–28, 268–69, 274
tsars, 95–103, 105, 107, 128, 157, 224–25
Turgot, Anne-Robert Jacques, 113–14
Turkey, 15

U

unemployment, 12, 18, 22, 58–59,
     61–62, 124, 142, 155, 159,
     162–63, 177, 185
unions
     trade, 19, 143, 147–49, 165–68,
          171
     labor, 40, 179
United Kingdom, 27, 30, 49–50,
     54, 71–72, 90–91, 108–10, 112,
     117–27, 129, 149, 154, 224, 237,
     247–48, 264
United States, 2–6, 21–31, 37–42,
     52–53, 56–61, 64–65, 129–44,
     153–54, 167–82, 189–90, 215,
     218–19, 244–46, 252–55, 266–76
Utah, 88, 138

V

Versailles, 110, 114–15, 146
violence, 20, 40–42, 66–67, 70–71,
     82, 115–16, 125, 193, 196, 198,
     222, 272
Voltaire, 112, 114

W

wages, 19, 51, 53, 56, 111, 147, 167,
     170, 175, 185, 203, 293
Wall Street, 260–61
Walpole, Horace, 125
Washington, DC, 134, 261
Washington, George, 248, 270–71, 274
wealth, 4, 12, 14–15, 21, 23, 44,
     53–54, 62, 100, 104–5, 121–22,
     133, 139–41, 192, 213–15, 234–35,
     250, 252–53
Weimar Republic, 159–64, 187, 240,
     270
welfare, economic, 201, 222, 225
welfare state, 39, 123, 184–86, 188–89

Wiener, Norbert, 211–12
Wilkerson, Isabel, 136
women, 54, 57, 86, 123, 187
workers, 18–19, 43–45, 50–51, 53–54,
     57–59, 62, 122–23, 143, 146–49,
     154, 161, 185, 187–88, 194,
     199–200, 202–6
world, developing, 152, 155
World War I, 20, 26–27, 29, 38,
     40–41, 103, 123, 154–58, 162,
     265–66
World War II, 20, 27, 29, 38, 65, 179,
     182, 266–68

Y

Yeltsin, Boris, 205–6

ABOUT THE AUTHOR

Manuel Hinds is a consultant to private and public institutions, including the World Bank, the Inter-American Development Bank, and the International Monetary Fund. He has served as minister of finance in El Salvador twice—first from 1979 to 1980, then between 1995 and 1999—and as division chief at the World Bank, working with more than thirty countries. He is the author of *The Triumph of the Flexible Society: The Connectivity Revolution and Resistance to Change* and *Playing Monopoly with the Devil: Dollarization and Domestic Currencies in Developing Countries* and coauthor of *Money, Markets, and Sovereignty*, 2010 winner of the Manhattan Institute's Hayek Prize. Hinds lives in San Salvador and has three daughters and five grandchildren.